# MOLLIE

## & OTHER
# WAR PIECES

# WITNESSES TO WAR

**LIVING THROUGH THE BLITZ**
*Tom Harrisson*

**INTO THE VALLEY**
*John Hersey*

**MOLLIE & OTHER WAR PIECES**
*A. J. Liebling*

**THIS IS LONDON**
*Edward R. Murrow*
*edited by Elmer Davis*

**ORWELL: THE WAR COMMENTARIES**
*edited by W. J. West*

**THE RED ORCHESTRA**
*Gilles Perrault*

# MOLLIE
# & OTHER
# WAR PIECES

A. J. LIEBLING

SCHOCKEN BOOKS / NEW YORK

With the exception of the foreword, most essays in this work
were originally published in *The New Yorker* in slightly
different form.

Library of Congress Cataloging-in-Publication Data
Liebling, A. J. (Abbott Joseph), 1904–1963.
Mollie and other war pieces/by A. J. Liebling.
[Witnesses to war]
p. cm.
Reprint. Originally published: New York:
Ballantine, 1964.
ISBN 0-8052-0957-3
1. World War, 1939–1945. I. Title.
D743.L53 1989

940.53—dc20                                                    89-42803

Display Typography by Eric Baker & Susie Oberhelm
Manufactured in the United States of America

🆂

# CONTENTS

FOREWORD                                                                    *vii*

I   **CONFUSION IS NORMAL IN COMBAT**                                         *1*
    *Quest for Mollie*                                                        *3*

II  **FOR BOOTS NORGAARD**                                                   *27*
    *The Foamy Fields*                                                       *28*
        P.S. on Rozanoff in 1954                                            *61*
    *Gafsa*                                                                  *67*
        The Eighth Army from Gabès—1943                                     *67*
        With Dr. Freeman in Africa                                          *75*
        The Chemounis Revisited                                             *82*
        Gafsa Revisited                                                     *87*

III **ENTR'ACTE**                                                           *93*
    *Run, Run, Run, Run*                                                    *95*
    *Notes from the Kidnap House—1944*                                     *107*

IV  **AND SO TO VICTORY**                                                  *115*
    *Cross-Channel Trip*                                                   *117*

V   **DIRECTION: PARIS**                                                   *149*
    *Letters from France*                                                  *152*

CONTENTS

*My Dear Little Louise*                                   165
*Letter from Paris*                                       171
*Day of Victory*                                          175


**VI   MASSACRE**                                         185
*The Events at Comblanchien—November, 1944*               187


**AFTERWORD**                                             209

# Foreword

ALL THE PIECES in this book are about things that happened between the beginning of 1943 and the end of 1944; most were written from the field, but some in 1945, when I was just home. The latest in date is the pseudo-short-story *Day of Victory*, which was written in the summer of 1946, in celebration of the second anniversary of the Liberation of Paris, of part of which it is an unofficial report. A pseudo-short-story is one in which fact is turned to fiction by changing the names of the actors and perhaps juggling a bit with details. I have no compunctions in including two such stories with the rest of the reports.

I covered bits of the war in 1939–40 in France, and in 1941 in Britain and on the high seas, but those seem in retrospect not merely previous but different wars, with a different feeling, and so I have not included them. Collectively, the wars were the central theme of my life from October, 1939, until the end of 1944, and I sometimes feel a deplorable nostalgia for them—as my friend the Count Rzewski once said about something else: "So disgusting, so deplorable, so human." The times were full of certainties: we could be certain we were right—and we were—and that certainty made us certain that anything we did was right, too. I have seldom been sure I was right since. It had attractive uncertainties, too; you never had to think about the future, because you didn't know if you would have one. Yet the risk was so disseminated over time that you seldom felt that *this* was the moment when the future might end.

I know that it is socially acceptable to write about war as an unmitigated horror, but subjectively at least, it was not true, and you can feel its pull on men's memories at the maudlin reunions of war divisions. They mourn for their dead, but also for war.

A. J. LIEBLING
1964

# PART I

## CONFUSION IS NORMAL IN COMBAT

## For Hal Boyle

FIRST SERVANT—Let me have war, say I, it exceeds peace as far as day does night. . . .

SECOND SERVANT—'Tis so, and as wars in some sort may be said to be a ravisher, so it cannot be denied but peace is a great maker of cuckolds.

FIRST SERVANT—Ay, and it makes men hate one another.

THIRD SERVANT—Reason, because they then less need one another.

—*Coriolanus*

(The Third Servant then says: "The war's for my money," but I feared some reader might mistake the appearance of this line unsoftened by parentheses for an endorsement of his declaration.)

# Quest for Mollie

MOLLIE is a part of the history of La Piste Forestière, and La Piste Forestière is perhaps the most important part of the history of Mollie. La Piste Forestière, or the Foresters' Track, is a dirt road that connects Cap Serrat, on the northern coast of western Tunisia, with Sedjenane, a town twenty miles inland. The country it runs through is covered with small hills, and almost all the hills are coated with a ten-foot growth of tall bushes and short trees, so close together that once you leave the road you can't see fifty feet in front of you. From the top of any hill you can see the top of another hill, but, because of the growth, you can't tell whether there are men on it. This made the country hard to fight in. The hillsides that have no trees are bright with wild flowers in the spring, and when some other war correspondents and I travelled back and forth along the Foresters' Track in jeeps, we sometimes used to measure our slow progress by reference to the almost geometrical patterns of color on such slopes. There was, for example, the hill with a rough yellow triangle of buttercups against a reddish-purple background of other blooms; it indicated that you were five miles from the road's junction with the main highway at Sedjenane. With luck you might reach the junction in two hours, but this was extremely unlikely, for the road was just wide enough for one truck—not for a truck and a jeep or even for a truck and a motorcycle. Only a man on foot or on a horse could progress along the margin of the road when there was a vehicle on it, and the horse would often have to scramble by with two feet off the road, like the sidehill bear of eastern Tennessee. When a jeep met a convoy, it sometimes had to back up for hundreds of yards to where there was room to get off the road and wait. Then, when all the heavy vehicles had passed, the jeep would resume its journey, perhaps to meet another convoy before it had recovered the lost yardage. Even when you got in behind trucks going your way, they were packed so closely together that they advanced at a crawl, so you did too. Bits of the war were threaded along the Foresters' Track like beads on a string, and the opportunity to become familiar with them was forced upon you. Mollie, for me, was the gaudiest bead.

The reason the Foresters' Track is such a miserable excuse for a road is that in normal times there is little need for it. There is a lighthouse at Cap Serrat and a forest warden's house about halfway between that and Sedjenane. The few Berbers in the district, who live in brush shelters in the bush, have no vehicles or need of a road. But in late April and early May of 1943, La Piste Forestière was an important military thoroughfare. The Allied armies, here facing east, lay in a great arc with their right flank at Sousse, on the Gulf of Tunis, and this little road was the only supply line for twenty miles of front; that is, the extreme left flank of the Allied line. The actual front line ran parallel to the road and only a few hundred yards east of it during the first days of the offensive that was to end the Allies' North African campaign, but because of the hills and the brush, people on the road couldn't see the fighting. However, American artillery placed just west of the road—it would have been an engineering feat to get it any considerable distance into the brush—constantly fired over our heads as our jeeps piddled along. The gunners hoped that some of their shells were falling on the Germans and Italians who were trying to halt our infantry's advance with fire from hidden mortars and machine guns. The Luftwaffe in Africa had predeceased the enemy ground forces; the budget of planes allotted it for the African adventure was exhausted, I suppose, and the German High Command sent no more. This was lucky for us, because one good strafing, at any hour, would have jammed the road with burned-out vehicles and Allied dead. By repeating the strafing once a day, the Germans could have kept the road permanently out of commission. The potential danger from the air did not worry us for long, however. You soon become accustomed to immunity, even when you cannot understand the reason for it.

Trucks left ammunition along the side of the road to be carried up to the fighting lines on the backs of requisitioned mules and horses and little Arab donkeys, a strangely assorted herd conducted by an equally scratch lot of soldiers. The Washington army had decided years before that the war was now one-hundred-per-cent mechanized, so the field army, quite a different organization, had to improvise its animal transport as it went along. The wounded were carried down to the road by stretcher bearers. Ambulances, moving with the same disheartening slowness as everything else, picked up the casualties and took them out to a clearing station near the yellow-triangle hill I have mentioned, where some of the viable ones were patched up for the further slow haul out. Cruder surgical units, strung out along the road, took such cases as they were equipped to handle. These units were always right by the side of the road, since in that claustrophobe's nightmare of a country there was no other place for them to be. The advanced units were French and had women nurses with them. A French doctor I knew used to say that it helped the men bear pain if nurses were looking at them. "Since we have so little anesthesia," he said, "we rely upon vanity." Sometimes I would sit in my jeep and watch that doctor work. He had broken down a few saplings and bushes by the side of the road to clear a space for his ambulance, and next to the ambulance he had set up a camp stool and a folding table with some instruments on it. Once a traffic jam stopped my jeep near his post when he had a tanned giant perched on the camp stool, a second lieutenant in the Corps Franc d'Afrique. The man's breasts were hanging off his chest in a kind of bloody ruff. "A bit of courage now, my son, will save you a great deal of trouble later on," the doctor said as he prepared to do something or other. I assumed, perhaps pessimistically, that he was going to hack off the bits of flesh as you would trim the ragged edges of an ill-cut page. "Go easy, Doctor," the young man said. "I'm such a softie." Then the traffic started to move, so I don't know what the doctor did to him.

The Corps Franc d'Afrique was a unit that had a short and glorious history. Soon after the Allied landings in North Africa, in October, 1942, the Corps Franc organized itself, literally, out of the elements the Darlanists in control of the North African government distrusted too much to incorporate into the regular French Army—Jews, anti-Nazis from concentration camps, de Gaullists, and other Allied sympathizers. A French general named Joseph de Goislard de Montsabert, who had helped plan the landings, had been thrown out by his collaborationist superiors, who, even after Darlan's agreement to play ball with the forces of democracy, had remained his superiors. De Montsabert, because he had a red face and snowy hair, was known to his troops as Strawberry in Cream. There had been, among the French in North Africa, a number of other professional officers and many reservists who, like the General, were apparently left out of the war because they were suspected of favoring de Gaulle or merely of being hostile to Germany. The Darlan regime had refused to mobilize the Jews because it clung to the Vichy thesis that they were not full citizens, and it did not want them to establish a claim to future consideration, and it was holding thousands of Spanish and German refugees and French Communists in concentration camps.

De Montsabert and a few of his officer friends, talking on the street in Algiers one rainy November day of that year, decided to start a "Free Corps" of men who wanted to fight but whom the government would not allow to. They took over a room in a schoolhouse on the Rue Mogador as headquarters and advertised in the *Echo d'Alger* for volunteers. The ad appeared once and then the Darlanist censorship, which was still operating under the Americans, like every other element of Vichy rule, suppressed it. But scores of volunteers had already appeared at the schoolhouse and de Montsabert sent them out with pieces of schoolroom chalk to write "Join the Corps Franc" on walls all over the city. Hundreds of new volunteers came in. General Giraud, who had arrived in Africa to command all the French but had subsequently accepted a rôle secondary to Darlan's, heard of the movement and interceded for it. Giraud, whatever his limitations, considered it natural that anybody in his right mind should want to fight the Germans. Darlan and his Fascist friends began to think of the Corps Franc as a means of getting undesirables out of the way, so the government recognized it but at the same time refused it any equipment. The Corps began life with a miscellany of matériel begged from the British and Americans. Its men wore British battle dress and French insignia of rank, lived on American C rations, and carried any sort of weapons they could lay their hands on. The most characteristic feature of their appearance was a long beard, but even this was not universal, because some of the soldiers were too young to grow one. After the Corps Franc's arrival in Tunisia, it added to its heterogeneous equipment a great deal more stuff it captured from the enemy. The Corps went into the line in February of 1943, in the zone north of Sedjenane, and it remained there into the spring.

Late April in Tunisia is like late June in New York, and heat and dust were great nuisances to our men when they were attacking. In February and March, however, coastal Tunisia is drenched with a cold and constant downpour. The Foresters' Track was two feet deep in water when the Corps Franc began to fight along it. There were two battalions to start with—about twelve hundred men—to cover a sector twenty miles long. A third and fourth battalion had been added by the time the Americans began their offensive. The Corps, in the beginning, had only two ambulances, converted farm trucks owned by a Belgian colonist in Morocco. The Belgian and his son had driven the trucks across North Africa to join the Corps. But the trucks were unable to negotiate the flooded Track, so the men of the Corps carried their wounded out to Sedjenane on their shoulders. I once asked my doctor friend why they had not used mules. "The mules rolled over in the water and crushed the wounded men," he said. "We know. We tried it with wounded prisoners."

Now that the great attack was on, there were other troops along the Track with the Corps—the Sixtieth Infantry of the American Ninth Division, part of the American Ninth Division's artillery, an American tank-destroyer battalion, some Moroccan units, and some American motor-truck and medical outfits. The medics and the artillery made the French feel pampered and their morale got very high. One hot morning, I passed a lean, elderly soldier of the Corps Franc who was burying two of his comrades. He looked about sixty—there was no age limit in the Corps—and had a long, drooping mustache of a faded biscuit color. He had finished one grave and was sitting down to rest and cool off before beginning the other. The two dead men lay with their feet to the road. Blueflies had settled on their faces. I told my jeep driver to stop and asked the gravedigger what men these were. "One stiff was an Arab from Biskra," the old soldier said, "and the other a Spaniard, a nihilist from Oran." I asked him how his work was going. He wiped the sweat from his forehead and said happily, "Monsieur, like on roller skates."

A quarter of the men in the Corps Franc were Jews. A Jewish lieutenant named Rosenberg was its posthumous hero by the time I arrived in the Foresters' Track country. He had commanded a detachment of twenty men covering the retreat of his battalion during a German counterattack in early March. This was a sequel to the counterattack against the Americans at Kasserine Pass in late February, and both assaults were prototypes, on a small scale, of the counteroffensive the Germans were to launch in Belgium at the end of 1944—the last flurry of the hooked and dying fish. Rosenberg, holding one of the innumerable little hills with his men, had decided that it was not fitting for a Jew to retire, even when the Germans looked as though they had surrounded his position. He and his men held on until the rest of the battalion had made its escape. Then he rose, and, intoning the "Marseillaise," led his men in an attack with hand grenades. He and most of his men were, of course, killed.

Besides the Jews, the Corps had hundreds of political prisoners from labor camps in southern Algeria—Spanish Republicans who had fled to Africa in 1939, anti-Nazi Germans who had come even before that, and French "Communists and de Gaullists," to employ the usual Vichy designation for dissidents. The political prisoners had been released upon agreeing to enter the Corps Franc, which they did not consider an onerous condition. There were also hundreds of Frenchmen who had joined because they distrusted the Vichy officers in the regular Army, or because they were "hard heads" who detested any species of regularity, or because they were too old or ill for more conventional fighting units. In the Corps Franc, they were at liberty to march and fight until they dropped. There were also a fair number of Mohammedans, good soldiers who had joined to earn the princely wage of twenty-three francs a day, ten times what they would have got if they had waited to be mobilized in their regular units. Whenever I had a chance, I asked Corps Franc soldiers who they had been in civilian life and why they had enlisted. I remember a former *carabiñero* who had fought in the Spanish Loyalist Army, and a baker of Italian parentage from Bône, in Algeria, who said, "I am a Communist. Rich people are poison to me."

Other members of the Corps who made a special impression on me were a former admiral in the Spanish Republican Navy, who was now a company commander and would not allow junior officers to shout at soldiers; a Hungarian poet who had been studying medicine at the University of Algiers; a sixteen-year-old Alsatian from Strasbourg who had run away from home to avoid having to become a German citizen; and a French captain, a shipping broker in civil life, who proclaimed himself a Royalist. The captain's sixteen-year-old son was also in the Corps; the boy was a motorcycle dispatch rider. I also remember two tough Parisians who had not seen each other since one had escaped from jail in Dakar, where they had both been imprisoned for trying to join the Free French in Brazzaville. The other had escaped later. "Say, it's you, old pimp!" one of the men shouted joyously. "And how did you get out of the jug, old rottenness?" the second man shouted back. Once I shared a luncheon of C-ration vegetable hash, scallions, and medlars with a little fifty-three-year-old second lieutenant, one of those Frenchmen with a face like a parakeet, who until 1942 had been vice-president of the Paris Municipal Council, in which he represented the *arrondissement* of the Opéra. He had got out a clandestine paper and had helped Jewish friends smuggle millions of francs out of France. Betrayed to the Gestapo, he had been arrested and put in Cherche-Midi Prison; he had escaped with the aid of a jailer and come to Africa and the Corps Franc. The middle-aged soldier who waited on us spoke French with a farce-comedy Russian accent; he had been a waiter at the Scheherazade, a night club in Montmartre, and had often served the lieutenant when he was a civilian. A handsome young Viennese half-Jew, who had been on the Austrian track team in the last Olympic Games, once asked me for some sulfanilamide. He had been in a labor camp for six months without seeing a woman but had been allowed one night's leave in Oran before being sent on to the front. He wanted the sulfanilamide, he said, so that he could treat himself; he was afraid that a doctor might order him away from the firing line. And in a hospital tent at the clearing station I came across a man with a French flag wrapped around his waist; the medics discovered it when they cut his shirt away. He was a hard-looking, blondish chap with a mouthful of gold teeth and a face adorned by a cross-shaped knife scar—the *croix de vache* with which procurers sometimes mark business rivals. An interesting collection of obscene tattooing showed on the parts of him that the flag did not cover. Outwardly he was not a sentimental type.

"Where are you from?" I asked him.

"Belleville," he said. Belleville is a part of Paris not distinguished for its elegance.

"What did you do in civilian life?" I inquired.

That made him grin. "I lived on my income," he said.

"Why did you choose the Corps Franc?"

"Because I understood," he said.


The American soldiers interspersed with the men of the Corps Franc along the Foresters' Track found them a fantastic lot. Most of the men then in the Ninth Division came from New York, New Jersey, or New England, and their ideas of North Africa and Frenchmen had been acquired from films with Ronald Colman as Beau Geste or Charles Boyer as Charles Boyer. They thought the Frenchmen very reckless. The Ninth had had its first experience in battle on the road to Maknassy, in southern Tunisia, only a few weeks earlier, and it was not yet a polished division. The men of the Ninth in Germany later took risks as nonchalantly as any Corps Franc soldier used to, but at the time I am speaking of they would sometimes call the Frenchmen "those crazy headhunters." This term reflected a tendency to confuse the Corps Franc with the Moroccans in the same zone; the Moroccans are not headhunters, either, but there is a popular American belief that they are paid according to how many enemy ears they bring in.

There were two tabors, or battalions, of Moroccans in the zone; a tabor consists of several goums, or companies, and each soldier who is a member of a company is called a goumier. For the sake of simplicity and euphony, Americans called the Moroccan soldiers themselves goums. The goums used to ride along the side of the road on bay mules or gray horses—sure-footed, mountain-bred animals—until they got near the place where they were going to fight. Then they would dismount and go off into the brush on bare feet, and return with their booty when they had finished their business. The goum's sole outer garment is the *djellabah*, which looks like a long brown bathrobe with a hood. It is made of cotton, wool, linen, goats' hair, or camels' hair and usually has vertical black stripes. It sheds water, insulates against heat and cold, is a substitute for a pup tent at night, and serves as a repository for everything the goum gloms, like the capacious garment of a professional shoplifter. In their Moroccan homeland the goums live with their wives and children in their own villages and are supposed to pay themselves with the spoils of tribes that resist the French government. In Tunisia the spoils were pretty well confined to soldiers' gear. As a goum killed or captured more and more enemies, he would put on layer after layer of tunics and trousers, always wearing the *djellabah* over everything. The girth of the goums increased as the campaign wore on. This swollen effect gave a goum an air of prosperity and importance, in his opinion; his standing as a warrior, he thought, was in direct ratio to his circumference. A goum who was doing well often wore, between sorties, one German and one Italian boot and carried a string of extra boots over his saddlebow. The funny part of it was that a goum wearing six men's clothing could slip noiselessly through a thicket that was impassable to a skinny American. The French officers commanding the goums assured me that their men were not paid by the ear; if a goum occasionally had a few dried ears concealed in a fold of his *djellabah*, one officer explained, it was because goums had discovered that such souvenirs had a trade value in G.I. cigarettes and chewing gum. "Far from paying for ears," this officer said, "we have recently been offering a small reward for live prisoners for interrogation. It is evident that a prisoner without ears is not a good subject for interrogation, because he does not hear the questions plainly." To hold the goums' respect, the officers had to be able to march, climb, and fight with them, and a goum is as inexhaustible as a mountain sheep and about as fastidious as a hyena. Most goums come from the Atlas Mountains and few of them speak Arabic, much less French, so the officers have to be fluent in the southern Berber dialects, which are all that the men know. The goums are trying companions in minefields, because, as one officer remarked, "They say, 'If it is the will of God, we go up,' and then they just push forward." Neither they nor the Corps Franc had mine detectors. An American captain named Yankauer, who was the surgeon at the clearing station near the yellow-triangle hill, was once digging scraps of steel out of a goum who had stepped on a mine. The man let out one short squeal—there was no anesthetic—and then began a steady chant. Yankauer asked a goum officer, who was waiting his turn on the table, what the goum was saying. The officer translated, "He chants, 'God forgive me, I am a woman. God forgive me, I am a woman,' because, you see, he has cried aloud, so he is ashamed." The goums' chief weapons were curved knives and long rifles of the vintage of 1871, and one of the supply problems of the campaign for the American G-4 was finding ammunition for these antediluvian small arms. Colonel Pierre Magnan, who had succeeded de Montsabert in command of the Corps Franc, was the senior French officer in the zone. I was with him one day when the commander of a newly arrived tabor presented himself for orders. "How are you fixed for automatic weapons, Major?" Magnan asked. "We have two old machine guns," the goum officer said. Then, when he saw Magnan's glum look, he added cheerily, "But don't worry, my Colonel, we use them only on maneuvers."

Magnan was a trim, rather elegant officer who, before the Allied landings, had commanded a crack infantry regiment in Morocco. On the morning of the American landings, he had arrested General Noguès, the Governor General of Morocco, and then asked him to prevent any fighting between the French and Americans by welcoming the invading forces. Noguès had telephoned to a tank regiment to come and arrest Magnan. Magnan, unwilling to shed French blood, had surrendered to the tankmen and become a prisoner in his turn. The liberated Noguès had then ordered a resistance which cost hundreds of French and American lives. Magnan was kept in prison for several days after Noguès, who was backed by our State Department, had consented to be agreeable to the Allies. Magnan had then been released, but he was deprived of his command and consigned to the Corps Franc. He now commands a division in France, and de Montsabert has a *corps d'armée*, so the scheme to keep them down has not been precisely a success.

The Axis forces north of Sedjenane must have been as hard put to it for supply routes as we were. I don't remember the roads the Intelligence maps showed behind the enemy's lines, but they could not have been numerous or elaborate. The Germans did not seem to have a great deal of artillery, but they occasionally landed shells on our road. Once, I remember, they shot up a couple of tank destroyers shortly after the jeep I was in had pulled out to let them pass. Throughout, it was a stubborn, nasty sort of fighting in the brush, and casualties arrived in a steady trickle rather than any great spurt, because large-scale attacks were impossible.

Our men fought their way a few hundred yards further east each day, toward Ferryville and Bizerte. Eventually, when Rommel's forces crumpled, men of the Corps Franc, in trucks driven by American soldiers, got to Bizerte before any other Allied troops.

On Easter Sunday, which came late in April, I was out along the Track all day, riding in a jeep with Hal Boyle, a correspondent for the Associated Press. At the end of the afternoon we headed home, hoping to get back to the press camp before night so that we wouldn't have to buck a stream of two-and-a-half-ton trucks and armored vehicles in the blackout. Traffic seemed, if anything, heavier than usual along the Foresters' Track, as it always did when you were in a hurry. The jeep stopped for minutes at a time, which gave Boyle the opportunity to climb out and get the names and home addresses of American soldiers for his stories. Sometimes he would stay behind, talking, and catch up with the jeep the next time it was snagged. We could have walked along the Track faster than we rode. Finally we came to a dip in the road. Fifty yards below and to our right there was a shallow stream, and there was almost no brush on the slope from the road down to the water. This, for the Foresters' Track country, was a considerable clearing, and it was being used for a number of activities. Some goums were watering their mounts in the stream, some French and American soldiers were heating rations over brush fires, a number of vehicles were parked there, and Colonel Magnan and some officers were holding a staff meeting. As we approached the clearing, we were stopped again for a moment by the traffic. A dismal American soldier came out of the brush on our left, tugging a gaunt, reluctant white horse. "Come along, Horrible," the soldier said in a tone of intensest loathing. "This goddam horse got me lost three times today," he said to us, looking over his shoulder at the sneering, wall-eyed beast. He evidently thought the horse was supposed to guide him.

We moved downhill a bit and stopped again, this time behind an ambulance that was loading wounded. There was a group of soldiers around the ambulance. Boyle and I got out to look. There were four wounded men, all badly hit. They were breathing hard and probably didn't know what was going on. Shock and heavy doses of morphia were making their move easy, or at least quiet. The four men were all from the Sixtieth Infantry of the Ninth Division. A soldier by the road said that they had been on a patrol and had exchanged shots with a couple of Germans; the Germans had popped up waving white handkerchiefs, the Americans had stood up to take them prisoners, and another German, lying concealed, had opened on them with a machine gun. It was the sort of thing that had happened dozens of times to other units, and that undoubtedly has happened hundreds of times since. Such casualties, a Polish officer once said to me, are an entry fee to battle. That doesn't make them easy to take, however. The soldiers had been told about this particular trick in their training courses, but they had probably thought it was a fable invented to make them hate the enemy. Now the men around the ambulance had really begun to hate the enemy. While Boyle was getting the names and addresses of the men, I saw another American soldier by the side of the road. This one was dead. A soldier nearby said that the dead man had been a private known as Mollie. A blanket covered his face, so I surmised that it had been shattered, but there was no blood on the ground, so I judged that he had been killed in the brush and carried down to the road to await transport. A big, wild-looking sergeant was standing alongside him—a hawk-nosed, red-necked man with a couple of front teeth missing—and I asked him if the dead man had been in the patrol with the four wounded ones. "Jeez, no!" the sergeant said, looking at me as if I ought to know about the man with the blanket over his face. "That's Mollie. Comrade Molotov. The Mayor of Broadway. Didn't you ever hear of him? Jeez, Mac, he once captured six hundred Eyetalians by himself and brought them all back along with him. Sniper got him, I guess. I don't know, because he went out with the French, and he was found dead up there in the hills. He always liked to do crazy things—go off by himself with a pair of big field glasses he had and watch the enemy put in minefields, or take off and be an artillery spotter for a while, or drive a tank. From the minute he seen those frogs, he was bound to go off with them."

"Was his name really Molotov?" I asked.

"No," said the sergeant, "he just called himself that. The boys mostly shortened it to Mollie. I don't even know what his real name was— Warren, I think. Carl Warren. He used to say he was a Broadway big shot. 'Just ask anybody around Forty-fourth Street,' he used to say. 'They all know me.' Me, I'm from White Plains—I never heard of him before he joined up."

"I had him with me on a patrol that was to contact the French when the regiment was moving into this zone last Thursday," a stocky blond corporal said. "The first French patrol we met, Mollie says to me, 'This is too far back for me. I'm going up in the hills with these frogs and get me some Lugers.' He was always collecting things he captured off Germans and Italians, but the one thing he didn't have yet was a Luger. I knew if I didn't let him go he would take off anyway and get into more trouble with the C.O. He was always in trouble. So I said, 'All right, but the frogs got to give me a receipt for you, so I can prove you didn't go A.W.O.L.' One of the soldiers with me could speak French, so he explained it and the frog noncom give me a receipt on a piece of toilet paper and Mollie went off with them." The corporal fished in one of the pockets of his field jacket and brought out a sheet of tissue. On it, the French noncom had written, in pencil, *"Pris avec moi le soldat américain Molotov, 23 avril, '43, Namin, caporal chef."*

"Mollie couldn't speak French," the American corporal went on, "but he always got on good with the frogs. It's funny where those big field glasses went, though. He used to always have them around his neck, but some-body must have figured they were no more good to him after he was dead, so they sucked them up. He used to always say that he was a big-shot gambler and that he used to watch the horse races with those glasses."

By now the four wounded men had been loaded into the ambulance. It moved off. Obviously, there was a good story in Mollie, but he was not available for an interview. The driver of the truck behind our jeep was giving us the horn, so I pulled Boyle toward the jeep. He got in, still looking back at Mollie, who said nothing to keep him, and we drove away. When we had gone a little way, at our customary slow pace, a tall lieutenant signalled to us from the roadside that he wanted a hitch and we stopped and indicated that he should hop aboard. He told us his name was Carl Ruff. He was from New York. Ruff was dog-tired from scram-bling through the bush. I said something about Mollie, and Ruff said that he had not known him alive but had been the first American to see his body, on Good Friday morning. The French had led him to it. "He was on the slope of a hill," Ruff said, "and slugs from an automatic rifle had hit him in the right eye and chest. He must have been working his way up the hill, crouching, when the German opened on him and hit him in the chest, and then as he fell, the other bullet probably got him in the eye. He couldn't have lived a minute."

It was a month later, aboard the United States War Shipping Administra-tion steamer Monterey, a luxury liner that had been converted to war service without any needless suppression of comfort, that I next heard of Molotov, the Mayor of Broadway. The Monterey was on her way from Casablanca to New York. On the passenger list were four correspondents besides myself, a thousand German prisoners, five hundred wounded Americans, all of whom would need long hospitalization, and a couple of hundred officers and men who were being transferred or were on various errands. It was one of the advantages of being a correspondent that one could go to America without being a German or wounded, or without being phenomenally lucky, which the unwounded soldiers on our boat considered that they were. The crossing had almost a holiday atmosphere. We were homeward bound after a great victory in the North African campaign, the first the Allies had scored over Germany in a war nearly four years old. The weather was perfect and the Monterey, which was not overcrowded and had wide decks and comfortable lounges, had the aspect and feeling of a cruise ship. The wounded were glad, in their sad way, to be going home. The prisoners were in good spirits, too; they seemed to regard the journey as a Nazi Strength through Joy excursion. They orga-nized vaudeville shows, boxing matches, and art exhibitions, with the ener-getic coöperation of the ship's chaplain, who found much to admire in the

Christian cheerfulness with which they endured their increased rations. A couple of anti-Nazi prisoners had announced themselves on the first day out, but the German noncoms had knocked them about and set them to cleaning latrines, so order had soon been restored. "That's an army where they really have some discipline!" one of the American officers on board told me enviously. The prisoners had to put up with some hardships, of course. They complained one evening when ice cream was served to the wounded but not to them, and another time they didn't think the transport surgeon, a Jew, was "sympathetic" enough to a German officer with a stomach ache.

The hospital orderlies would wheel the legless wounded out on the promenade deck in wheelchairs to see the German boxing bouts, and the other wounded would follow them, some swinging along on crutches or hopping on one foot, some with their arms in slings or casts, some with their broken necks held stiffly in casts and harnesses. They had mixed reactions to the bouts. An arm case named Sanderson, a private who wore the Ninth Division shoulder patch, told me one day that he wished he could be turned loose on the prisoners with a tommygun, because he didn't like to see them jumping about in front of his legless pals. Another arm case, named Shapiro, from the same division, always got a lot of amusement out of the show. Shapiro was a rugged-looking boy from the Brownsville part of Brooklyn. He explained how he felt one day after two Afrika Korps heavy-weights had gone through a couple of rounds of grunting, posturing, and slapping. "Every time I see them box, I know we can't lose the war," he said. "The Master Race—phooey! Any kid off the street could of took the both of them."

Shapiro and Sanderson, I learned during one ringside conversation with them, had both been in the Sixtieth Infantry, Molotov's old regiment. They had been wounded in the fighting around Maknassy, in southern Tunisia, early in April, the first serious action the regiment had been in. Molotov had been killed late in April, during the drive on Bizerte, and until I told them, the boys hadn't heard he was dead. I asked them if they had known him.

"How could you help it?" Shapiro said. "There will never be anybody in the division as well known as him. In the first place, you couldn't help noticing him on account of his clothes. He looked like a soldier out of some other army, always wearing them twenty-dollar green tailor-made officers' shirts and sometimes riding boots, with a French berrit with a long rooster feather that he got off an Italian prisoner's hat, and a long black-and-red cape that he got off another prisoner for a can of C ration."

"And the officers let him get away with it?" I asked.

"Not in the rear areas, they didn't," Shapiro said. "But in combat, Mollie was an asset. Major Kauffman, his battalion commander, knew it, so he would kind of go along with him. But he would never have him made even a pfc. Mollie couldn't of stood the responsibility. He was the greatest natural-born foul-up* in the Army," Shapiro added reverently. "He was court-martialled twenty or thirty times, but the Major always got him out of it. He had the biggest blanket roll in the Ninth Division, with a wall tent inside it and some Arabian carpets and bronze lamps and a folding washstand and about five changes of uniform, none of them regulation, and he would always manage to get it on a truck when we moved. When he pitched his tent, it looked like a concession at Coney Island. I was with him when he got his first issue of clothing at Camp Dix in 1941. 'I've threw better stuff than this away,' he said. He never liked to wear issue. He was up for court-martial for deserting his post when he was on guard duty at Fort Bragg, but the regiment sailed for Morocco before they could try him, and he did so good in the landing at Port Lyautey that they kind of forgave him. Then he went over the hill again when he was guarding a dock at Oran in the winter, but they moved us up into the combat zone before they could try him then, so he beat that rap, too. He was a very lucky fellow. I can hardly think of him being dead."

"Well, what was so good about him?" I asked.

Sanderson, who was a thin, sharp-faced boy from Michigan, answered me with the embarrassed frankness of a modern mother explaining the facts of life to her offspring. "Sir," he said, "it may not sound nice to say it, and I do not want to knock anyone, but in battle almost everybody is frightened, especially the first couple of times. Once in a while you find a fellow who isn't frightened at all. He goes forward and the other fellows go along with him. So he is very important. Probably he is a popoff, and he kids the other guys, and they all feel better. Mostly those quiet, determined fellows crack up before the popoffs. Mollie was the biggest popoff and the biggest screwball and the biggest foul-up I ever saw, and he wasn't afraid of nothing. Some fellows get brave with experience, I guess, but Mollie never had any fear to begin with. Like one time on the road to Maknassy, the battalion was trying to take some hills and we were getting no place. They were just Italians in front of us, but they had plenty of stuff and they were in cover and we were in the open. Mollie stands right up, wearing the cape and the berrit with the feather, and he says, 'I bet those Italians would surrender if somebody asked them to. What the hell do they want to fight for?' he says. So he walks across the minefield and up the hill to the Italians, waving his arms and making funny motions, and they shoot at him for a while and then stop, thinking he is crazy. He goes up there yelling *'Veni qua!,'* which he says afterward is New York Italian for 'Come here!,' and *'Feeneesh la guerre!,'* which is French, and when he gets to the Italians he finds a soldier who was a barber in Astoria but went home on a visit and got drafted in the Italian Army, so the barber translates for him and the Italians say sure, they would like to

* A euphemism, of course.

surrender, and Mollie comes back to the lines with five hundred and sixty-eight prisoners. He had about ten Italian automatics strapped to his belt and fifteen field glasses hung over his shoulders. So instead of being stopped, we took the position and cleaned up on the enemy. That was good for the morale of the battalion. The next time we got in a fight, we said to ourselves, 'Those guys are just looking for an easy out,' so we got up and chased them the hell away from there. A disciplined soldier would never have did what Mollie done. He was a very unusual guy. He gave the battalion confidence and the battalion gave the regiment confidence, because the other battalions said, 'If the Second can take all those prisoners, we can, too.' And the Thirty-ninth and the Forty-seventh Regiments probably said to themselves, 'If the Sixtieth is winning all them fights, we can also.' So you might say that Mollie made the whole division." I found out afterward that Sanderson had oversimplified the story, but it was essentially true and the tradition endures in the Ninth Division.

"What kind of a looking fellow was Mollie?" I asked.

"He was a good-looking kid," Shapiro said. "Medium-sized, around a hundred and sixty pounds, with long, curly blond hair. They could almost never get him to have his hair cut. Once, when it got too bad, Major Kauffman took him by the hand and said, 'Come along with me. We'll get a haircut together.' So he sat him down and held onto him while the G.I. barber cut both their hair. And everything he wore had to be sharp. I remember that after the French surrendered to us at Port Lyautey, a lot of French officers gave a party and invited a couple of officers from the battalion to it, and when the officers got there they found Mollie was there, and the Frenchmen were all bowing to him and saluting him. He was dressed so sharp they thought he was an officer, too—maybe a colonel."

Another boy, a badly wounded one in a wheelchair, heard us talking about Mollie and rolled his chair over to us. "It was the field glasses I'll always remember," he said. "From the first day we landed on the beach in Morocco, Mollie had those glasses. He told some fellows once he captured them from a French general, but he told some others he brought them all the way from New York. He told them he used to watch horse races with the glasses; he was fit to be tied when he got to Morocco and found there was no scratch sheets. 'Ain't there no way to telegraph a bet on a race?' he said, and then he let out a howl. 'Vot a schvindle!' That was his favorite saying—'Vot a schvindle!' He was always bitching about something. He used to go out scouting with the glasses, all alone, and find the enemy and tip Major Kauffman off where they were. He had a lot of curiosity. He always had plenty of money, but he would never tell where he got it from. He just let people understand he was a big shot—maybe in some racket. When we was down at Fort Bragg, he and another fellow, a sergeant, had a big Buick that he kept outside the camp, and they used to go riding all around the country. They used to get some swell stuff."

"He never shot crap for less than fifty dollars a roll when he had the dice," Shapiro said, "and he never slept with any woman under an actress." The way Shapiro said it, it was as if he had said, "He never saluted anybody under the rank of brigadier general."

During the rest of the voyage, I heard more about Mollie. I found nobody who was sure of his real name, but the majority opinion was that it was something like Carl Warren. "But he wasn't American stock or Irish," Sanderson said one day in a group discussion. "He seemed to me more German-American." Another boy in the conversation said that Mollie had told him he was of Russian descent. Sanderson was sure that Molotov wasn't Russian. "Somebody just called him that because he was a radical, I guess," he said. "He was always hollering he was framed." "He used to have a big map of the eastern front in his tent in Morocco," another soldier said, "and every time the Russians advanced he would mark it with pins and holler, 'Hey, Comrade, howdya like that!'" One boy remembered that Mollie had won fifteen hundred dollars in a crap game at Fort Bragg. "He had it for about three days," he said, "and then lost it to a civilian. When he got cleaned in a game, he would never borrow a buck to play on with. He would just leave. Then the next time he played, he would have a new roll. Right after we landed in Morocco, he was awful flush, even for him, and he told a couple of guys he'd climbed over the wall of an old fort the French had just surrendered and there, in some office, he found a briefcase with fifty thousand francs in it. The next thing he done was hire twelve Arabs to cook and clean and wash dishes for him."

"I was inducted the same time with him, at Grand Central Palace," an armless youngster said, "and him and me and the bunch was marched down to Penn Station to take the train. That was way back in January, 1941," he added, as if referring to a prehistoric event. "He was wearing a blue double-breasted jacket and a dark-blue sport shirt open at the neck and gray flannel trousers and a camel's-hair overcoat. They took us into a restaurant on Thirty-fourth Street to buy us a feed and Mollie started buying beers for the whole crowd. 'Come on, Comrades,' he says. 'Plenty more where this comes from.' Then he led the singing on the train all the way down to Dix. But as soon as he got down there and they took all his fancy clothes away from him, he was licked. 'Vot a schvindle!' he says. He drew K.P. a lot at Dix, but he always paid some other guy to do it for him. The only thing he could ever do good outside of combat was D.R.O. —that's dining-room orderly at the officers' mess. I've seen him carry three stacks of dishes on each arm."

When I told them how Mollie had been killed, Shapiro said that that was just what you'd have expected of Mollie. "He never liked to stay with his own unit," he said. "You could hardly even tell what battalion he was in."

I was not to see the Army's official version of what Mollie had done in the fight against the six hundred Italians until the next summer, when I caught up with the Second Battalion of the Sixtieth Infantry near Marigny, in Normandy. Mollie's protector, Major Michael S. Kauffman, by then a lieutenant colonel, was still commanding officer. "Mollie didn't capture the lot by himself," Kauffman said, "but he was instrumental in getting them, and there were about six hundred of them all right. The battalion S-2 got out a mimeographed training pamphlet about that fight, because there were some points in it that we thought instructive. I'll get you a copy." The pamphlet he gave me bears the slightly ambitious title "The Battle of Sened, 23 March, '43, G Co. 60th Infantry Dawn Attack on Sened, Tunisia." The Sened of the title was the village of Sened, in the high *djebel* a couple of miles south of the Sened railroad station. It was country I remembered well: a bare plain with occasional bunch grass, with naked red-rock hills rising above it. The Americans had fought there several times; I had seen the taking of the railroad station by another regiment at the beginning of February, 1943, and it had been lost and retaken between then and March 23rd.

On the first page of the pamphlet there was a map showing the Italian position, on two hills separated by a narrow gorge, and the jump-off position of the Americans, two much smaller hills a couple of miles to the north. Then there was a list of "combat lessons to be learned," some of which were: "A small aggressive force can knock out a large group by determined action," "Individuals, soldiers with initiative, aggressiveness, and courage, can influence a large battle," and "Confusion is normal in combat." I have often since thought that this last would make a fine title for a book on war. The pamphlet told how an Italian force estimated at from thirty men to three thousand, according to the various persons interviewed in advance of the fight by S-2 ("Question civilians," the pamphlet said. "Don't rely on one estimate of enemy strength. Weigh all information in the light of its source."), had taken refuge in the village of Sened. G Company, about a hundred and fifty men, had been ordered to clean out the Italians. It had artillery support from some guns of the First Armored Division; in fact, a Lieutenant Colonel MacPherson, an artillery battalion commander, was actually the senior American officer in the action. This colonel, acting as his own forward observer, had looked over the situation and at four in the afternoon of March 22nd had ordered the first platoon of the company to attack. It was soon apparent, judging by the defenders' fire, that the lowest estimate of the enemy's strength was very wrong and that there were at least several hundred Italians on the two hills. Then, in the words of the pamphlet, "Private Molotov"—even his officers had long since forgotten his civilian name—"crawls to enemy position with Pfc. De Marco (both are volunteers) and arranges surrender conference. C.O. refuses to surrender and fire fight continues. Individual enemy riflemen begin to throw down their arms. First platoon returns to Sened Station at dark with 147 prisoners, including 3 officers."

"De Marco was a friend of Molotov's," Colonel Kauffman told me. "It was Mollie's idea to go up to the enemy position, and De Marco did the talking. It must have been pretty effective, because all those Italians came back with them."

"G Company," the pamphlet continued, "attacks again at dawn, first and third platoons attacking. Entrance to town is deep narrow gorge between two long ridges. Town lies in continuation of gorge, surrounded on all sides by 1,000–2,000 foot *djebels* as shown in sketch. (Possible enemy escape route was used by Ancient Romans as park for wild animals used in gladiatorial matches.) Approach to gorge entrance is terraced and well concealed by a large olive-tree grove; five (5) or six (6) field pieces in grove have been knocked out by previous day's artillery fire."

Although the pamphlet didn't say so, the olive groves had once covered all the plain. That plain is now given over to bunch grass, but it was carefully irrigated in the days of the Roman Empire. The "wild animals used in gladiatorial matches" were for the arena at the splendid stone city of Capsa, now the sprawling, dried-mud Arab town of Gafsa, fifteen miles from Sened.

"Company attacks as shown on sketch," the pamphlet continued, "third platoon making steep rocky climb around right, first platoon (Molotov's) around left. Light machine guns and mortars follow close behind by bounds, grenadiers move well to front with mission of flushing enemy out of numerous caves where he has taken up defensive positions. Left platoon, commanded by Sergeant Vernon Mugerditchian, moves slowly over ground devoid of concealment, and finally comes to rest. Molotov goes out alone, keeping abreast of faster moving platoon on right, and assists Lt. Col. MacPherson in artillery direction by shouting."

The combined artillery and infantry fire made the Italians quit. The pamphlet says, in closing, "Italian captain leads column of prisoners out of hills, bringing total of 537 (including officers). Total booty includes 2 large trucks, 3 small trucks, several personnel carrier motorcycles, 200 pistols, machine guns, rifles, and ammunition."

"Mollie liked to go out ahead and feel he was running the show," Colonel Kauffman said. "We put him in for a D.S.C. for what he did, but it was turned down. Then we put in for a Silver Star, and that was granted, but he was killed before he ever heard about it. He was a terrible soldier. He and another fellow were to be tried by a general court-martial for quitting their guard posts on the docks at Oran, but we had to go into action before court could be held. The other fellow had his court after the end of the campaign and got five years."

The officers of the battalion, and those at division headquarters, knew that I was going to write a story about Mollie sometime. Whenever I would encounter one of them, in a country tavern or at a corps or Army headquarters, or on a dusty road behind the lines, during our final campaign before Germany's surrender, he would ask me when I was going to "do Mollie." I am doing him now.


Even after I had been back in the States for a while that summer of 1943, I had an intermittent interest in Mollie, although La Piste Forestière assumed a curious unreality after I had been living on lower Fifth Avenue a couple of weeks. I asked a fellow I knew at the Times to check back through the casualty lists and see if the death of a soldier with a name like "Carl Warren" had been reported, since I knew the lists gave the addresses of the next of kin and I thought I might be able to find out more about Mollie. The Times man found out that there hadn't been any such name but that there was often a long interval between casualties and publication. I took to turning mechanically to the new lists as they came out and looking through the "W"s. One day I saw listed, among the Army dead, "Karl C. Warner, sister Mrs. Ulidjak, 230 E. Eightieth Street, Manhattan." The juxtaposition of "a name like Warren" with one that I took to be Russian or Ukrainian made me suspect that Warner was Molotov, and it turned out that I was right.

A couple of days later, I went uptown to look for Mrs. Ulidjak. No. 230 is between Second and Third Avenues, in a block overshadowed by the great, brute mass of the Manhattan Storage & Warehouse Company's building at the corner of Eightieth. Along the block there were a crumbling, red-brick elementary school of the type Fusion administrations like to keep going so that they can hold the tax rate down, a yellowish, oldfashioned Baptist church, some boys playing ball in the street, and a banner, bearing a number of service stars, hung on a line stretched across the street. As yet, it had no gold stars. No. 230 is what is still called a "new-law tenement," although the law governing this type of construction is fifty years old: a six-story walkup with the apartments built around air shafts. Ulidjak was one of the names on the mailboxes in the vestibule. I pushed the button beside it, and in a minute there was an answering buzz and I walked upstairs. A thin, pale woman with a long, bony face and straight blond hair pulled back into a bun came to the apartment door. She looked under thirty and wore silver-rimmed spectacles. This was Mrs. Ulidjak, Private Warner's sister. Her husband is in the Merchant Marine. She didn't seem startled when I said I was a correspondent; every American expects to be interviewed by a reporter sometime. Mrs. Ulidjak had been notified of her brother's death by the War Department over a week before, but she had no idea how it had happened or where. She said he had been in the Sixtieth Infantry, all right, so I was sure Warner had been Mollie. "Was he fighting the Japs?" she asked me. When I told her no, she seemed slightly disappointed. "And you were there?" she asked. I said I had been. Then, apparently trying to visualize me in the context of war, she asked, "Did you wear a helmet, like Ernie Pyle? Gee, they must be heavy to wear. Did it hurt your head much?" When I had reassured her on this point, she led me into a small sitting room with a window opening on a dark air shaft. A young man and a young woman, who Mrs. Ulidjak said were neighbors, were in the room, but they went into the adjoining kitchen, apparently so that they would not feel obliged to look solemn.

"Was your name Warner, too, before you were married?" I asked Mrs. Ulidjak.

"No," she said, "Karl and I were named Petuskia—that's Russian—but he changed to Warner when he came to New York because he thought it sounded sweller. We were from a little place called Cokesburg, in western Pennsylvania. He hardly ever came up here. He had his own friends."

"Did he go to high school in Cokesburg?" I asked.

The idea amused Mrs. Ulidjak. "No, just grammar school," she said. "He was a pit boy in the coal mines until we came to New York. But he always liked to dress nice. You can ask any of the cops around the Mall in Central Park about him. Curly, they used to call him, or Blondy. He was quite a lady's man."

Then I asked her the question that had puzzled Mollie's Army friends: "What did he do for a living before he went into the Army?"

"He was a bartender down to Jimmy Kelly's, the night club in the Village," Mrs. Ulidjak said.

She then told me that her brother's Christian name really was Karl and that he was twenty-six when he was killed, although he had looked several years younger. Both parents are dead. The parents had never told her, as far as she could remember, what part of Russia they came from. When I said that Mollie had been a hero, she was pleased, and said he had always had an awful crust. She called the young neighbors, who seemed to be of Italian descent, back into the sitting room and made me repeat the story of how Mollie captured the six hundred Italians (I hadn't seen the official version of his exploit yet and naturally I gave him full credit in mine). "Six hundred wops!" Mrs. Ulidjak exclaimed gaily. She got a lot of fun out of Mollie's "big shot" stories, too. She showed me a large, expensive-looking photograph of him "addressing" a golf ball. He was wearing light-colored plus-fours, white stockings, and brogues with tassels, and there was a big, happy grin on his face that made it plain that he was not going to hit the ball but was just posing. He had a wide, plump face with high cheekbones and square white teeth, and the hair about which I had so often heard looked at least six inches long. "He had a room at 456 West Forty-fourth Street, and a little Jewish tailor down in that neighborhood made all those nice things for him special," she said admiringly. She had never heard him called Molotov.

I went over to West Forty-fourth Street a few days later. The 400 block, between Ninth and Tenth Avenues, looks more depressing than the one the Ulidjaks live on. It is mostly shops dealing in the cheap merchandise that is used as premiums, and stores that sell waiters' supplies, and lodging houses favored by waiters and cooks. It was evident from the look of the house at No. 456 that though Mollie had spent a disproportionate share of his income on clothes, he had wasted nothing on his living quarters. No one at No. 456 remembered Mollie. The tenants and the janitor had all come there since his time. I couldn't find the little tailor. But on the north side of Forty-fourth Street, near Ninth Avenue, there is a building occupied by the Warner Brothers' Eastern offices, and I was sure that this had given Mollie the idea of calling himself Warner.

That evening I went down to Jimmy Kelly's, on Sullivan Street. Kelly's is the kind of club that never changes much but that you seldom remember anything specific about unless you have had a fight there. I had been there a few times in the late thirties, but I couldn't remember the bartender's face. Kelly's has a dance floor a little bigger than two tablecloths, and there is always a show with young, sometimes pretty girls imitating the specialties that more famous and experienced performers are doing at clubs uptown, and a master of ceremonies making cracks so old that they have been used in Hollywood musicals. The man behind the bar the night I showed up said he had been there several years and had known his predecessor, whose name was not Molotov. He had never heard of a bartender named Molotov or Warner or Mollie or Karl at Kelly's. After I had had a couple of Scotches and had told him the story, he said he wondered if the fellow I meant hadn't been a busboy. The description seemed to fit one who had worked there. "We all used to call this kid Curly," he said, "but Ray, the waiter who is the union delegate, might remember his real name."

Ray was a scholarly-looking man with a high, narrow forehead and shell-rimmed spectacles. "Curly's name *was* Karl C. Warner," he said after he had been told what I wanted to know. "I remember it from his union card. He was a man who would always stand up for his fellow-worker. Waiters and Waitresses Local No. 1 sent him down here in the summer of 1940 and he worked until late the next fall. He was outspoken but a hard worker and strong—he could carry three stacks of dishes on each arm. A busboy has a lot to do in a place like this when there is a rush on—clearing away dishes, setting up for new parties, bringing the waiters their orders—and a stupid boy can spoil the waiters' lives for them. We had another boy here at the same time, an Irish boy, who kidded Curly about the fancy clothes he wore, so they went down in the basement and fought for a couple of hours one afternoon. Nobody won the fight. They just fought until they were tired and then stopped. Curly had wide interests for a busboy," Ray continued. "When there was no rush on, he would sometimes stop by a customer's table, particularly if it was some man who looked important, and talk to him for ten minutes or so. The customers didn't seem to mind. He had a nice way about him. He had a kind of curiosity."

The Army stories about Mollie's wealth made Ray and the bartender laugh. "He used to come back here now and then during the first year he was in the Army," Ray said, "and always he would borrow ten or twenty dollars from one of us waiters. We would lend it to him because we liked him, without expecting to get it back." A busboy at Kelly's is paid only nominal wages, Ray told me—just about enough to cover his laundry bill—but the waiters chip in a percentage of their tips for the boys. "I guess Curly averaged about forty a week here," he said. "If he was anxious to get extra money, he might have had a lunch job someplace else at the same time, but I never heard about it. A tailor like he had probably made those suits for about twenty-five per. What else did he have to spend money on? His night life was here. He used to tell us he had worked at El Morocco, but we used to say, 'What's the difference? Dirty dishes are the same all over.' "

At the union headquarters, which are on the twelfth floor of a loft building on West Fortieth Street, Mollie was also remembered. The serious, chunky young woman in the union secretary's office said, "Warner was always a dissident. He would speak up at every meeting and object to everything. But we all liked him. He stopped paying dues a few months before he went into the Army, but at Christmastime in 1941 he came back here and said he heard that union members in the services were getting a present from the local, so he wanted one, too. So we gave it to him, of course. The secretary will be interested to know he is dead."

The young woman called the secretary, a plump, olive-complexioned man, from his desk in an inner room and said to him, "You remember Karl Warner, the blond boy with curly hair? He has been killed in Africa. He was a hero."

"Is that so?" the secretary said. "Well, get a man to put up a gold paper star on the flag in the members' hall right away and draw up a notice to put on the bulletin board. He is the first member of Local No. 1 to die in this war."

I thought how pleased Mollie would have been to be restored to good standing in the union, without even having paid up his dues. Then I thought of how much fun he would have had on the Mall in Central Park, in the summertime, if he could only have gone up there with his Silver Star ribbon on, and a lot of enemy souvenirs. I also thought of how far La Piste Forestière was from the kitchen in Jimmy Kelly's.

When I walk through the West Side borderland between Times Square and the slums, where Mollie once lived, I often think of him and his big talk and his golf-suit grin. It cheers me to think there may be more like him all around me—a notion I would have dismissed as sheer romanticism before World War II. Cynicism is often the shamefaced product of inexperience.

He has become a posthumous pal, though I never knew him when he was alive. He was full of curiosity—he would have made a great explorer —and fond of high living, which is the only legitimate incentive for liking money. He had faith in the reason of his fellow-man, as when he sensed that the Italians at Sened were no more eager to fight than he was. The action that earned him his Silver Star cost no lives. It saved them. He bragged, but when challenged he would not back off. The brag was like the line a deckhand throws over a bollard—it pulled performance after it. I lived with him so long that I once half-convinced myself he was not dead. This was when I began to write a play about him, and was reminded by more experienced hands that it is customary for the protagonist of a work of that nature to remain alive until the last act.

"Suppose," I said, "that the corpse with the face shot away that I saw by La Piste was not Mollie at all, but that Mollie had put his uniform and dog-tags on a dead goumier and gone over the hill wearing a Moroccan *djellabah*, to wage a less restricted kind of war, accumulating swag as he went? And suppose he was living in Morocco now, with a harem, a racing stable, and a couple of Saharan oil wells? And suppose he returned to New York as a member of the Moroccan, or the Mauretanian, Delegation to the United Nations, or, better yet, a Delegate from the Touareg state that is sure to be formed sooner or later? The last would afford him the advantage of a veil covering his face below the eyes, to conceal his grin.

Mollie would like the fancy togs, and if any old rival, perhaps the Irish busboy, recognized him in the last scene and twitted him with his defection, he could pull out from his flowing sleeves hundreds of dried Nazi ears to prove he had waged war effectually to the last. If Allah has so willed it, the thing is.

Or suppose he had switched uniforms with a dead German, and thereafter, as a secret agent, confounded all the Wehrmacht's plans? He liked to operate in disguise, as he proved when he fooled the French officers at Casablanca, and superior officers of foreign powers confided in him on sight. I like him better as a Touareg, and I think he would have liked

Touaregs better as company. I dropped the play because that was all the plot I could think of.

Long after I abandoned thought of writing about Mollie again, I had a letter from a lady in Mechanicsburg, Pennsylvania, that cleared up the question of how Mollie transmuted his last name. It had nothing to do with Warner Brothers—a warning, this, against adopting mere plausibility in place of valid evidence. She wrote that her brother, a Mr. Karl Warner, had come to Cokesburg as boss of a construction job in about 1932, and had given the Petuskia boy a job as watchman, in defiance of all local counsel. Young Petuskia was considered a bad risk. The boy proved honest, and afterward wanted to pull up stakes and follow the construction gang when it left town. Warner told him he was too young. The Mechanicsburg lady was sure the boy had subsequently taken the Warner name in honor of her brother.

I am sure she is right, but it sounds like a detail out of an old-fashioned boys' book.


The air vendetta that is described in the next set of pieces took place in an earlier phase of the war in North Africa—all, in fact, during the month of January, 1943. I wrote the stories in my room at the Hotel Aletti, in Algiers, in early February. There were no facilities for sending despatches from the rudimentary air fields, several hundred miles away, where the fighting happened. This was one of the good points of being a correspondent—you could leave the discomfort of the scene of combat without being wounded.

Headquarters were so far from our war that the censor officers read our despatches like notes on an unknown world. For the staff it was rather like running a war in Ohio from a hotel in Washington, except that their hotel was better. It was the Saint George, up on the hill. But the Aletti was a fine place too—you could have a bath, though seldom a hot one, in a bathtub, and receive female visitors if they stood in well with the concierge. In town there was a great deal of Algerian wine, which is maligned in France by the very blenders who import it in vast quantities to give body to their thin vintages, and there was excellent food to be had if you knew where to look for it, in the Street of the Gate of Weeping, in the establishment of a Swiss who considered himself, as a neutral, immune from wartime food regulations. The fish and the small birds were almost literally beyond price, and there was a wine so kind that if I had a daughter, I would give her its name—Miliana.

In the twilight, as we walked to our dinners, German planes would come like swallows out of Sicily, far away, and jettison their bombs before reaching the center of our magnificent anti-aircraft display, like a beehive drawn in lines of orange tracer. If Headquarters hadn't been there, we wouldn't have had such a pretty beehive, and the pilots wouldn't have flinched so soon. My debts to the Supreme Command are therefore double—it stayed in a safe place and it kept it safer.

Then, in the dark after the third armagnac, we would steal away to a place of enchantment called the Sphinx, where girls would act charades that graying members of the American Legion still dream of with nostalgia in Terre Haute. It was a schizoid existence: in Tunisia, with your belly pressed to the ground, the Hotel Aletti seemed a mirage, but when you were in Algiers, you wondered whether you had lived on the Foamy Fields or imagined them.

# PART II

## FOR BOOTS NORGAARD

# The Foamy Fields

IF THERE is any way you can get colder than you do when you sleep in a bedding roll on the ground in a tent in southern Tunisia two hours before dawn, I don't know about it. The particular tent I remember was at an airfield in a Tunisian valley. The surface of the terrain was mostly lime-stone. If you put all the blankets on top of you and just slept on the canvas cover of the roll, you ached all over, and if you divided the blankets and put some of them under you, you froze on top. The tent was a large, circular one with a French stencil on the outside saying it had been rented from a firm in Marseilles and not to fold it wet, but it belonged to the United States Army now. It had been set up over a pit four feet deep, so men sleeping in it were safe from flying bomb frag-ments. The tall tent pole, even if severed, would probably straddle the pit and not hit anybody. It was too wide a hole to be good during a strafing, but then strafings come in the daytime and in the daytime nobody lived in it. I had thrown my roll into the tent because I thought it was vacant and it seemed as good a spot as any other when I arrived at the field as a war correspondent. I later discovered that I was sharing it with two enlisted men.

I never saw my tentmates clearly, because they were always in the tent by the time I turned in at night, when we were not allowed to have lights on, and they got up a few minutes before I did in the morning, when it was still dark. I used to hear them moving around, however, and some-times talk to them. One was from Mississippi and the other from North Carolina, and both were airplane mechanics. The first night I stumbled through the darkness into the tent, they heard me and one of them said, "I hope you don't mind, but the tent we were sleeping in got all tore to

"The Foamy Fields" was written and originally published during World War II. After the war, Liebling revealed in footnotes and postscript some identities, locations, and additions that had to remain secret or were unknown when the piece first appeared. Here we print the full postwar text.—Editor

pieces with shrapnel last night, so we just moved our stuff in here." I had been hearing about the events of the previous evening from everybody I met on the field. "You can thank God you wasn't here last night," the other man said earnestly. The field is so skillfully hidden in the mountains that it is hard to find by night, and usually the Germans just wander around overhead, dropping their stuff on the wrong hillsides, but for once they had found the right place and some of the light anti-aircraft on the field had started shooting tracers. "It was these guns that gave away where we was," the first soldier said. "Only for that they would have gone away and never knowed the first bomb had hit the field. But after that they knew they was on the beam and they come back and the next bomb set some gasoline on fire and then they really did go to town. Ruined a P-38 that tore herself up in a belly landing a week ago and I had just got her about fixed up again, and now she's got shrapnel holes just about everywhere and she's hopeless. All that work wasted. Killed three fellows that was sleeping in a B-26 on the field and woke up and thought that was no safe place, so they started to run across the field to a slit trench and a bomb got them. Never got the B-26 at all. If they'd stayed there, they'd been alive today, but who the hell would have stayed there?"*

"That shrapnel has a lot of force behind it," the other voice in the tent said. "There was a three-quarter-ton truck down on the field and a jaggedy piece of shrapnel went right through one of the tires and spang through the chassix. You could see the holes both sides where she went in and come out. We was in our tent when the shooting started, but not for long. We run up into the hills so far in fifteen minutes it took us four hours to walk back next morning. When we got back we found we didn't have no tent." There was a pause, and then the first soldier said, "Good night, sir," and I fell asleep.

When the cold woke me up, I put my flashlight under the blankets so I could look at my watch. It was five o'clock. Some Arab dogs, or perhaps jackals, were barking in the hills, and I lay uncomfortably dozing until I heard one of the soldiers blowing his nose. He blew a few times and said, "It's funny that as cold as it gets up here nobody seems to get a real cold. My nose runs like a spring branch, but it don't never develop."

When the night turned gray in the entrance to the tent, I woke again, looked at my watch, and saw that it was seven. I got up and found that the soldiers had already gone. Like everyone else at the field, I had been sleeping in my clothes. The only water obtainable was so cold that I did not bother to wash my face. I got my mess kit and walked toward the place, next to the kitchen, where they were starting fires under two great caldrons to heat dish water. One contained soapy water and the other rinsing water. The fires shot up from a deep hole underneath them, and a group of soldiers had gathered around and were holding the palms of

---

* The B-26 was Lieutenant-General James Doolittle's personal plane. He was on a tour of inspection, and the three soldiers were members of his crew.

their hands toward the flames, trying to get warm. The men belonged to a maintenance detachment of mechanics picked from a number of service squadrons that had been sent to new advanced airdromes, where planes have to be repaired practically without equipment for the job. That morning most of the men seemed pretty cheerful because nothing had happened during the night, but one fellow with a lot of beard on his face was critical. "This location was all right as long as we had all the planes on one side of us, so we was sort of off the runway," he said, "but now that they moved in those planes on the other side of us, we're just like a piece of meat between two slices of bread. A fine ham sandwich for Jerry. If he misses either side, he hits us. I guess that is how you get to be an officer, thinking up a location for a camp like this. I never washed out of Yale so I could be an officer, but I got more sense than that."

"Cheer up, pal," another soldier said. "All you got to do is dig. I got my dugout down so deep already it reminds me of the Borough Hall station. Some night I'll give myself a shave and climb on board a Woodlawn express." Most of the men in camp, I had already noticed, were taking up excavation as a hobby and some of them had worked up elaborate private trench systems. "You couldn't get any guy in camp to dig three days ago," the Brooklyn soldier said, "and now you can't lay down a shovel for a minute without somebody sucks it up."

Another soldier, who wore a white silk scarf loosely knotted around his extremely dirty neck, a style generally affected by fliers, said, "What kills me is my girl's brother is in the horse cavalry, probably deep in the heart of Texas, and he used to razz me because I wasn't a combat soldier."

The Brooklyn man said to him, "Ah, here's Mac with a parachute tied around his neck just like a dashing pilot. Mac, you look like a page out of *Esquire*."

When my hands began to feel warm, I joined the line which had formed in front of the mess tent. As we passed through, we got bacon, rice, apple butter, margarine, and hard biscuits in our mess tins and tea in our canteen cups. The outfit was on partly British rations, but it was a fairly good breakfast anyway, except for the tea, which came to the cooks with sugar and powdered milk already mixed in it. "I guess that's why they're rationing coffee at home, so we can have tea all the time," the soldier ahead of me said. I recognized the bacon as the fat kind the English get from America. By some miracle of lend-lease they had now succeeded in delivering it back to us; the background of bookkeeping staggered the imagination. After we had got our food, we collected a pile of empty gasoline cans to use for chairs and tables. The five-gallon can, known as a flimsy, is one of the two most protean articles in the Army. You can build houses out of it, use it as furniture, or, with slight structural alterations, make a stove or a locker. Its only rival for versatility is the metal shell of the Army helmet, which can be used as an entrenching tool, a shaving bowl, a wash basin, or a cooking utensil, at the discretion of the owner. The helmet may also serve on occasion as a bathtub. The bather fills it with water, removes one article of clothing at a time, rubs the water hastily over the surface thus exposed, and replaces the garment before taking off another one.*

There was no officers' mess. I had noticed Major George Lehmann, the commanding officer of the base, and First Lieutenant McCreedy, the chaplain, in the line not far behind me. Major Lehmann is a tall, fair, stolid man who told me that he had lived in Pittsfield, Massachusetts, where he had a job with the General Electric Company. When I had reported, on my arrival at the field, at his dugout the evening before, he had hospitably suggested that I stow my blanket roll wherever I could find a hole in the ground, eat at the general mess shack, and stay as long as I pleased. "There are fighter squadrons and some bombers and some engineers and anti-aircraft here, and you can wander around and talk to anybody that interests you," he had said.

Father McCreedy is a short, chubby priest who came from Bethlehem, Pennsylvania, and had been assigned to a parish in Philadelphia. He always referred to the pastor of this parish, a Father McGinley, as "my boss," and asked me several times if I knew George Jean Nathan, who he said was a friend of Father McGinley. Father McCreedy had been offici- ating at the interment of the fellows killed in the raid the evening before, and that was all he would talk about during breakfast. He had induced a mechanic to engrave the men's names on metal plates with an electric needle. These plates would serve as enduring grave markers. It is part of a chaplain's duty to see that the dead are buried and to dispose of their effects. Father McCreedy was also special-services officer of the camp, in charge of recreation and the issue of athletic equipment. "So what with one thing and another, they keep me busy here," he said. He told me he did not like New York. "Outside of Madison Square Garden and the Yankee Stadium, you can have it." He wore an outsize tin hat all the time. "I know a chaplain is not supposed to be a combatant," he said, "but if parachute troops came to my tent by night, they'd shoot at me because they wouldn't know I was a chaplain, and I want something solid on my head." He had had a deep hole dug in front of his tent and sometimes, toward dusk, when German planes were expected, he would stand in it waiting and smoking a cigar, with the glowing end of it just clearing the hole.

When I had finished breakfast and scrubbed up my mess kit, I strolled around the post to see what it was like. As the sun rose higher, the air grew warm and the great, reddish mountains looked friendly. Some of them had table tops, and the landscape reminded me of

---

* This is known as a whore's bath. The impelling reason for exposing only one surface at a time was cold, not modesty.

Western movies in Technicolor.* I got talking to a soldier named
Bill Phelps, who came from the town of Twenty-nine Palms, California. He was working on a bomber that had something the matter with
its insides. He confirmed my notion that the country looked like the
American West. "This is exactly the way it is around home," he said, "only
we got no Ayrabs." A French writer has described the valley bottoms in
southern Tunisia as foamy seas of white sand and green alfa grass. They
are good, natural airfields, wide and level and fast-drying, but there is
always plenty of dust in the air. I walked to a part of the field where there
were a lot of P-38's, those double-bodied planes that look so very futuris-
tic, and started to talk to a couple of sergeants who were working on one.
"This is Lieutenant Hoelle's plane," one of them said, "and we just finished putting a new wing on it. That counts as just a little repair job out
here. Holy God, at home, if a plane was hurt like that, they would send it
back to the factory or take it apart for salvage. All we do here is drive a
two-and-a-half-ton truck up under the damaged wing and lift it off, and
then we put the new wing on the truck and run it alongside the plane
again and fix up that eighty-thousand-dollar airplane like we was sticking
together a radio set. We think nothing of it. It's a great ship, the 38.
Rugged. You know how this one got hurt? Lieutenant Hoelle was strafing
some trucks and he come in to attack so low he hit his right wing against
a telephone pole. Any other plane, that wing would have come off right
there. Hitting the pole that way flipped him over on his back, and he was
flying upside down ten feet off the ground. He gripped that stick so hard
the inside of his hand was black and blue for a week afterward, and she
come right side up and he flew her home. Any one-engine plane would
have slipped and crashed into the ground, but those two counter-rotating
props eliminate torque." I tried to look as though I understood. "Lieutenant Hoelle is a real man," the sergeant said.**
     I asked him where Hoelle and the other P-38 pilots were, and he
directed me to the P-38 squadron's operations room, a rectangular struc-
ture mostly below ground, with walls made out of the sides of gasoline
cans and a canvas roof camouflaged with earth. A length of stovepipe
stuck out through the roof, making it definitely the most ambitious struc-
ture on the field.


Hoelle was the nearest man to the door when I stepped down into the
operations shack. He was a big, square-shouldered youngster with heavy

* This use of the familiar false as touchstone of the unfamiliar real recurred often
both in writing and conversation during World War II. "Just like a movie!" was a
standard reaction. It assured the speaker of the authenticity of what he had just
experienced.
** These praises of the Lightning now look as old-fashioned as a cavalryman's praise of
the Anglo-Arab charger, and the mechanic's talk about an eighty-thousand-dollar
airplane, sounds like a reference to the good nickel cigar.

eyebrows and a slightly aquiline nose. I explained who I was and asked him who was in charge, and he said, "I am. I'm the squadron C.O. My name's Hoelle." He pronounced it "Holly." There was a fire in a stove, and the shack was warm. Two tiny black puppies lay on a pilot's red scarf in a helmet in the middle of the dirt floor, and they seemed to be the centre of attention. Six or eight lieutenants, in flying togs that ranged from overalls to British Army battle dress, were sitting on gasoline cans or sprawled on a couple of cots. They were all looking at the puppies and talking either to them or their mother, a small Irish setter over in one corner, whom they addressed as Red. "One of the boys brought Red along with him from England," Hoelle said. "We think that the dog that got her in trouble is a big, long-legged black one at the airport we were quartered at there."

"These are going to be real beautiful dogs, just like Irish setters, only with black hair," one of the pilots said in a defensive tone. He was obviously Red's master.

"This is a correspondent," Hoelle said to the group, and one of the boys on a cot moved over and made room for me. I sat down, and the fellow who had moved over said his name was Larry Adler but he wasn't the harmonica player and when he was home he lived on Ocean Parkway in Brooklyn. "I wouldn't mind being there right now," he added.

There was not much in the shack except the cots, the tin cans, a packing case, the stove, a phonograph, a portable typewriter, a telephone, and a sort of bulletin board that showed which pilots were on mission, which were due to go on patrol, and which were on alert call, but it was a cheerful place. It reminded me of one of those secret-society shacks that small boys are always building out of pickup materials in vacant lots. Adler got up and said he would have to go on patrol. "It's pretty monotonous," he said, "like driving a fast car thirty miles an hour along a big, smooth road where there's no traffic. We just stooge around near the field and at this time of day nothing ever happens."

Another lieutenant came over and said he was the intelligence officer of the squadron. Intelligence and armament officers, who do not fly, take a more aggressive pride in their squadron's accomplishments than the pilots, who don't like to be suspected of bragging. "We've been out here for a month," the intelligence officer said, "and we have been doing everything—escorting bombers over places like Sfax and Sousse, shooting up vehicles and puncturing tanks, going on fighter sweeps to scare up a fight, and flying high looking for a target and then plunging straight down on it and shooting hell out of it. We've got twenty-nine German planes, including bombers and transports with troops in them and fighters, and the boys have flown an average of forty combat missions apiece. That's more than one a day. Maybe you'd like to see some of the boys' own reports on what they have been doing."

I said that this sounded fine, and he handed me a sheaf of the simple statements pilots write out when they put in a claim for shooting down a German plane. I copied part of a report by a pilot named Earnhart, who I thought showed a sense of literary style. He had had, according to the intelligence officer, about the same kind of experience as everybody else in the squadron. Earnhart had shot down a Junkers 52, which is a troop-carrier, in the episode he was describing, and then he had been attacked by several enemy fighters. "As I was climbing away from them," he wrote, "a 20-millimetre explosive shell hit the windshield and deflected through the top of the canopy and down on the instrument panel. Three pieces of shell hit me, in the left chest, left arm, and left knee. I dropped my belly tank and, having the ship under control, headed for my home base. On the way I applied a tourniquet to my leg, administered a hypodermic, and took sulfanilamide tablets. I landed the ship at my own base one hour after I had been hit by the shell. The plane was repaired. Claim, one Ju 52 destroyed." The intelligence officer introduced Earnhart to me. He was a calm, slender, dark-haired boy and he persisted in addressing me as sir. He said he came from Lebanon, Ohio, and had gone to Ohio State.

Still another lieutenant I met was named Gustke. He came from De-troit. Gustke had been shot down behind the German lines and had made his way back to the field. He was a tall, gangling type, with a long nose and a prominent Adam's apple. "I crash-landed the plane and stepped out of it wearing my parachute," he told me, "and the first thing I met was some Arabs who looked hostile to me, and as luck would have it I had forgotten to bring along my .45, so I tripped my parachute and threw it to them, and you know how crazy Arabs are about cloth or anything like that. They all got fighting among themselves for the parachute, and while they were doing that I ran like hell and got away from them. I got to a place where there were some Frenchmen, and they hid me overnight and the next day put me on a horse and gave me a guide, who brought me back over some mountains to inside the French lines. I had a pretty sore ass from riding the horse."

A pilot from Texas named Ribb, who stood nearby as Gustke and I talked, broke in to tell me that they had a fine bunch of fellows and that when they were in the air they took care of each other and did not leave anybody alone at the end of the formation to be picked off by the enemy. "In this gang we have no ass-end Charlies," he said feelingly.

I asked Lieutenant Hoelle what was in the cards for the afternoon, and he said that eight of the boys, including himself, were going out to strafe some German tanks that had been reported working up into French territory. "We carry a cannon, which the P-40's don't, so we can really puncture a tank the size they use around here," he said. "We expect to meet some P-40's over the target, and they will stay up high and give us cover against any German fighters while we do a job on the tanks. Maybe I had better call the boys together and talk it over."

A couple of pilots had begun a game of blackjack on the top of the packing case, and he told them to quit, so he could spread a map on it. At that moment an enlisted man came in with a lot of mail and some Christmas packages that had been deposited by a courier plane. It was long after Christmas, but that made the things even more welcome, and all the pilots made a rush for their packages and started tearing them open. Earnhart, who was going on the strafe job, got some National Biscuit crackers and some butterscotch candy and a couple of tubes of shaving cream that he said he couldn't use because he had an electric razor, and the operations officer, a lieutenant named Lusk, got some very rich homemade cookies that an aunt and uncle had sent him from Denver. We were all gobbling butterscotch and cookies as we gathered round the map Hoelle had spread. It was about as formal an affair as looking at a road map to find your way to Washington, Connecticut, from New Milford. "We used to make more fuss over briefings in England," the intelligence officer said, "but when you're flying two or three times a day, what the hell?" He pointed out the place on the map where the tanks were supposed to be, and all the fellows said they knew where it was, having been there before. Hoelle said they would take off at noon. After a while he and the seven other boys went out onto the field to get ready, and I went with them. On the way there was more talk about P-38's and how some Italian prisoners had told their captors that the Italian army could win the war easy if it wasn't for those fork-tailed airplanes coming over and shooting them up, a notion that seemed particularly to amuse the pilots. Then I went to the P-38 squadron mess with Adler, who had just returned from patrol duty and wasn't going out on the strafe job, and Gustke, who was also remaining behind. This mess was relatively luxurious. They had tables with plates and knives and forks on them, so they had no mess tins to wash after every meal. "We live well here," Adler said. "Everything high-class."

"The place the planes are going is not very far away," Gustke said, "so they ought to be back around half past two."

When we had finished lunch, I took another stroll around the post. I was walking toward the P-38 squadron's operations shack when I saw the planes begin to return from the mission. The first that came in had only the nose wheel of its landing gear down. There was evidently something the matter with the two other wheels. The plane slid in on its belly and stopped in a cloud of dust. Another plane was hovering over the field. I noticed, just after I spotted this one, that a little ambulance was tearing out onto the field. Only one of the two propellers of this plane was turning, but it landed all right, and then I counted one, two, three others, which landed in good shape. Five out of eight. I broke into a jog toward the operations shack. Gustke was standing before the door looking across the field with binoculars. I asked him if he knew whose plane had belly-landed, and he said it was a Lieutenant Moffat's and that a big, rough Texas pilot the other fellows called Wolf had been in the plane that had come in with one engine out. "I see Earnhart and Keith and Carlton, too," he said, "but Hoelle and the other two are missing."

A jeep was coming from the field toward the operations shack, and when it got nearer we could see Wolf in it. He looked excited. He was holding his right forearm with his left hand, and when the jeep got up to the shack he jumped out, still holding his arm.

"Is it a bullet hole?" Gustke asked.

"You're a sonofabitch it's a bullet hole!" Wolf shouted. "The sonofa-bitching P-40's sonofabitching around! As we came in, we saw four fight-ers coming in the opposite direction and Moffat and I went up to look at them and they were P-40's, coming away. The other fellows was on the deck and we started to get down nearer them, to about five thousand, and these sonofabitching 190's came out of the sun and hit Moffat and me the first burst and then went down after the others. There was ground fire coming up at us, too, and the sonofabitches said we was going to be over friendly territory. I'm goddam lucky not to be killed."*

"Did we get any of them?" Gustke asked.

"I know I didn't get any," Wolf said, "but I saw at least four planes burning on the ground. I don't know who the hell they were."

By that time another jeep had arrived with Earnhart, looking utterly calm, and one of the mechanics from the field. "My plane is all right," Earnhart told Gustke. "All gassed up and ready to go. They can use that for patrol."

The telephone inside the shack rang. It was the post first-aid station calling to say that Moffat was badly cut up by glass from his windshield but would be all right. The mechanic said that the cockpit of Moffat's plane was knee-deep in hydraulic fluid and oil and gas. "No wonder the hydraulic system wouldn't work when he tried to get the wheels down," the mechanic said. The phone rang again. This time it was group opera-tions, calling for Earnhart, Keith, and Carlton, all three of them un-wounded, to go over there and tell them what had happened. The three pilots went away, and a couple of the men got Wolf back into a jeep and took him off to the first-aid station. Hoelle and the two other pilots were still missing. That left only Gustke and me, and he said in a sad young voice, like a boy whose chum has moved to another city, "Now we have lost our buddies."

A couple of days later I learned that Hoelle had bailed out in disputed territory and made his way back to our lines, but the two other boys are either dead or prisoners.

* Normal confusion.

NOT many Mondays ago I was standing in a chow line with my mess tins
at an airfield* in southern Tunisia, waiting to get into a dugout where
some mess attendants were ladling out a breakfast of stew and coffee. The
field is enormous, a naturally flat airdrome of white sand and alfa grass
that doesn't hold rainwater long enough to spoil the runways—terrain of
the kind a French writer once said looked like foamy seas. All around the
field there are bulky, reddish mountains. To the east, the sun was just
coming up over one of them, and the air was very cold. The mess shack
was covered on top and three sides by a mound of earth. It served officers
and men of a squadron of P-40 fighters, and on that particular Monday
morning I stood between a corporal named Jake Goldstein, who in civilian life had been a Broadway songwriter, and a private named John
Smith, of New Hope, Pennsylvania, who used to help his father, a con-
tractor, build houses. Goldstein told me about a lyric he had just written
for a song to be called "Bombs." "The music that I think of when it goes
through my head now," he said, "is kind of a little like the old tune called
'Smiles,' but maybe I can change it around later. The lyric goes:

> There are bombs that sound so snappy,
> There are bombs that leave folks sad,
> There are bombs that fell on dear old Dover,
> But those bombs are not so bad.

The idea is that the real bad bomb is when this girl quit me and blew up
my heart."

"It sounds great," I told the Corporal.

"It will be even bigger than a number I wrote called 'What Do You
Hear from Your Heart?'" Goldstein said. "Probably you remember it.
Bing Crosby sang it once on the Kraft Cheese Hour. If you happen to
give me a little writeup, remember that my name in the songwriting
business is Jack Gould." Private Smith started to tell me that he had once
installed some plumbing for a friend of mine, Sam Spewack, the writer, in
New Hope. "His wife, Bella, couldn't make up her mind where she
wanted the can," Smith said, "so I said—"

I never heard any more about Bella Spewack's plumbing, because
Major Robert Christman, the commanding officer of the squadron, came
up to me and said, "Well, it's a nice, quiet morning." He had his back to
the east. I didn't get a chance to answer him, because I started to run like
hell to get to the west side of the mound. A number of soldiers who had
been scattered about eating their breakfast off the tops of empty gasoline
cans had already started running and dropping their mess things. They
always faced eastward while they ate in the morning so that they could

* This time it was Thélepte, in Tunisia.

see the Messerschmitts come over the mountains in the sunrise. This morning there were nine Messerschmitts. By the time I hit the ground on the lee side of the mound, slender airplanes were twisting above us in a sky crisscrossed by tracer bullets—a whole planetarium of angry worlds and meteors. Behind our shelter we watched and sweated it out. It is nearly impossible to tell Messerschmitts from P-40's when they are maneuvering in a fight, except when one plane breaks off action and leaves its opponent hopelessly behind. Then you know that the one which is distanced is a P-40. You can't help yelling encouragement as you watch a fight, even though no one can hear you and you cannot tell the combatants apart. The Messerschmitts, which were there to strafe us, flew right over the mess shack and began giving the runways and the planes on the field a going-over.

We had sent up four planes on patrol that morning and they tried to engage the strafing planes, but other Germans, flying high to protect the strafers, engaged the patrol. Some "alert" planes that we had in readiness on the perimeter of the field took off in the middle of the scrap, and that was a pretty thing to watch. I saw one of our patrol planes come in and belly-land on the field, smoking. Then I saw another plane twisting out of the sky in a spin that had the soldiers yelling. We all felt that the spinning plane was a Messerschmitt, and it looked like a sure thing to crash into one of the mountains north of us. When the plane pulled out and disappeared over the summit, the yell died like the howl at Ebbets Field when the ball looks as if it's going into the bleachers and then is snagged by a visiting outfielder. It was a Messerschmitt, all right. A couple of minutes later every one of the German planes had disappeared, with our ships after them like a squad of heavy-footed comedy cops chasing small boys.

The fellows who had ducked for cover hoisted themselves off the ground and looked around for the mess things they had dropped. They were excited and sheepish, as they always are after a strafe party. It is humiliating to have someone run you away, so you make a joke about it. One soldier yelled to another, "When you said 'Flop!' I was there already!" Another, who spoke with a Brooklyn accent, shouted, "Jeez, those tracers looked just like Luna Park!"*

We formed the chow line again and one fellow yelled to a friend, "What would you recommend as a good, safe place to eat?"

"Lindy's, at Fifty-first Street," the other soldier answered.

"The way the guys ran, it was like a Christmas rush at Macy's," somebody else said.

Everybody tried hard to be casual. Our appetites were even better than they had been before, the excitement having joggled up our internal

---

* See note on p. 32. Luna was an amusement park at Coney Island, so famous that it gave its name to imitations all over Europe. Fireworks were a nightly feature, but they were pretty pallid compared to any respectable anti-aircraft barrage. Luna is no more.

secretions. There were arguments about whether the plane that had escaped over the mountain would crash before reaching the German lines. I
was scraping the last bits of stew from my mess tin with a sliver of hard
biscuit when a soldier came up and told me that Major——,* whom I
had never met, had been killed on the field, that five men had been
wounded, and that one A-20 bomber had been ruined on the ground.

After I had washed up my tins, I walked over to the P-40 squadron
operations shack, because I wanted to talk to a pilot familiarly known as
Horse about a fight he had been in two days before. The day it had
happened I had been visiting a P-38 squadron's headquarters on the field.
I had seen eight P-38's go out to attack some German tanks and only five
come back, two of them badly damaged. A lot of Focke-Wulf 190's had
attacked the P-38's over the target, and Horse and three other P-40 pilots,
who were protecting the 38's, had been up above the 190's. Horse was a
big fellow with a square, tan face and a blond beard. He came from
a town called Quanah, in Texas, and he was always showing his friends a
tinted picture of his girl, who was in the Waves. Horse was twenty-five,
which made him practically a patriarch in that squadron, and everybody
knew that he was being groomed to command a squadron of his own
when he got his captaincy. He was something of a wit. Once I heard one
of the other boys say that now that the field had been in operation for six
weeks, he thought it was time the men should build a sit-down latrine.
"The next thing we know," Horse said, "you'll be wanting to send home
for your wife."

I found Horse and asked him about the fight. He said he was sorry that
the 38's had had such a bad knock. "I guess maybe it was partly our
fault," he said. "Four of our ships had been sent out to be high cover for
the 38's. They didn't see any 38's or Jerries either, so when their gas was
beginning to run low they started for home.** Myself and three other
fellows had started out to relieve them and we passed them as they came
back. The 38's must have arrived over the tanks just then, and the 190's
must have been hiding at the base of a cloud bank above the 38's but far
below us. When we got directly over the area, we could see tracers flying
way down on the deck. The 190's had dived from the cloud and bounced
the 38's, who never had a chance, and the 38's were streaking for home.
We started down toward the 190's, but it takes a P-40 a long time to get
anywhere and we couldn't help. Then four more 190's dived from way up
top and bounced us. I looped up behind one of them as he dived. My two
wing men were right with me. I put a good burst into the sonofabitch and

* We were not allowed by the censor to mention names of casualties until they had
appeared in the lists published at home. Now I cannot fill in this blank, because I
forget the poor gentleman's name.
** See note p. 36 on confusion.

he started to burn, and I followed him down. I must have fired a hundred and twenty-five rounds from each gun. It was more fun than a county fair. Gray, my fourth man, put a lot of lead into another 190, and I doubt if it ever got home. The other two Jerries just kept on going."

The P-40 operations shack was set deep in the ground and had a double tier of bunks along three of its walls. Sand and grass were heaped over the top of the shack, and the pilots said that even when they flew right over it, it was hard to see, which cheered them considerably. The pilots were flying at least two missions a day and spent most of the rest of the time lying in the bunks in their flying clothes, under as many coats and blankets as they could find. The atmosphere in the shack was a thick porridge of dust diluted by thin trickles of cold air. Major Christman, the squadron leader, once said in a pleased tone, "This joint always reminds me of a scene in 'Journey's End.'"* The pilots, most of whom were in their earliest twenties, took a certain perverse satisfaction in their surroundings. "Here we know we're at war," one of them said to me. "Not that I wouldn't change for a room and bath at a good hotel."

During most of my stay at the field I lived not in the Journey's End shack but in one known as the Hotel Léon because technically it belonged to a French lieutenant named Léon,** a liaison officer between the French forces and our fliers. It was the newest and finest dugout on the field, with wooden walls and a wooden floor and a partition dividing it down the middle, and the floor was sunk about five feet below ground level. When I arrived at the field, there were plans to cover the part of the shack that projected above ground with sand, in which Léon intended to plant alfa. I was travelling with an Associated Press correspondent named Norgaard, and soon after our arrival Léon, a slender man with a thin, intelligent face and round, brown eyes, welcomed us to his palace. We put our stuff into the shack and emerged to find Léon throwing a modest shovelful of sand against one of the walls. Norgaard offered to help him. "There is only one shovel," Léon said with relief, pressing it into Norgaard's hands. "It is highly interesting for our comfort and safety that the house be covered entirely with sand. I am very occupied." Then he walked rapidly away, and Norgaard and I took turns piling sand around the Hotel Léon for endless hours afterward. Léon always referred to a telephone switchboard as a switching board, oil paper as oily paper, a pup tent as a puppy tent, and a bedding roll as a rolling bed.

After my talk with Horse, I walked over to the Hotel Léon and found it

---

* See note p. 32 on citations of the fictitious as criteria of reality.
** I suppressed his last name, Caplan, because he might have had relatives in France, who, if my piece in the *New Yorker* had reached France (highly unlikely), might have been made to suffer. Léon, when I saw him long after the war, was the number two man in the French Shell Oil Company—a *potentat petrolier*.

crowded, as it usually was. Only Léon and Norgaard and I, together with Major Philip Cochran and Captain Robert Wylie, lived in the hotel, but during the day Cochran and Léon used it as an office, and that was why it was crowded. When I first came to the field, it had been operating for six weeks practically as an outpost, for there was just a unit of American infantry, fifty miles to the southeast, between it and the region occupied by Rommel's army. Cochran, though only a major, had run the field for almost the entire period, but by the time I arrived he had reverted to the status of operations officer. The shack had telephone lines to detachments of French troops scattered thinly through the hills to our east, and they called up at all hours to tell Léon where German tanks were moving or to ask our people to do some air reconnaissance or drop bags of food to a platoon somewhere on a mountain. The French had no trucks to transport food. Sometimes Cochran flew with American transport planes to tell them where to drop parachute troops and sometimes he flew with bombers to tell them where to drop bombs. Because of Cochran's and Léon's range of activities, they always had a lot of visitors.

Attached to the partition in the shack were two field telephones, one of which answered you in French and the other in English. Two soldier clerks, who were usually pounding typewriters, sat on a bench in front of a shelf along one wall. One of them was Corporal Goldstein, the songwriter. The other was a private first class named Otto, who wore metal-rimmed spectacles with round lenses and belonged to the Pentecostal brethren, an evangelical sect which is against fighting and profanity. Otto owned some barber tools, and he cut officers' hair during office hours and enlisted men's at night. That morning he was cutting the hair of Kostia Rozanoff,* the commandant of the Lafayette Escadrille, a French P-40 outfit that was stationed at the field. Rozanoff was a blond, round-headed Parisian whose great-grandfather was Russian. Otto, perhaps taking a cue from the shape of Rozanoff's skull, had clipped him until he looked like Erich Von Stroheim, but there was no mirror, so Rozanoff was happy anyway. Cochran, dressed in a dirty old leather flying jacket, had just come back from a mission in the course of which he thought he had destroyed a 190, and was trying to tell about that while nearly everybody else in the shack was trying to tell him about the morning's strafing. Also in the shack was Colonel Edson D. Raff, the well-known parachutist, who had once unexpectedly found himself in command of all the American ground forces in southern Tunisia and for weeks had successfully bluffed enemy forces many times larger. He had flown in from his post in Gafsa in a small plane which he used as his personal transport. He was crowded in behind Otto's barbering elbow and was trying to talk to Cochran over Rozanoff's head. Raff is short and always wears a short carbine slung over his left shoulder, even indoors. He invariably flies very low in his plane

---

* Rozanoff survived to fly jets. He will recur.

to minimize the risk of being potted by a Messerschmitt. "I have one foot trailing on the ground," he says.

Lieutenant Colonel William Momyer, the commanding officer of the field, was sitting between Rozanoff and Corporal Goldstein, telling about a mission he had been on himself that morning, escorting a lot of A-20's over Kebili, a town where the Italians had begun to repair a dynamited causeway across the Chott Djerid. "I bet the wops will never get any workmen to go back to that place," Momyer said. "We scared hell out of them." Momyer had shot down a Junkers 88 and a Messerschmitt within a week. He was hot.

Among the others in the shack that morning were Norgaard, the Associated Press man, and a tall P-40 pilot named Harris, who kept asking Léon whether any French unit had telephoned to report finding the Messerschmitt he had been shooting at during the strafing episode, because he was sure it must have crashed. It was the Messerschmitt we had seen pull out of the spin over the mountain. The English-speaking telephone rang and Captain Wylie answered it. He has the kind of telephone voice that goes with a large, expensive office, which he probably had in civilian life. It was somebody up the line asking for Major ——, the officer who had just been machine-gunned in the strafing. "Major —— has been killed," Wylie said. "Is there anything I can do for you?"


There was a variety of stuff on the field when I was there. In addition to Christman's P-40 squadron and the Lafayette Escadrille, there was a second American P-40 squadron commanded by a Major Hubbard, which had a full set of pilots but only five ships. This was because the powers that be had taken away the other ships and given them to the Lafayettes in the interest of international good will. Hubbard's pilots were not sore at the Lafayettes, but they didn't think much of the powers that be. There was also a bomber squadron. The people on our field were not by any means sitting targets. They constantly annoyed the Germans, and that is why the Germans were so keen on "neutralizing" the field. But they didn't come back that day, and neither lunch nor dinner was disturbed.

The guests of the Hotel Léon often didn't go to the mess shack for dinner, because Léon would prepare dinner for them on the premises. He was a talented cook who needed the stimulation of a public, which was, that Monday evening, us. He also needed Wylie to keep the fire in the stove going, Cochran to wash dishes, and me and Norgaard to perform assorted chores. He got eggs from the Arabs and wine from a nearby French engineer unit, and he had gathered a choice assortment of canned goods from the quartermaster's stores. He also bought sheep and pigs from farmers. Léon's idea of a campaign supper was a *soufflé de poisson,* a *gigot,* and an *omelette brûlée à l'armagnac.* He made the *soufflé* out of canned salmon. The only trouble with dining at Léon's was that dinner was seldom ready before half past eight and it took until nearly midnight to clean up afterward.

During that Monday dinner we speculated on what the enemy would do next day. Norgaard said it was hell to have to get up early to catch the Germans' morning performance, but Cochran, the airfield's official prophet, and a successful one, said, "They'll want to make this one a big one tomorrow, so you can sleep late. They won't be over until two-thirty in the afternoon." Momyer, who was having dinner at the hotel that night, agreed that there would be something doing, but he didn't predict the time of day. Léon said, "I think also that there is something cooking in." Momyer decided to maintain a patrol of eight planes over the field all day. "Of course, maybe that's just what they want us to do, use our planes defensively, so we will fly less missions," he said, "but I think this time we ought to do it."

I had such faith in Cochran that it never occurred to me that the Germans would attack us before the hour he had named, and they didn't. The only enemy over the field the following morning was Photo Freddie, a German reconnaissance pilot who had become a local character. He came every morning at about forty thousand feet, flying a special Junkers 86 job so lightened that it could outclimb any fighter. The anti-aircraft guns would fire, putting a row of neat, white smoke puffs a couple of miles below the seat of Freddie's pants, the patrol planes would lift languidly in his direction, like the hand of a fat man waving away a fly, and Photo Freddie would scoot off toward Sicily, or wherever he came from, to develop his pictures, thus discovering where all the planes on the field were placed. The planes were always moved around after he left, and we used to wonder what the general of the Luftwaffe said to poor Freddie when the bombers failed to find the planes where he had photographed them. Now and then some pilot tried to catch Photo Freddie by getting an early start, climbing high above the field, and then stooging around until he appeared. Freddie, however, varied the hour of his matutinal visits, and since a P-40 cannot fly indefinitely, the pilot would get disgusted and come down. I do not think anybody really wanted to hurt Freddie anyway. He was part of the local fauna, like the pet hens that wandered about the field and popped into slit trenches when bombs began to fall.

At about twenty minutes past two that afternoon Norgaard and I returned to the Hotel Léon to do some writing. An Alsatian corporal in the French army was working in front of the shack, making a door for the entrance. The corporal had been assigned by the French command to build Léon's house, and he was a hard worker. He always kept his rifle by him while he was working. He had a long brown beard, which he said he was going to let grow until the Germans were driven out of Tunisia. Only Goldstein and Otto were inside the hut this time. I said to Goldstein,

"Why don't you write a new number called 'One-Ninety, I Love You'?" Otto, who had been reading the *Pentecostal Herald*, said, "I do not think that would be a good title. It would not be popular." At that precise moment all of us heard the deep woomp of heavy ack-ack. It came from one of the British batteries in the mountains around the field. We grabbed our tin hats and started for the doorway. By the time we got there, the usual anti-aircraft show was on. In the din we could easily distinguish the sound of our Bofors guns, which were making their peculiar seasick noises —not so much a succession of reports as one continuous retch. The floor of the shack, as I have said, was five feet below ground level and the Alsatian had not yet got around to building steps down to the entrance, so we had a nice, rectangular hole just outside from which to watch developments. The Germans were bombing now, and every time a bomb exploded, some of the sand heaped against the wooden walls was driven into the shack through the knotholes. The only trouble was that whenever a bomb went off we pulled in our heads and stopped observing. Then we looked out again until the next thump. After several of these thumps there was a straight row of columns of black smoke a couple of hundred yards to our right. I poked my head above ground level and discovered the Alsatian corporal kneeling and firing his rifle, presumably at an airplane which I could not see. The smoke began to clear and we hoisted ourselves out of the hole to try and find out what had happened. "I do not think I touched," the Alsatian said. A number of dogfights were still going on over the mountains. Scattered about the field, men, dragging themselves out of slit trenches, were pointing to the side of a mountain to the north, where there was smoke above a downed plane.

Léon had a little and old Citroën car, which he said had become, through constant association with the United States Army, "one naturalized small jeeps." He had left it parked behind the shack, and as Norgaard and I stood gawping about, Léon came running and shouted that he was going out to the fallen plane. We climbed into the naturalized jeeps and started across the field toward the mountainside. At one of the runways, we met a group of P-40 pilots, including Horse, and I yelled to them, "Was it theirs or ours?" "Ours, I think," Horse said. We kept on going. When we reached the other side of the field, we cut across country, and Léon could not make much speed. A couple of soldiers with rifles thumbed a ride and jumped on the running boards. As we went out across plowed fields and up the mountain toward the plane, we passed dozens of soldiers hurrying in the same direction.

When we arrived where the plane had fallen, we found three trucks and at least fifty men already there. The plane had been a Messerschmitt 109 belonging to the bombers' fighter escort. Flames were roaring above the portion deepest in the earth, which I judged was the engine. Screws, bolts, rings, and unidentifiable bits of metal were scattered over an area at least seventy-five yards square. Intermingled with all this were widely scattered red threads, like the bits left in a butcher's grinder when he has finished preparing an order of chopped steak. "He never even tried to pull out," a soldier said. "He must have been shot through the brain. I seen the whole thing. The plane fell five thousand feet like a hunk of lead." There was a sour smell over everything—not intolerable, just sour. "Where is the pilot?" Norgaard asked. The soldier waved his hand with a gesture that included the whole area. Norgaard, apparently for the first time, noticed the red threads. Most of the soldiers were rummaging amid the wreckage, searching for souvenirs. Somebody said that the pilot's automatic pistol, always the keepsake most eagerly sought, had already been found and appropriated. Another soldier had picked up some French and Italian money. How these things had survived the pilot's disintegration I do not know. While the soldiers walked about, turning over bits of the plane with their feet, looking for some object which could serve as a memento, an American plane came over and everybody began to run before someone recognized it for what it was. Just as we came back, a soldier started kicking at something on the ground and screaming. He was one of the fellows who had ridden out on our running boards. He yelled, "There's the sonofabitch's God-damn guts! He wanted my guts! He nearly had my guts, God damn him!" Another soldier went up to him and bellowed, "Shut up! It ain't nice to talk that way!" A lot of other men began to gather around. For a minute or so the soldier who had screamed stood there silently, his shoulders pumping up and down, and then he began to blubber.

Léon picked up a large swatch of the Messerschmitt's tail fabric as a trophy, and as the soldiers walked away from the wreck most of them carried either similar fragments or pieces of metal. After a while Norgaard and I climbed into Léon's car and the three of us started back toward the field. When we arrived, we learned that a lieutenant named Walter Scholl, who had never been in a fight before, had shot down the Messerschmitt. He was the fellow who, in the Cornell-Dartmouth football game of 1940, threw the famous fifth-down touchdown pass for Cornell, the one that was completed for what was considered a Cornell victory until movies of the game showed that it shouldn't have been Cornell's ball at all and the decision had to be reversed. But this was one win that they couldn't take away from him. Two other pilots had shot down two Junkers 88 bombers. One of our planes on the ground had been destroyed, and a slit trench had caved in on two fellows, nearly frightening them to death before they could be dug out.

NORGAARD often said that the country reminded him of New Mexico, and with plenty of reason. Both are desert countries of mountains and mesas, and in both there are sunsets that owe their beauty to the dust in the air. The white, rectangular Arab houses, with their blue doors, are like the houses certain Indians build in New Mexico, and the Arabs' saddle blankets and pottery and even the women's silver bracelets are like Navajo things. The horses, which look like famished mustangs, have the same lope and are similarly bridlewise; burros are all over the place, and so is cactus. These resemblances are something less than a coincidence, because the Moors carried their ways of house-building and their handicraft patterns and even their breed of horses and method of breaking them to Spain, and the Spaniards carried them to New Mexico eight hundred years later.° All these things go to make up a culture that belongs to a high plateau country where there are sheep to furnish wool for blankets and where people have too little cash to buy dishes in a store, where the soil is so poor that people have no use for heavy plow horses but want a breed that they can ride for long distances and that will live on nearly nothing.

"This horse is young," an Arab once said to Norgaard and me as he showed us a runty bay colt tied in front of a combined general store and barbershop in a village about a mile from the airfield. "If I had had a little barley to feed him, he would be bigger, but what barley we had we have ourselves eaten. It is a poor country."

We used to go down to this village to get eggs when we were too lazy to make the chow line for breakfast or when we felt hungry at any time of day. We'd take them back to the shack and cook them. Solitary Arabs squat along the roadside all over North Africa, waiting for military vehicles. When one comes into sight, the Arab pulls an egg out from under his rags and holds it up between thumb and forefinger like a magician at a night club. The price of eggs—always high, of course—varies in inverse ratio to the distance from a military post. Near big towns that are a long way from any post the Arabs get only five francs (ten cents at the new rate of exchange) for an egg, but in villages close to garrisons eggs are sometimes hard to find at any price. Norgaard and I followed a standard protocol to get them. First we went into the general store and barbershop, which was just a couple of almost empty rooms that were part of a mud house, and shook hands with all the male members of the establishment. Naturally, we never saw any of the females. Then we presented a box of matches to the head of the house, an ex-soldier who spoke French, and he invited us to drink coffee. The Arabs have better coffee and more sugar than the Europeans in North Africa. While we drank the coffee, we sat with the patriarch of the family on a white iron bed of European manufacture. The patriarch had a white beard and was always knitting socks; he stopped only to scratch himself. Once, as we were drinking coffee, we watched our French-speaking friend shave a customer's head. He simply started each stroke at the top of the cranium and scraped downward. He used no lather; the customer moistened his own poll with spittle

---

° The cactus, though, was imported *from* Latin America into North Africa, where it is considered a prime fodder plant, particularly appreciated by camels.

after each stroke of the razor. Once, when the customer made a particularly awful face, all the other Arabs sitting around the room laughed. During the coffee-drinking stage of the negotiations we presented the Arabs with a can of fifty English cigarettes. After that they presented us with ten to fifteen eggs. Soldiers who were not such good friends of theirs usually got twenty eggs for fifty cigarettes, but it always costs something to maintain one's social life. One day I asked the barber why the old man scratched himself, and he said, laughing, "Because of the black spots. We all have them, and they itch." With much hilarity the Arabs showed us the hard, black spots, apparently under their skins, from which they were suffering. I judged the trouble to be a degenerate form of the Black Death, tamed during the centuries by the rugged constitutions of our hosts. Norgaard thought that the spots were just chiggers.

The Germans had come over our airfield on a Monday morning and strafed it and they had come back on Tuesday afternoon and bombed the place. They were going to start an offensive in southern Tunisia, we later learned, so they wanted to knock out this, the most advanced American field. On Wednesday morning the Germans made no attack. That afternoon Norgaard and I decided that we needed some eggs, so we walked down to the Arab village. I carried the eggs home in my field hat, a visored cap which has long flaps to cover your neck and ears when it is cold and which makes a good egg bag. We got back to the Hotel Léon between five and six o'clock. Major Cochran was out flying, and Léon was out foraging. Jake and Otto had gone to chow. There was less than an hour of daylight left.

Cochran, with his fine instinct for divining what the Germans were likely to do, had been sure that they would come over for the third day in succession, and Lieutenant Colonel William Momyer, the commanding officer of the field, had maintained a patrol of P-40's over the field all day. Cochran was among those taking their turns on patrol duty now. In forty minutes more all the planes would have to come down, because the field had no landing lights. And nothing had happened yet.

The walk had made Norgaard and me hungry and we decided to have our eggs immediately. We threw some kindling wood in the stove to stir the fire up and I put some olive oil in the mess tin in which I was going to scramble the eggs. The olive oil belonged to Léon. I took the lid off the hole in the top of the stove, put the mess tin over the hole, and broke all the eggs into the oil. I think there were eleven of them. They floated around half submerged, and although I stirred them with a fork, they didn't scramble. We decided that I had used too much oil, so we added some cheese to act as a cement. Before the cheese had time to take effect, we heard a loud explosion outside—plainly a bomb—and felt the shack rock. Norgaard grabbed his tin hat and ran out the door to look, and I was just going to follow him when I reflected that if I left this horrible brew on the stove hole a spark might ignite the oil and thus set fire to the shack. I carefully put the mess on a bench and replaced the lid on the stove. I put on my helmet and followed Norgaard out into a kind of foxhole outside our door. More bombs exploded and then all we could hear was the racket of the Bofors cannon and .50 calibre machine guns defending the field. I went back inside, removed the stove lid, and put the eggs on again. Just as some warmth began to return to the chill mess, another stick of bombs went off. In the course of the next minute or so, I repeated my entire routine. Before I finished cooking dinner, I had to repeat it three times more. Finally the eggs and the cheese stuck together after a fashion and I drained the oil off. Then, since no bombs had dropped for a couple of minutes, I poured half the concoction into Norgaard's canteen cup, I put what was left in my mess tin, and we ate.

After we had eaten, we left the shack and started toward the large, round pit, some fifty yards away, which served as a control room for the field. Night had closed in. There had been no firing now for ten minutes, but as we approached the pit, our anti-aircraft opened up again, firing from all around the field simultaneously. The Bofors tracer shells, which look like roseate Roman candles, reminded me of the fireworks on the lagoon at the World's Fair in Flushing. The burst ended as abruptly as it had begun, except that one battery of .50's kept on for an extra second or two and then stopped in an embarrassed manner.

We saw a lot of our pilots clustered around the pit. A corporal named Dick usually stood in the pit talking to our planes in the air by radio telephone, but Major Robert Christman, the C.O. of one of the post's fighter squadrons, was in Dick's place. I recognized Christman's voice as he spoke into the telephone, asking, "Did you see the gunfire? Did you see the gunfire?" You wouldn't ask a Jerry that if you were shooting at him, so I knew they were firing the anti-aircraft guns to light one or more of our planes home. Christman asked again, "Did you see the gunfire? Did you see the gunfire?" Then he said to somebody else in the pit, probably Dick, "Hold this a minute." He stuck his head up over the side of the pit and shouted in the direction of a nearby dugout, "They say they saw the fire! Cochran's going to lead in and land to show the other ship the way! Lord, how that Cochran swears when he's excited! Tell the ack-ack to hold everything!" The switchboard through which the control room communicated with all the ack-ack batteries was in the dugout. Nothing was convenient on that field. It sometimes seemed that one of the pilots had scratched the whole thing out of the ground with a broken propeller blade after a forced landing.

We could see a plane showing red and green lights slowly circling over the field, descending gradually in long, deliberate spirals, as if the pilot wanted somebody to follow him. Then there was a blast of machine-gun fire and a fountain of tracers sprayed up from a distant edge of the field. "God damn them!" Christman yelled. "Tell them to hold that fire! What do they want to do—shoot Phil down?" The plane coasted slowly, imperturbably lower. It was Cochran's firm belief, I knew, that the ack-ack on the field had never hit anything, so he probably wasn't worried. The plane skimmed over the surface of the field. There was one pitiful red light on the field for it to land by. "He'll never make it that way," a pilot near me said. "What the hell is he doing? He'll overshoot. No, there he goes up again."

In a minute Christman, back at the phone once more, said, "Cochran went up because the other fellow couldn't see him. The other ship says he saw the gunfire, though. Now he wants a burst on the southern edge of the field only." Somebody in the switchboard dugout yelled, "Come on now! Battery C only, Battery C only! Everybody else *hold* it!" All the guns on the field immediately fired together. I could hear Momyer's voice yelling in the dugout, "God damn it, I'll have them all court-martialled!" Christman shouted, "He says he saw it and now he can see Cochran! He's coming in!" Cochran was again circling in the blackness above the field. The pilot next to me said, "This is sure sweating it out." I recognized him, partly by his voice and partly by the height of his shoulders, as Horse, the big Texan who wore a square beard.

"Did we get any of theirs?" I asked Horse.

"Yes, sir," Horse said. "Bent got one for sure. He's in already. And a French post has telephoned that another one is down near there in flames and that pilot out there with Cochran had one smoking. He must have chased it so far he couldn't get back before dark. Must have forgot himself. I don't rightly know who he is."

The ack-ack batteries fired again. They apparently did what was wanted this time, because nobody cursed. Christman called up from the pit, "They want one more burst, all together, and then they're coming in!" The message was relayed and the ack-ack fired another salvo. Now there were two planes, both showing lights, moving in the sky above the field, one high and one low. "Cochran's coming in," Horse said. "Look at him. Just like it was day and he could see everything." The lower pair of lights drifted downward, straightened out and ran forward along the field, and stopped. The other lights slowly followed them down, seemed to hesitate a moment, then slanted toward the ground, and coasted into a horizontal. "Good landing," Horse said. "We sure sweated that one." The second pilot to land turned out to be a lieutenant named Thomas, who had become too absorbed in the pursuit of a Junkers 88 to turn back until he had shot it down. That made three Junkers for us, each carrying a crew of four men. I learned that the German bombs had spoiled, to use the airmen's term, two of our planes on the field. A couple of minutes later a jeep that had gone out to meet Cochran's plane brought him to where the rest of us were standing. He is a short, box-chested man, and the two or three flying jackets he was wearing made him look shorter and stockier than he really is. He was feeling good. "I'm sorry I cursed you out, Bob! I was excited!" he yelled down into the control pit to Christman. Momyer, who had come out of the dugout, made as if to grab Cochran and hug him, but stopped in astonishment when he heard Cochran being so polite. It seemed to remind him of something. Looking rather thoughtful, he went back into the dugout and called up the lieutenant colonel in command of the ack-ack, which he had been abusing. "Thank you very much, Colonel," I heard him say. "Your boys certainly saved the day."

That evening was a happy one. Léon's shack was crowded with pilots talking about the successful fight and scrambling eggs and eating them out of mess tins. Cochran felt so good that he decided to have his first haircut since he had left New York three months before, so he sent over to the enlisted men's quarters for Otto to do the job. Otto is a young man with reddish hair and white eyebrows and a long nose, and he had a habit of getting interested in a conversation between two senior officers and breaking into it. Once, hearing Colonel Edson D. Raff, the parachute-troop commander, telling Lieutenant Colonel Momyer that he could take Tunis with no more than four hundred and fifty men, Otto blurted out, "How can you be so sure?" Aside from this failing he is a good soldier and when he gives a haircut he really cuts off hair, so nobody can say he is looking for a return engagement in the near future.

It was well after dark when Léon came in from his foraging, which had been a success too. "I have bought three small peegs," he announced triumphantly, "and when they are theek enough we shall eat them." He had left them in the care of a *hôtelier* in a town a few miles away. They were subsequently taken, and presumably eaten, by the Germans. At the time, however, Léon thought it a safe *logement* for the pigs. "I have also talked with the aide of General Koeltz," Léon said to Cochran and Momyer, "and he says that in the case any pilot sees any trucks moving on the road of which we have spoken yesterday, he is allowed to shoot without permission." While Otto cut Cochran's hair, we added up the box score of the three-day German attack on the field. The home team felt that it had done pretty well. During the Monday strafing the Germans had spoiled one of our planes on the field and another in the air and had killed one officer, a major, with machine-gun bullets. We had merely damaged one of their fighters. On Tuesday, while they had spoiled two more of our planes on the ground with bombs, we had shot down a Messerschmitt 109 and two Junkers 88's. That meant that we had lost a total of three planes but only one life while they had lost three planes and nine lives. One of our missions had also destroyed a Focke-Wulf 190 on Monday morning and a Messerschmitt had been badly damaged in the dogfight that had accompanied the strafing of our field. Wednesday evening we had destroyed three more planes and twelve men, and the Germans had succeeded only in damaging two planes on the ground, which gave us an imposing lead. "They won't be over tomorrow morning," Cochran said. "Maybe not all day. They'll want to think things over and try something big to make up for their losses and get the lead back. They'll be like a guy doubling his bet in a crap game."

That field had been fought over many times before in the course of history and a corner of it had been the site of a Numidian city. Bent, a pilot who talked with a British accent and had once done some digging among old ruins in England, said that every time he flew over that corner he could plainly see the gridiron pattern of the ancient streets on the ground. Horse, the bearded pilot, was irreverent about Bent's claims. "Maybe a couple of thousand years from now," he said, "people will dig around this same field and find a lot of C-ration cans that we've left and attribute them to archeology. They'll say, 'Those Americans must surely have been a pygmy race to wear such small helmets. It scarcely seems possible they had much brains. No wonder they rode around in such funny airplanes as the P-40.'"*

Another officer who turned up in Léon's shack that evening was Major (afterward Lieutenant Colonel) Vincent Sheean, who always points out these days that he was once a correspondent himself. He said he had been driving in a jeep on a road near the field when the bombing started, so he had stopped and jumped into a ditch. Sheean had come down from the second highest headquarters of the African Air Forces to see that the French pilots of the Lafayette Escadrille, which had recently arrived at our field, received understanding and kind treatment from their American comrades. A couple of the Lafayette pilots happened to be in the shack when he arrived; they had received so much kind treatment that they could hardly remember the words of "Auprès de Ma Blonde," which they were trying to teach to Momyer on a purely phonetic basis.

The next day, Thursday, was as quiet as Cochran had said it would be. The Germans left us completely alone. In the morning the Lafayette Escadrille fellows went on their first mission, covering a French local offensive in a mountain pass, and returned without meeting any enemy aircraft.

The exposed position of our mess shack had begun to worry Major Christman's men after the strafing we had received the Monday before, and he had ordered the chow line transferred to a place called the Ravine, a deep, winding gulch on the other side of the high road along one end of the field. Most of the men lived in the Ravine and felt safe there. They had scooped out caves in its sides and used their shelter halves to make doors. One stretch of the gully was marked by a sign that said "Park

* I was back in 1956, but even the C-ration cans are gone. The natives of those parts are extremely poor, and may have thought even tin cans worth salvaging.

Avenue." Sheean and I stood in the chow line for lunch and then took an afternoon stroll along Park Avenue. Afterward I went back to Léon's shack to write a letter and found it crowded, as usual. An engineer officer who had been at the field a couple of days was asking Cochran how he could be expected to get on with the construction job he had been sent there to do if new bomb holes appeared on the field every day and his detachment had to fill them up. "We've been filling up bomb holes ever since we been here, and it looks like we won't get a chance to do anything else," the engineer said. "My colonel sent me down here to build revetments for airplanes and he's going to expect me back soon." Another visitor, a captain in the Royal Engineers, asked him if there were any unexploded bombs on the runways. Men on the field always referred to this British captain as the booby-trap man, the planting of fiendish traps for the enemy being his specialty, and added with respect, "Even the parachute troops say he's crazy." He had made several jumps with Colonel Raff's parachutists to install his humorous devices in places where he thought German soldiers would later get involved with them. The American officer told him that there were several unexploded bombs on the runways and that he had marked off their positions with empty oil drums.

"But haven't you removed the fuses?" the booby-trap man asked with obvious astonishment.

"To hell with that!" his American colleague said with feeling. "They won't do any harm if they do go off. It's a big field."

"Oh, but they'll make quite a lot of noise," the booby-trap man said, still vaguely unhappy.

The American officer looked at the booby-trap man and Cochran as if they were both lunatics and went out of the hut without saying anything more. "How *extraordinary!*" the booby-trap man said. "He didn't even seem interested." He sounded hurt, like a young mother who has just learned that a visitor does not care for babies.

The booby-trap man looked like a conventional sort of Englishman, with a fair, boyish face and a shy smile. He spoke with the careful accent of the north countryman who has been to a university and he did not himself use the term "booby trap." He preferred to call his darlings, variously, trip mechanisms, push mechanisms, pull mechanisms, and anti-personnel switches. Trip mechanisms, for instance, are the ones soldiers inadvertently set off by stumbling over a concealed wire, and pull mechanisms are those they explode by picking up some innocent-seeming object like a corned-beef tin. The captain was an amateur botanist and seldom went out without a couple of pocketfuls of small devices to set about the countryside in likely spots as he ambled along collecting specimens of Tunisian grasses. I asked him that afternoon how he had started on what was to become his military career, and he said with his shy smile, "I expect it was at public school, when I used to put hedgehogs in the other boys' beds. After a while the hedgehogs began to pall and I invented a system for detuning the school piano, so that when the music master sat down to play 'God Save the King' it sounded god-awful."

"I sometimes try to imagine what your married life will be like, Captain," Cochran said. "Someday the baby will be in the crib and your wife will go to pick it up and the whole house will blow up because you've wired the baby to a booby trap."

"I trust I shall be able to restrain my professional instincts to fit the circumstances of domestic life," the booby-trap man said rather stiffly. He was a man who really took his branch of warfare seriously.

SLEEP in the Hotel Léon was usually interrupted in the gray hour before dawn by the jangle of a field telephone that spoke French. Then Léon would sit up and pull the telephone from the holster in which it hung at the foot of his bed. He slept wearing all the clothes he possessed, which included several sweaters, a long military overcoat, and a muffler. When he grabbed the phone, he would say, "*Allo! Oui?*" (The rest of us sometimes would sing "Sweet Allo, Oui" to the tune of "Sweet Eloise.") The French voice at the other end of the phone was almost always audible, and, so that the half-awake American officers in the shack would get the idea of what was going on, Léon would reply in a hybrid jargon. He would say, for example, "One *ennemi appareil* flying sousewest over point 106? *Merci, mon capitaine.*" Then he would hang up and fall back into bed, muttering, "*Imbécile*, why he don't fly west? He will be losted."

A partition divided Léon's shack into a bedroom, in which four of us slept side by side, and an office, in which only two slept. In the bedroom were Léon, Major Cochran, Norgaard, and myself. Captain Robert Wylie and Vincent Sheean slept in the office. We would try to ignore Léon's first morning call, but before long there would be another; Cochran would be asking what was going on, and we would hear the roar of the motors down on the field being warmed up for the dawn patrol and the morning missions. Then we would hear Wylie clattering around our stove in his G.I. shoes and there would be a glow in the shack when he put the match to the paper with which he started the fire. Wylie, who wasn't a flying officer, always tried to have the shack warm by the time Cochran got up, and he wanted the Major to stay in bed until the last minute. He was as solicitous as a trainer with a favorite colt, and the rest of us benefited from the care he took of Cochran, because we didn't get up early, either. Wylie is a wiry man with a high forehead and a pepper-and-salt mustache. He wears glasses and looks like an advertising artist's conception of an executive who is in good humor because he has had an excellent night's sleep owing to Sanka. He is a highly adaptable man. After Wylie had puttered around for a while, we would sit up one by one and stretch and complain about being disturbed or about the cold and then go outside to wash. Mornings on which the anti-aircraft opened up against early visitors, the tempo was accelerated. Cochran undressed at night by loosening the knot in his tie and drew it tight again in the morning as a sign that he was dressed. These were symbolic gestures he never omitted.

On the morning of the fifth and last day of our small private war, it was the anti-aircraft that brought us out of bed. We scrambled for the door, lugging our tin hats, our toothbrushes, and our canteens. The Germans were already almost over our field, but they were quite high, since our patrol planes had engaged them on the way in and they could not break off the fight to strafe us. The German planes were single-engined fighters, which sometimes carry wing or belly bombs, but this time they were not bombing. Some of the defending planes were marked with the tricolor *cocarde* of the French Army. It was, I suppose, a historic combat, because the pilots of the Lafayette Escadrille, which was stationed at the field, were making the first French air fight against the Germans since the armistice of 1940. The Escadrille, which had been equipped with a number of our Curtiss P-40's in Morocco, had been with us only a few days.

As we watched, a plane fell, apparently far on the other side of a ridge of mountains near the field, and we yelled happily, thinking it was a Messerschmitt. After the fight we were to learn that it had been a P-40 with a French sergeant pilot. Cochran kept up an expert running commentary on what all the pilots were trying to do, but he frequently didn't know which were French and which German. During the battle we simultaneously watched and brushed our teeth. A couple of the French planes landed on the field while the others were still fighting, so we knew that they must have been shot up. Finally, one group of planes above the field started away and the others chased them, but the first planes simply outclimbed their pursuers and left them behind; then there was no longer any doubt about which were Messerschmitts and which were Curtisses. One German plane remained over the field, at perhaps thirty thousand feet, even after the rest of the invaders had disappeared. "That's what kills me," Cochran said, pointing to the lone plane. "There's that sucker stooging around and casing the joint for a future job and he's so high nobody can bother him." Finally the stooge, evidently having found out all he wanted to know, took his leisurely departure.

A group of P-40's rose to relieve the Lafayettes, and the French planes came buzzing in like bees settling on a sugared stick. In a few minutes Kostia Rozanoff, commandant of the Escadrille, and his pilots had gathered in Léon's shack to discuss the fight. All of them had had combat experience in 1939 and 1940, but the engagement this morning had been the *rentrée*, and they were as excited as if they had never seen a Messerschmitt before. Despite the fact that they were old hands, Cochran said, they had fought recklessly, climbing up to meet the Messerschmitts instead of waiting until the Germans dived. "If they don't dive," Cochran had frequently warned his own pilots, "you just don't fight." The French

pilots' ardor had got them a beating, for besides the pilot whom we had
seen fall and who, Rozanoff said, had not bailed out and was quite certainly killed, the two planes that had landed during the combat were
riddled and would be of no use except for salvage, and one of their pilots
had been wounded. The Germans apparently had suffered no damage
at all. Rozanoff, a chunky, blond man who gets his name, as well as his
coloring and his high cheekbones, from his Russian ancestry, is thirty-
seven and has a deep voice, like Chaliapin's. He said that the pilot who
had been killed was his wing man and he could not understand how he
had failed to see the Messerschmitt that had attacked him from the rear.
"I cry him turn," Rozanoff kept saying. "I turn. He turns not. Poor little
one."

It was extremely sad that the first Escadrille combat had not been a
victory; it would have been such a fine story to bolster French morale all
over the world. I remembered the sergeant pilot, who had been a likable
fellow. An officer of the district gendarmerie brought the sergeant's wed-
ding ring back to the field later in the morning.


My friend Norgaard and I had chosen that Friday for our departure
from the field. We were going in to the big city, where the censors and
the cable offices were, to write some stuff and get it off. There was air
transportation between our field and the more settled places to the west,
where staff officers and diplomats lived, but the service did not run on a
formal schedule. Big Douglas transports skimmed in over the mountains
once and sometimes twice a day, carrying mail and supplies, and they
usually had room for passengers going back. They came at a different
hour each day to make it as hard as possible for the Germans to waylay
them. When they came, they stayed merely as long as was necessary, and
the only way to be sure of a ride was to have your bedding roll made up
and to stay near the landing field waiting for the transports to appear.
When they did, an officer would drive you and your luggage out to them
in a jeep and you would get your stuff aboard. Norgaard and I hung
around in front of our shack that morning, waiting. As the day wore on, a
strong wind came up and blew great clouds of sand. At about eleven
o'clock two transports arrived, escorted by some Spitfires. Cochran had
planned to drive us down to the transports, but he was called to the
telephone, and Christman said that he would drive us instead.

When we arrived where the transports were standing on the runway,
the transport captain, whose name, I noted from the leather strip on the
breast of his flying jacket, was Lively, came over to the jeep and asked
where his Spits could get gas. His ship was named the Scarlett O'Hara.
He and Christman started discussing what was the quickest way to get
the gas. Christman and Norgaard and I stayed in the jeep. Dust was

blowing over the field a mile a minute. Suddenly Christman looked over his shoulder, called on God, and vanished. Within a moment Lively was also gone. I turned around to speak to Norgaard, and discovered that he too had evaporated. I hate to sit in an empty jeep when I don't know why the other passengers have jumped. I do not remember actually getting out myself, but I know that I was already running when I heard somebody yell, "Hit the dirt!" Under the circumstances, this sounded so sensible that I bellyflopped to the ground, and I landed so hard that I skinned my knees and elbows. No surface in the world offers less cover than a runway. I regretted that my body, which is thick, was not thinner. I could guess what had happened: German strafers had ridden in on the dust storm and nobody had seen them until they opened fire. I knew that the very nasty noises above me were being made by airplane cannon and that the even nastier ones close to me came from the detonation of the small explosive shells they fire. The strafers, I figured, were heading for the transports—large, expensive, unarmored jobs that you could punch holes in with a beer-can opener. I was therefore in line with the target and was very sorry to be where I was.

As soon as there was a lull in the noises overhead, I got up and ran toward the edge of the runway to get away from the transports, but more noises came before I made it, so I flopped again. After they had passed, I got up and ran off the runway. I saw a soldier in a fine, large hole nearly six feet deep. He shouted, "Come right in, sir!" You can have Oscar of the Waldorf any time; I will always remember that soldier as my favorite host. I jumped in and squeezed up against him. Almost immediately the noises came a third time and two transport pilots jumped down on my back. I was astonished that I had been able to outrun such relatively young men. I was 38.

By this time all of our machine guns along the edges of the field were firing away, and there was a fourth pass, as the fliers say, and a loud crash, as if one of the Germans had dropped a bomb. A minute or two later the noise began to die down. Looking up from the bottom of the hole, we could see a man descending in a parachute. The big, white chute was swaying this way and that in the wind. The man had an awful time landing. We could see that even from a distance. The chute dragged him and bounced hell out of him after he landed. Afterward, word got around the field that he was an American. I didn't find out until a couple of days later, though, that the man with the chute had been Horse. In landing, he hit his head against the ground and suffered a concussion of the brain. They put him in an ambulance and started for the nearest hospital, which was forty miles by road, but he had bad luck. The Germans had been strafing that road, too, that morning, and when the ambulance got within five miles of the hospital, it was blocked by two burning ammunition trucks. The shells on the trucks were exploding. The squadron surgeon and the ambulance-driver put Horse on a stretcher and carried him around the trucks to a safe point on the other side, and an ambulance from the hospital came out to pick him up, but by the time it got there he was dead.*

When the shooting at the field was over, the pilots and the soldier and I got out of the hole and walked back toward the transports, which were still there. Norgaard climbed out of another hole not far away. He said that when he had jumped out of the jeep he had crawled under it, and there he had found a transport lieutenant who had had the same idea. They had given up the jeep after the first pass and run for it, just as I had already done. We stared at the parallel furrows the Messerschmitt cannon had plowed down the runway, as if they had been the teeth of a rake, and ourselves the field mice between them. The transport boys borrowed our jeep to get gas for the Spits, which had been immobilized during the raid because their tanks were empty. When the boys came back, we climbed into one of the transports. The big planes took off almost immediately. "Leave them laughing," Norgaard said to me when he recovered sufficient breath to say anything.


We learned later that the strafing had been done by eight Messerschmitts flying in four loose pairs, and that was why there had been four passes. Another Messerschmitt, making a run by itself, had dropped one bomb, ineffectually. There had also been a high cover of Messerschmitts; one of them had accounted for Horse. We were told that Cochran had said, with a hint of admiration in his voice, "It is getting so that the Germans patrol our field for us." A lot of Air Force generals who were on a tour of inspection visited the field shortly after we left, said that the situation was very grave, and left, too. This point in the war over the field may be compared to the one in a Western movie at which the villain has kicked hell out of the heroine and just about wrestled her to the brink of ruin in a locked room.**

At about two-thirty that same afternoon the Lafayette Escadrille was patrolling the field, in the company of two pilots from the American P-40 squadron commanded by Major Hubbard. This squadron had its full complement of pilots but only five planes. The pilots took turns flying the five ships, so they were not getting a great deal of practice. Nevertheless, Hubbard's squadron had already scored two victories that week. The two American pilots in the air were Hubbard and a man named Beggs. Two of their mates, Boone and Smith, were on the ground on alert call, sitting in their planes ready to reinforce the patrol if they were called.

* Horse's square name was Alton B. Watkins, but hardly anybody at Thélepte knew. Father McCreedy buried him under a metal plate marked "Horace."
** See note on p. 32.

This field didn't have one of those elaborate radio airplane-detectors that warn swank airdromes of the approach of enemy aircraft. It had to rely on its patrol system and on tips that watchers telephoned in. The tipsters were not infallible, as Norgaard and I had noticed that morning, and in the afternoon they slipped up again. Ten Junkers 88 bombers unexpectedly appeared, flying toward the field at three thousand feet. There was an escort of four fighters, unusually small for so many bombers, flying high above them and, as someone described it to me, acting oddly uninterested. The Frenchmen on patrol, also flying high, made one swipe at the escort and it disappeared, not to be seen again. Nine of the bombers were flying in three loose V's and one ship was trailing the third V. Hubbard took the bomber on the right of the first V and shot it down. Beggs got the middle one and a Frenchman knocked down the one on the left. The other Junkers had begun to drop their bombs. Boone and Smith came up off the field through the falling bombs to join the battle. Hubbard shot down another plane, and Boone, who had never fired a shot at a man or a plane before, came up behind one Junkers and blasted it out of the sky; it caromed against another Junkers on the way down, which gave Boone two planes with one burst of fire. He went on to destroy two more. Smith, opening fire at extreme range for fear that he would be shut out, blew the rudder off another Junkers, which also crashed. The tenth Junkers headed for home, but it never got there; the French picked off that one. It was the jack pot, ten out of ten. It was also the end of the five-day war over our airfield. No producer of Westerns ever wound up a film more satisfactorily.[*] The Germans stayed away, in fact, for nineteen days and then came back only once, for a quick sneak raid.

Of the ten German bomber crews, only four men came out of the fight alive and two of these died in the hospital. The two others said that the ten bombers had been escorted by four Italian Macchi C. 202 fighters, which had deserted them. Why the Luftwaffe should have entrusted four Macchis with the protection of ten Junkers 88's is harder to explain than the result. The Germans, fortunately for our side, sometimes vary their extreme guile with extreme stupidity.

I didn't have a chance to return to the airfield for about ten days, and then I stopped in on my way down to Gafsa, where the Americans were supposed to be launching a ground offensive. Captain Wylie, who told me about the big day at the field, said that Boone had come into the operations shack looking rather incredulous himself. "Probably I'm crazy," he had said to Wylie, "but I think I just shot down four planes."[**] The Frenchmen thought up a gag. They said it was a victory for three nations

---

[*] See note on p. 32. From here on, I will cease to call attention to this phenomenon.
[**] His luck did not last. He was killed a couple of weeks later.

—"The Americans shot down seven planes, we shot down two, and the Italians shot down the tenth so the crew couldn't tell on them."

The Americans left the field undefeated, for the two P-40 squadrons were relieved not long afterward by other outfits and sent back from the fighting zone to rest. Christman's squadron had been fighting there steadily for two months. I met the fellows from Christman's bunch again while I was trying to get a ride into civilization from another airfield, a bit west of the one where they had been stationed. A lot of trucks drove up and deposited the officers and men of the squadron on the field, with their weapons, their barracks bags, and their bedding rolls. Christman was there, and Private Otto, the squadron barber, and Corporal Jake Goldstein, the reformed songwriter. I renewed my acquaintance with a pilot named Fackler, whom I remembered especially because he had once, finding himself flying formation with two Messerschmitts who thought he was another Messerschmitt, shot one of them down, and I again met Thomas, the Oklahoma boy who had been lost in the air one night and had been lighted home by the fire of the field's anti-aircraft guns, and a non-flying lieutenant named Lamb, who used to practice law in New York, and a dozen others. I felt as if I had known them all for a long time.

Eleven transports came in to take the squadron west, and I arranged to travel in one of them. I was in the lead ship of the flight, and the transport major who commanded it told me that his orders were to drop the squadron at a field only about an hour's flight away. Then the transports would go on to their base, taking me along with them. It was pleasant to see the faces of the P-40 boys aboard my transport when it took off. They didn't know anything about the field they were going to, but they knew that they were going for a rest, so they expected that there would at least be huts and showers there. They looked somewhat astonished when the transports settled down in a vast field of stubble without a sign of a building anywhere around it. There were a few B-25 bombers on the field and in the distance some tents. A transport sergeant came out of the pilot's compartment forward in our plane and worked his way toward the tail of our ship, climbing over the barracks bags heaped in the space between the seats. "I guess this is where you get out," he told the P-40 fellows.

A couple of soldiers jumped out and the rest began passing out bags and rifles to them. Pretty soon all the stuff was piled outside the plane and the soldiers were standing on the field, turning their backs to a sharp wind and audibly wondering where the hell the barracks were. A jeep with an officer in it drove out from among the tents and made its way among the transports until it arrived at our ship. The transport major talked to the officer in the jeep, and then they both drove over to the transport Christman was travelling in and picked him up, and the three of them drove back to the tents. Some soldiers who had been near the jeep had heard the field's officer say that nobody there had been notified that they were coming. The transport major had replied that all he knew was that he had orders to leave them there. The soldiers who had heard the conversation communicated the news to the others by Army telegraphy. "Situation normal!"* one soldier called out, and everybody laughed. Soldiers are fatalistic about such situations.

Some time before a report had circulated among the men that the squadron was to go back to the United States. Now I heard one soldier say, "This don't look like no United States to me."

Another one said, "When we get back there, Freddie Bartholomew will be running for President." He didn't seem sore.

Somebody said, "I hear they're going to start us here and let us hack our way through to South Africa."

Somebody else began a descant on a favorite Army fantasy: what civilian life will be like after the war. "I bet if my wife gives me a piece of steak," he said, "I'll say to her, 'What the hell is this? Give me stew.' "

Another one said, "I bet she'll be surprised when you jump into bed with all your clothes on."

The delicacy of their speculations diminished from there on.

After a while the jeep came back. The transport major got out and said, "There seems to be some mistake. You'd better put your stuff back in the ship." We all got back into the planes, and the major told me that this obviously wasn't the place to leave the men but that he would have to wait until base operations could get headquarters on the telephone and find out their destination. We sat in the planes for an hour; then another officer came out in a jeep and said that nobody at headquarters knew anything about the squadron, so the major had better not take it any place else. The major told his sergeant to instruct the men to take their luggage off the planes. "We enjoy doing this. It's no trouble at all," one of the soldiers in my plane said. The transports took off and left them standing there. I learned later that they eventually got straightened out. After two or three days someone at headquarters remembered them; the pilots were sent to western Morocco and the ground echelon was moved to another field.

All this happened what seems now to be long ago, in the pioneer days of the American Army in Tunisia. The old field, from which I had watched the five-day war, was never knocked out from the air, but it was taken by German ground troops with tanks, and then the Americans took it back and went on. The Hotel Léon, if the Germans hadn't burned it, was certainly full of booby traps for the Americans when they got there. I shouldn't like to have slept in it. Léon is now in a large Algerian city, where he has been assigned to a calmer liaison job. Cochran was promoted and decorated and posted to a new command.**

* See note on confusion p. 36.
** He is now back in Erie, Pa.

## P. S. ON ROZANOFF IN 1954

THERE are lines you pick up from a particular person that become parts of your habitual repertory. They have associations that keep them bright for you, but they sound so flat you feel called upon to explain what once made them seem funny. For example, I sometimes say between drinks: "It is better as a kick in za pants, so say my grandmozaire."

This expression never tickles anybody else, but it evokes the image of a round, pink Slavic face with a roof of yellow hair like the down on an Easter chick—the face of Kostya, le Commandant Rozanoff—and a conversational voice precisely like the old basso Chaliapin's.

Rozanoff would knock off three ounces of straight whiskey in a gulp. He was what old bartenders call a lip drinker: When he had got the edge of the vessel against his lower lip, he would throw his head back and the drink over his tongue and down. Then he would intone his cherished line of what he believed to be American, and hold out his canteen cup for more whiskey. The rest of his English was negligible. I forget how the alternation began—with the jest or the gesture—but it usually continued until the pink face blurred before my eyes. He was invincible.

Rozanoff fondled the illusion that all Americans drank their whiskey straight and in the manner he practiced. Like the grandmozaire gag, it was part of the tradition of his squadron in the Armée de l'Air, les Sioux, pronounced, under another misapprehension, "Syukes." (They assumed, apparently, that Americans would sound the "x," and they wanted to say it the American way.) The original members of the squadron, in World War I, had been American volunteers, and after they went, the squadron had kept the name, the insigne, and its concepts of American customs. The insigne, an Indian head in full war bonnet, was painted on the American P-40 that Rozanoff got out of when I first met him—at Thélepte, in January, 1943. "Rozanoff," he said, shaking hands, and then, before even declaring himself conventionally enchanted: "These machines respond to the controls too slowly, and then react too violently." He had been a test pilot before the war, and the habit stuck. When I met Rozanoff, he commanded a group of nine French pilots who had been assigned new P-40s at Casablanca. From Casa, they had flown toward the front, with a stop at Algiers to refuel. But only seven arrived at Thélepte.

Rozanoff told me that evening that he was thirty-eight, and when I relayed the information to some of our young pilots, they were gloomy, because we were short of planes at that field and they thought it wasteful to let a man so old fly a new fighter. "His reflexes are just too slow for three hundred miles an hour," they said. (They were flattering the P-40 slightly.) Ten years later, I read in a French magazine that Rozanoff, the leading test pilot of France, had hit eight hundred and thirty-seven in a Mystère IV, the new French jet. He had pierced the sound barrier—

horizontally, not diving—five times in a single flight. Most of the young pilots who had survived the war considered themselves middle-aged by that time. It cheered me no end, especially considering the training regime of the Commandant, who had in the intervening years become the Colonel.

A few weeks ago, I saw on page 6 of the Sunday New York *Times* a headline that puzzled me for a moment:

### FRENCH JET CRASH
### PERILS MINISTERS

I don't like "perils" as a verb, although as I have ascertained it is in Webster's Unabridged. What was more important, I couldn't understand at first glance how a jet crash could "peril" a passenger. It would kill him. This was a momentary obtuseness. The Ministers had not been in the plane. The bank of the head explained:

PLANE PARTS FALL NEAR PLEVEN
AND BRITISH SUPPLY CHIEF—
NOTED PILOT IS KILLED

The lead said parts of the plane had fallen "about fifty yards" from the statesmen, which didn't excite me unduly. But the second paragraph began, "Col. Constantin Rozanoff, 49 years old, who was at the controls of the Mystère IV, France's latest jet, met instant death." Kostya is the diminutive for Constantin. I remembered Kostya had told me his grandparents were Russian and he was French. The *Times* said he was a native of Poland; his birth may have occurred during the family's westward migration.

Kostya had been showing off the plane before the visiting officials, including a British air marshal. I imagine he had wanted the R.A.F. to be stunned with admiration. Skimming the ground, he would have allowed a clearance of about one centimetre, if I knew him. I was happy to see he had not been at fault personally. "The plane encountered a strong gust of wind, one wing touched the ground, and the craft crashed, exploded, and burst into flames. Parts were hurled in all directions." It would have pained Kostya to think he was losing his touch, but winds at an altitude of almost nothing are unpredictable. From an air-mail copy of *Le Monde* that I saw a couple of days later, I learned that the French had been showing the British their jets with a view to selling them some. Kostya had been doing eleven hundred kilometres—six hundred and eighty-four miles—an hour.

While I was still reading the *Times* story, however, I didn't know about Kostya's added incentive. There was a picture that showed him wearing one of the enormous helmets that make all jet pilots look like hydrocephalics. The Indian head, his old talisman, was clearly visible on its front. Kostya was sitting in a cockpit, reaching down over the side, and some joker was handing him up a building brick, to celebrate his first crash through the "wall" of sound.

The joke was in Rozanoff's own vein. I remembered the time in Africa when a French division commander, General Welvert, fifty miles away, learned of the presence of Kostya and his pilots at the American field, and decided this gave him a private air force. The General telephoned an order for le Commandant Rozanoff to wait on him immediately. Rozanoff was too busy, fighting two or three times a day; besides, he had no idea of putting himself under the orders of a ground-force general. When Rozanoff didn't show up, the General sent over a message, by hand, ordering him to consider himself under arrest. Kostya got down into his hole so that only his head showed above ground at the entrance. He held two sticks vertically in front of his face and made a horrendous grimace. One of his pilots took a photograph of him that way, and they sent it over to the *divisionnaire* with the message "The Commandant Rozanoff in prison, at the orders of General Welvert." Old Welvert had had no right to send for him, of course. It was a time when all French generals were trying to accumulate as much authority as possible against the day when Giraud's people and de Gaulle's people would have to share the marbles. That was a day Welvert never lived to see; he was killed by a mine in the spring offensive. (An Algerian infantryman in one of his battalions was named Ahmed Ben Bella.)

Nobody could say Kostya didn't have a sense of humor. During the winter of the war that turned out not to be phony, he once told me, the French shot down a Messerschmitt of a new mark in the area between the two armies in Lorraine. The pilot had bailed out before the plane hit. By a lucky chance, it was not a complete wreck. The Army of the Air had a curiosity to examine a Messerschmitt of this latest edition; Rozanoff therefore went out into the disputed land to repair the plane. He worked at night under a tarpaulin, to hide his light, and slept under the wings by day. After several nights, he had repaired the engine, and one dawn he took off for France. But as he prepared to land on the airfield at Toul, the French ack-ack opened up and shot the unannounced Messerschmitt full of holes. He had to bail out, like the German pilot before him, and the plane crashed "in much worse state than before"—an irretrievable mess. He thought it very funny. "It is better as a kick in za pants," he said, and we had a drink on his adventure.

Kostya lived through a difficult time at Thélepte, until the victory over the ten bombers made everybody happy. He and his brother pilots had been, as I've said, members of the old Armée de l'Air. They had flown their planes to Africa after the debacle of 1940 in the belief the French government would continue the war. But when Pétain surrendered the empire, they had not skipped out to join de Gaulle. So their will to fight the Germans was still in question when I first met them. The seven out of nine who arrived at the field with the P-40s must have suspected the reason for the non-appearance of the two others, but they dared not admit their suspicion, even to themselves. Consequently, Rozanoff made constant inquiries about the two men, unreported since Algiers. Was it possible, he would ask, that there had been an unobserved air action deep in Allied territory in which they had been shot down, or that they had made a forced landing in the mountains and nobody had found them? "They were experienced pilots," he would say. "They had plenty of fuel. It is inconceivable that they lost their way." In fact, as we learned later, the two men had flown their planes to Vichy France and delivered them to the Pétainists.

I gather my memories of Rozanoff as the infantrymen gathered up the pilot's ring and papers. He was a barrel-chested man, and even in 1943 the barrel had begun to slip. The piece in *Le Monde* said that with the years he had developed *"une certaine corpulence."* He wore a dirty leather flying jacket, like everybody else at Thélepte, but he topped it with a visored blue cap circled with gold braid. His movements were brusque, his forms of speech were vigorous rather than graceful. *"Il manque d'élégance,"* the French liaison officer at the field complained, and I was constrained to agree.

In the early spring of 1944, I was coming out of a newsreel theatre in Piccadilly when I saw a French aviator in a bus queue. I was with a pretty girl in a becoming blue uniform, and this type in the bus queue made her the eye. I regarded him with resentment, and then I saw it was Kostya, in a blue uniform storm coat, blue trousers, black shoes—completely regulation. He was a lieutenant colonel. He told me that after the African campaign he had been promoted and attached to the staff of the new French Air Force, which incorporated both de Gaullist and Giraudist elements. De Gaulle had by that time solidly established his leadership. Kostya said that he was testing planes again, and was happy. We made a date to have lunch at the *popote* of the staff, which was in South Kensington.

The lunch was gay. We drank a fair amount of cognac, and then I invited Kostya and some other officers, one of whom was the novelist Joseph Kessel, to accompany me to a remarkable club of which I was a member. The club was called Frisco's; it was in Sackville Street, in a bomb-damaged retail shop whose glassless windows were masked with heavy cardboard. The secretary and proprietor was Frisco, an American Negro legally named Bingham. Like hundreds of other such clubs in London, it was licensed to sell to members and guests during the afternoon hours, when ordinary pubs were shut. Its remarkable feature was the amount of whiskey Frisco was able to lay hands on in a period when even the best hotel bars gave clients a grim choice between gin and sobriety. In 1944, Frisco's was usually full of colored American soldiers, who ran a continuous jam session on an old piano. The secretary took on all comers at darts, and since he had the advantage of thirty years' expatriate practice, he cleaned up.

Kostya, rendered ecstatic by the presence of so much whiskey, shouted, "It is better as a kick in za pants, so say my grandmozaire!" as soon as he got his hand around a glass. Then he emptied the glass. His war cry rang out again, above the notes of "Don't Get Around Much Any More" in intricate syncopation from the old piano. At first, his cries were intermittent but regular, like the call of the bobwhite. Then they became more rapid and, finally, just about continuous. Kessel and I tried to fly on his wings, but he lost us. After the fourth drink, Kessel was flying blind, and I, a mere groundling, was in a spin. "Better as a kick, better as a say, better as my grandmozaire's pants." It was all a blur.

There was a crash. I had preceded Kostya through the sound barrier by eight years.

I never saw him again, and now I never will.

THE NEXT pieces are about ground fighting, or what passed for it, in the first month of our maiden effort in Africa. The troops, pacific by nature, eased themselves into it like an old man with chilblains getting into a hot bath.

Gafsa, the center of these operations, is one of the oldest continuously inhabited places on earth, which is a reflection on human selectivity, because it is a desolation; it was the seat of a prehistoric culture called by archaeologists the Gafsan, which has left stone artifacts as evidence of the near-idiocy of the first inhabitants. Norman Douglas, who visited it in 1911, quoted an Arab song about it that begins:

"Gafsa is miserable; its water is blood . . ."

During all its long, ignoble history this has been so. Sallust tells how Marius, the Roman general, took it by night marches across the desertic steppe to the north, followed by a surprise attack. The steppe offered a formidable barrier to large bodies of troops, because camels had not been introduced into North Africa, and water supply was a problem. Marius solved it by having his soldiers drive cattle before them to the last spring. There he had them slaughter the beasts, skin them, fill the hides with water, and begin their march burdened only with these and meat, a concentrated ration, travelling across the high steppe in the cold nights and laying up in the heat of the day. There was no air observation and they cut the throats of the few travellers they met. He achieved complete surprise, and when the Gafsans came out to work their gardens in their oasis, the Romans rushed them so fast they had no chance to shut the city gates behind them.

Marius, following a colonialist tradition already old, denounced the Gafsans as treacherous and uncivilized, before putting the men to the sword and selling the women and children into slavery. But the city grew up again as a Roman garrison and colony, and was fought over by Moslem princelings all through the Middle Ages because by then the camels had come to North Africa, and it lay across a great caravan route. And in time Major-General Terry Allen of the First Division captured the city by the same maneuver—a night march across the desert, this time in trucks and jeeps, to avert annoyance by the *Luftwaffe*. He did this, however, before the third episode in the following narration, when the First Division, which was precocious compared to all others, had already found its stride. Gafsa is about 50 miles southeast of Cochran's old field at Thélepte.

# Gafsa

THE Anglo-American North African campaign is sure to furnish a lot of historical controversy sooner or later, so there is no harm in correcting the record on one point immediately. The junction of the American Second Corps and the British Eighth Army, fighting its way north from Mareth, was copiously reported in newspapers in this country last April. Most of the reporters said that the meeting took place on the Gafsa-Gabès road. According to their stories, the historic moment came when an American motorized patrol met a British motorized patrol. Actually, the Eighth Army and the Second Corps joined up more than two months before the motorized incident, in the hall of the Hôtel de France, a two-story palace in Gafsa. I know, because I was there. In fact, I might say that I introduced them.

Gafsa, called Capsa by the Numidians, is a very ancient town on a very slight hill in south-central Tunisia. Warm springs gush from the foot of the hill, below a fifteenth-century Arab citadel, which was wrecked by our engineers during the fighting last February. The citadel was still intact when I first saw the place. The climate of Gafsa, even in late January, when Norgaard and I reached it, is warm and dry. There is an oasis around the town, which used to be an important knot in the web of caravan routes between the Sahara and the Mediterranean. Last winter Gafsa had, and by now probably has again, ten thousand inhabitants, of whom five or six hundred are Europeans, eight hundred are native Jews, and the rest Moslems who call themselves Arabs but are predominantly of Berber stock, like most North Africans. The Europeans are administrators or railroad workers. The Jews, whose ancestors came there not long after the Destruction of the Temple, are traders and traditionally middlemen between the Christians and the Moslems.

When Norgaard and I arrived in Gafsa, a battalion of American infantry was stationed there, together with several batteries of French seventy-fives, a battalion of Senegalese, and some Algerian *tirailleurs*. The

Americans, who belonged to the First Division, were the only ground troops we had south of the town of Sbeitla, which was sixty miles away. They had been there for a month and were quite at home in the place, which, as almost every enlisted man you talked to was certain to say, looked like a set in a Beau Geste movie. Old Jews sold surprisingly good native pastries and Arabs peddled dates in the square in front of the American barracks. The soldiers had adopted Arab kids as mascots and clothed them in G.I. shirts and shoes. There was a great outdoor Roman swimming pool, filled by warm running water from the springs. The water contained a good deal of sulphur, but it was nevertheless pleasant to bathe in, and the Americans spent a lot of time swimming in it. The French soldiers preferred to dangle fishing lines in a nearby spring-fed stream and catch little, extremely voracious blue fish,* which apparently were used to living in hot, sulphurous water.

There was also a clean Arab bath, in a narrow Arabian Nights alley, where the attendants would stretch you on the floor and twist your arms and legs out of joint and then pound you with a hot brick before allowing you to steam yourself in peace. I remember seeing, at the bath, an English captain I knew, a booby-trap expert, pink and jolly in the steam, wearing a towel around his loins. A couple of weeks later he accidentally blew himself up with an extremely special mine he had just devised. He simply vanished. Somehow I always think of him flying toward heaven draped in a towel and deeply embarrassed.** Gafsa also had a bordello offering a dozen girls whom a friend of mine described as "sort of French" and a madam who was a de Gaulliste. When a British lieutenant general came to town for a look around, the much-junior American officer who was his host wanted to give him a touch of real luxury—sheets to sleep between. He borrowed a pair from the madam.

Norgaard and I had gone to Gafsa because it was the American-held point nearest to Montgomery's advancing army and it seemed a likely place to witness the joining of the two forces. We expected the Americans either to hold on to the town until Montgomery arrived or else to launch an offensive from it in order to join him. The latter course presupposed heavy reinforcements, and we thought that we sensed their coming.

The Americans in Gafsa had carried out numerous raids against the Italian detachments that occasionally appeared in the no man's land to the east, between Gafsa and Maknassy. Neither adversary had any fixed garrison in this flat, desolate stretch of about seventy miles between the two towns. Once the fellows from Gafsa had bagged eighty-four prisoners. That was reckoned a big haul for southern Tunisia in January.

* Tilapia.
** This never happened, although when I wrote this piece, I fully believed it had. One more instance of confusion—I had the story from a "reliable source" who knew us both.

Captured Italian carbines and automatic pistols, if you had a chance to get them back to Algiers, attracted much attention. Even the stars which Italian soldiers wear on their lapels had a certain curiosity value. If you gave one to an Army nurse at an evacuation hospital, she would be quite happy, for which reason few stars ever got back as far as Algiers, and nurses at base hospitals to the west didn't get to see any until April or May. But by then there were so many Italian prisoners that the stars were no longer chic.

Norgaard and I had been told, by Léon Caplan, to look up a friend of his at Gafsa, a French captain named O'Neill. O'Neill, whose family had emigrated to France from Ireland in the seventeenth century, pronounced his name "Onay." He looked like a conventional O'Neill—blue-eyed, florid, and saddle-nosed—but he spoke English, which he had learned at a *lycée*, with a heavy French accent. Captain O'Neill commanded a battery of three guns which had been buried in a cache after the fall of France and thus concealed from the German Armistice Commission. All three guns had to be hauled by one old motor truck that burned alcohol, so the battery travelled in installments, one gun at a time. They could shoot well enough, O'Neill said, but they never arrived anywhere in time to shoot at an enemy. O'Neill invited us to dine at the battery mess with him, his two lieutenants, and a chaplain attached to the unit.

We showed up at the mess, which was in a shed built onto the side of a one-story house, ahead of O'Neill and his officers, who were accustomed to dining late. American Army chow is usually dished up early. The owner of the house, a young native Jew who wore a European business suit and a blue beret, invited us in for an apéritif while we waited. He had delicate Arabian features, and eyes as blue as O'Neill's, and he spoke excellent French. The Jew's house was large and square, with thick, mud walls to insulate it from the summer sun. It was built around a small circular court that let in air and daylight. The house looked ageless, like most of the others in town—the Numidians had probably built in exactly the same fashion—but the rooms leading off the court were wired for electric light and filled with heavy, gaudy contemporary furniture from some factory in Europe. The Jew's ancient, bearded father, who spoke no French, and the younger man's small, comely, brunette wife and their gray-eyed daughter kissed our hands. The French took over Tunisia in 1881, and in the old man's youth there had been no French-language schools in the country, but in the son's there had been. The younger man poured sweet wine for us and gave us olives and sliced turnips pickled in lemon juice. The family name, he told us, was Chemouni. When a servant who had been left on watch outside came in and told us that O'Neill had arrived, we left the Chemounis, feeling faintly embarrassed by their fervor. I remembered them a few weeks later, when I heard that we had abandoned Gafsa to the advancing Germans and Italians.

O'Neill's mess was the most exiguous I have encountered in the French

Army. We had a thin soup and a few scraps of breast of lamb, finishing off with some black imitation coffee sweetened with gray Arab loaf sugar. There was a bottle of rough red wine, and Norgaard and I had brought over three cans of American fruit for dessert. One of O'Neill's lieutenants was a hawk-nosed, Assyrian-bearded man who walked with a pronounced limp, assisting himself with a spiked cane. He was a French colonist who had farmed an oasis on the edge of the Sahara. The other was a handsome, wavy-haired young Parisian, a Regular Army officer who had escaped from the Occupied Zone in France and made his way to Africa in 1941. He spoke most nostalgically of Fouquet's, a restaurant which I had never admired but which, I had to agree, would have looked good in Africa. The chaplain, a young man with scraggly whiskers, was merely shy and hungry.

After dinner, Norgaard and I walked to the office of the American signals officer, in the Hôtel de France, to get the dope on how to send messages out of Gafsa. (They would have to go first by Army courier to where the censors were.) The hotel was a rectangular, flat-topped, yellow stucco building two stories high. It was neater and more modern than, I think, most Americans would imagine a hotel in Gafsa to be. There was running water in all the rooms and there were at least two bathtubs in the house. The American commandant, Lieutenant Colonel (now Colonel) Bowen,* had taken it over as a headquarters and lived upstairs. The signals officer presided over his telephones on the street floor, in what had once been the hall and dining room. We were talking to him when a French officer appeared in the doorway leading from the street and asked for Colonel Bowen. Apparently the signals man couldn't understand French, so when the officer asked for Bowen again, I took it upon myself to say, "He is upstairs. What do you want him for?"

"It is the British officers from the Eighth Army at Gabès," the Frenchman said. "Those he requested to see."

"The Eighth Army at Gabès?" I said, startled, because two days before I had heard that the Eighth was still a hundred miles south of there. I took this to mean that Montgomery had moved north that hundred miles in forty-eight hours, breaking the Mareth Line en route. That would have been a record even for him.**

"They are officers, three of them, from the Eighth Army, and they come from Gabès," the Frenchman said, "but the Army itself is not there. They say they come from a patrol that got up there somehow. They came into our lines at Kriz, on the Chott Djerid." His voice was quite matter-of-fact. "If you will show them to Colonel Bowen, I will leave them with you," he

* And now (1962) Major-General.
** Our image of Montgomery then was of a dashing fellow. That was before we had to work with him.

said, and ducked out into the dark without waiting for an answer. That was how I came to introduce the Eighth Army to the Second Corps.

A moment after the Frenchman disappeared, the three British officers came through the doorway. They walked with mincing steps, lifting each foot quickly as if they were glad to get it off the floor and putting it back reluctantly. Their shoes were wrapped in rags, and I deduced that their feet must be masses of blisters. Two of the men wore long beards and one, whose head was wrapped in a blood-soaked bandage, looked as if he badly needed a shave. All three were wearing khaki battle-dress pants and shirts, from which great swatches of material were missing, evidently torn off to make bandages. One of the men with beards carried a goatskin water sack, with the long hair outside; it reminded me of Robinson Crusoe. Their faces were sunken and their eyes seemed preternaturally large, and in one case really protuberant. The eyes of this fellow were round and sky-blue and his hair and whiskers were very fair. His beard began well under his chin, giving him the air of an emaciated and slightly dotty Paul Verlaine. "We walked forty miles farther than we should have," he said to me apologetically, "because some Arabs told us the Germans had taken Gafsa and that two thousand Americans were prisoners. But we knew that the French were at Kriz and Tozeur, so we went around that way. We've been walking for five nights and five days." Some soldiers who had drifted into the room brought in chairs for them and they sat down, looking about them a trifle incredulously, as if they had not really expected to get out of whatever awful scrape they had been in. A sergeant went upstairs to inform Bowen of their arrival. The soldiers gave the British officers cigarettes and offered to bring them food and water. The officers said that the French at Kriz and Tozeur had already given them as much as they could handle for a while, and they were no longer thirsty or hungry. The least bearded man passed his hand over his head, and Norgaard asked him, "Grazed by a bullet?"

The man shook his head slowly—you could almost hear it ring—and said, "No. An Arab hit me with a stone. They tried to strip us of our clothes, and when we fought they tried to kill us. We ran. We had no weapons, you see."

"Have any others come in?" the fair man asked us. "Have you heard anything about Big Dave?"

The signals officer said, "No, you're the first British who've come into our lines."

The man with the bandaged head said, in a discouraged voice, "Big Dave must have been killed. There was all that shooting back in the wadi." He looked on the verge of falling asleep.

The fair man said, in a tone of sudden energy, as if he were trying to carry out a duty before he too caved in, "It's very important that we put out a radio warning to all our people behind the German lines that the enemy may have got our code. We must change the code."

"Are you *really* from the Eighth Army?" I asked the man with the goatskin sack.

He said they were.

"When did you leave the Eighth?" I asked.

"November seventeenth," he said. This was January twenty-eighth. "We've been living behind the enemy lines ever since. We were supposed to stay out four weeks longer, but we had a bit of hard luck."

A lieutenant came down the stairs and said that Colonel Bowen wanted to see the men, and they climbed up, holding on to the banister and resting as much weight on their hands as possible. I could hear the fair man saying, "We've got to put out that warning immediately." After a few minutes the lieutenant came down again and sent one of the men out to get the medics' ambulance. "The Colonel doesn't know quite what to make of them," he said. "They seem to be all right, but he says they might be spies. So he wants to send them up to G-2 at Corps tonight. They'll be comfortable in the ambulance."

Corps, as Norgaard and I knew, was near Tebessa, in Algeria, a hundred miles away. Driving over the narrow road, partly through rocky hills, without lights, an ambulance would be lucky to make it in six hours. Norgaard and I had one jeep, with an Army driver, between us. We decided that we ought to follow the ambulance to Tebessa. We hurried over to barracks to get our bedrolls and our driver, whose name was Eddie. He was a good-natured pfc from Queens who had been impressed by the tales of war he had heard in Algiers and was now being stuffed with horror stories by the infantrymen with whom he had taken up quarters in Gafsa. He looked relieved when we told him we were getting out of there, even though it meant a cold night drive. It didn't take long to roll our bedding and get it into the rear seat of the jeep. When three men carry three bedrolls in a jeep, it means that the men all ride in the front seat.

When we got back to the Hôtel de France, we learned that the ambulance had not yet arrived. We found the three officers from the Eighth Army in the kitchen, drinking hot coffee and surrounded by officers and men who were asking them about the desert. I spoke to the man with the bandaged head, and he told me that the fair-haired chap, Sadler, was the only commissioned officer of the three, a lieutenant. The two others were sergeants. They all belonged to an organization known as the SAS, which stood for Special Air Service. I asked him if it had anything to do with the RAF and he said no, it was an air service in a negative way. "You see, when we were first formed, we used to specialize in destroying German airplanes on the ground," he said. "Get back of their lines, get onto an airfield at night—do in a sentry, you know, or something of that sort; it's easy—and then attach pencil bombs to as many planes as we could get to. The bombs are timed to go off in a short time. We do a bunk, the bombs go off, and all the planes burn. Quite a good idea. Colonel Stirling, the one we call Big Dave, really thought of it first. Bright chap.

"They used to drop us by parachute behind the lines and let us find our way back," he continued, gravely sipping his coffee. "Worked well in places like Crete and Greece, but no future in it in Africa. Distances too great, you know. Easy to drop your men near an airport but impossible for them to walk back. So Colonel Stirling thought of using jeeps. Wonderful things, jeeps, absolutely fine. They go anywhere in desert country. Our fellows swing wide of the actual fighting area, come in behind the enemy lines, and then simply live in the desert for weeks, annoying them. One chap in SAS has got a hundred and twenty planes with his own hands. Big Dave must have got nearly a hundred. But Jerry got onto that airport dodge. Now there are too many guards and too many booby traps. So on this last trip out we stayed away from airfields and did just mines, traffic disruption, and general confusion. Sometimes we made Jerry and the Eye-ties think that they had been flanked in force and that a whole motorized column was operating in their rear. We made a whole Italian division pull out of one area, frightened stiff. Glorious fun, really."

I asked the sergeant where he was from and he said Nottingham. He told me that his name was Cooper and that he was twenty years old. He said he had been at school when war broke out and had enlisted in the Scots Guards. "I didn't like that," he said, "drill and spit and polish, all that. Big Dave was an officer in the Scots Guards himself, and he mustn't have liked it either. Then I went into the Commandos when they were started, and they were quite good at first, but they got formalized. Became too smart, you know—show yourself in London bars, Captain Lord Thisandthat, meet Leftenant the Right Hon., Lady Ursula's brother. So I became a parachutist and then I went into this thing. This is heaven," he said, absent-mindedly touching his bandaged head and then looking at his fingers to see if any blood had soaked through. "Extra pay and no drill or any of that foolishness." Cooper said he was a gunner and land navigator. He and his companions took their bearings in the desert just as if they were aboard ship, he said.

The other sergeant, the one with the goatskin sack, was a Free Frenchman who had been in the French Legation at Cairo when France fell. He was a navigator and an expert in Arabic. He told me his name was Taxis and that he was the old man of the group—thirty-one. He said that the disposition of the Tunisian Arabs was very bad. "You must never drive out in the desert without a gun," he said, "and the pilots must never forget to carry their pistols when they fly over the desert, in case they are forced to land." The Arabs who had tried to rob the men of their clothes had not acted like the Arabs in storybooks, who respect the laws of hospitality. They had invited the three ragged men to eat and then had pointed out a place in a wadi that they had said was safe to sleep in. When the men were dozing off, they had attacked them with stones.

"Our particular SAS lot started out with thirty men and a dozen jeeps," Cooper said. "It's wonderful what you can get on a jeep. We mount a heavy and a light machine gun on each one, besides radio equipment, and then we tie supplies and tins of extra petrol onto them until the springs barely clear the ground. They're the finest combat vehicle developed in this war. When you come to a deep wadi, where you can't progress farther, you can lower them into the wadi by ropes and get them out the same way on the other side. When a jeep breaks down seriously, we take the best of its tires and motor parts and use them as replacements on other jeeps, and the petrol helps too. So you have fewer and fewer jeeps as you go along. When your own petrol begins to run out, you raid an enemy petrol dump or shoot up some enemy trucks and take what they have. You lose all sense of strangeness, really, after a while. It seems as normal to go to an Eye-tie dump for your petrol as to one of our own places.

"We went along for weeks without any trouble. Big Dave himself commanded the party. When we started, the Eighth was still near Alamein and we operated for a while in true desert. We would always hide out in the daytime and sleep, and then do all our moves by night. When we got up into this semi-hill country, we would find deep wadis or crevices to hide away in. We would come out onto the roads by night and shoot up the enemy convoys. We weren't the only party out, of course. There were dozens of others, mostly LRDP, but all doing the same sort of thing, approximately. LRDP means Long Range Desert Patrol. They're very similar to us, but there are more of them. Altogether, we made a shambles of the enemy's line of supply. Their convoys became afraid to move by night at all, and when they used the roads by day, our fighter planes shot them up, so they had trouble both ways. One of our best tricks was to come onto a road and move along it *toward* the front, so they would never suspect us of being intruders. A string of empty lorries would come back from the front, having unloaded, and we would flash our lights at them for the right of way. They would flash back and then we would open fire with our machine guns, right at the lights. We got thirty-seven lorries that way one evening, left them flaming on the road. Once we had a battle with some Italian armored cars. We chased them with our jeeps. I suppose they thought we were at least light tanks, in the dark. We never had a casualty in six weeks, until the thing in the wadi north of Gabès."

"One of the most amusing bits was the mines," Sadler said.

"Yes, I nearly forgot," Cooper said. "Naturally, Jerry was preparing his retreat, and as our people got nearer, the German sappers would lay mines along the shoulders of the roads and in fields that columns would be likely to take a cut through. Their own people could keep on using the roads until the last minute because the engineers had marked the lanes through the mines. We used to go out sometimes to places where they had been working and take up their mines and then replace them in a slightly altered pattern. It must have been disconcerting when their lorries hit their own stuff.

"But we got to feeling too safe. We had gone so long unobserved that we thought it would last forever. Our party split up a couple of times and toward the end there were just fifteen in our particular group, travelling with four jeeps. We were lying up in a deep wadi about ten miles north of Gabès, a place with cliff walls four hundred feet high. I was fast asleep under my blankets when I heard the first shots. Germans with tommy guns were coming up both ends of the wadi. Some Arabs must have spotted us going in there and told Jerry. There wasn't a chance to fight our way out of that position. I managed to climb up a cliff, but I had no chance to get a weapon or a heavy coat. Sadler and Taxis got away by the same method, and we joined after we got to the top of the cliff. We waited around to see if any of the others would get away, but nobody did. There was a lot of shooting in the wadi and then silence. After a time, we began to walk."

The ambulance had finally pulled up in front of the Hôtel de France. A captain who had been deputed to escort the three suspicious characters to Corps was waiting at the kitchen door, and the three men got up and hobbled out to their conveyance. Norgaard and I went out after them and climbed into our jeep with Eddie and followed them up to Tebessa. It was the coldest, and it seemed the longest, ride I have ever had. We rode with our windshield down, on the theory that this would make it a trifle easier to see through the blackness, and we had a wind in our faces all the way. Norgaard and Eddie alternated driving, and I was always in the middle, with my arms stretched out behind them. I felt like a figurehead on a ship, driving chest first into a gale. The fellows lying inside the ambulance were of course more comfortable. Occasionally, when one of them sat up to smoke a cigarette and used a cigarette lighter, we could see a bearded face gleam through a rear window. Otherwise the ambulance was just a patch of blackness slightly more solid than the dark around it.

We got to Corps, which was eight miles outside of Tebessa, at two o'clock in the morning. A G-2 officer came out of the staff tent and climbed into the ambulance to talk to the Eighth Army officers. He had a bottle of whiskey with him, which was an excellent idea, because they were pretty well done in by that time. After half an hour he climbed out and told us that he thought they were all right.

### WITH DR. FREEMAN IN AFRICA

NORGAARD and I went back to Gafsa within a week, and by the time we got there a big military action for that stage of the war was already going on. It was an offensive in the direction of Maknassy, the first all-American venture of the Tunisian campaign.

Sened, thirty miles east of Gafsa, was the first objective. The bulk of Rommel's army was only a little west of Tripoli, and there was nothing but a long, thinly held, tempting corridor between him and von Arnim. The Americans making the attack believed that they could go on from Sened to Maknassy and from Maknassy to the coast of the Gulf of Gabès, cutting Rommel's line of supply and retreat. The major general in command* told the war correspondents that he was going on to Maknassy, at least, and "draw the pucker string tight." We understood from his manner that he meant to go farther than that if he got the chance.

Norgaard and I had an Army jeep, and we drove out from Gafsa to see the battle. We had formerly had an Army driver, but on this trip Norgaard himself drove. The battle was in its second day. A battle, in the sort of open, desert warfare that was going on then, is not an easy thing to find, and we often had to stop to ask directions. We made our first stop beside two American Negro soldiers, sitting with their legs dangling into two parallel slit trenches cut in the dead-looking terrain. Each man was eating a mixture of cold meat and beans out of a small, shiny tin can which reflected the sun's rays a distance of several miles in that flat country** and each turned his face upward periodically, with mouth full, to stare into the hot, aluminum-colored sky. I got out of the jeep and walked up to the end of one trench, and its proprietor, a tan man, looked at me, but the other soldier continued to stare at the sky. Then the tan man looked up at the sky and his companion looked at me. "We was dive-bummed yesterday," this second soldier, a very dark man, said to me. "Driving the infantry up to the line in two-and-a-half-ton trucks. Dive-bumming makes me sick to my stomach."

I tried to sound hearty and casual as I asked, "What outfit you men out of?"

"The Rolling Umpty-seventh," the tan man said, while the dark man took his turn looking at the sky. The Umpties are a motor-truck regiment which I had already met under happier circumstances, in England.

"How you doing?" I asked, for want of a better question.

"Really, sir, I don't belong on this battlefield at all," the tan soldier answered. "I'm strictly a non-combat man."

I thought to myself that we were two of a kind.

I asked the men how far ahead the front was. I put into my voice the implication that I wanted to rush right into the middle of things. The men didn't know exactly where the battle was. Soldiers seldom do.

I walked back from the twin slit trenches to the jeep. "They don't know where the battle is," I said to Norgaard. "Maybe we had better go farther ahead." He said all right, so we started off across the sand again. We took

---

* General Lloyd Fredendall.
** A khaki C-ration can came in later. Nobody in the Source of Supplies, apparently, had had the imagination to foresee the tactical disadvantages of the bright ones.

to the desert, keeping away from the main road between Gafsa and Sened, because there were trucks on it and trucks attract strafers. The line of telephone poles beside the road gave us our direction. When we had gone a short way, we saw a pair of jeeps coming toward us over the sand, and we stopped. There were a couple of American officers and eight men in the jeeps, all belonging to a tank-destroyer battalion that had lost its equipment earlier in the campaign. They were serving as battlefield military police, guiding traffic and waiting for prisoners to take charge of.

The officers didn't know exactly where the front was either. They invited us to have a can of coffee beside a mud house, a mile or so away, where the M.P.'s had set up headquarters, and we all drove there together. There were a few scraggly olive trees around the house and a low mud wall around the trees, presumably to prevent the sand's blowing away from their roots. One of the soldiers poured some gasoline into a couple of empty ration cans and lighted it. He laid two strips of metal across the top of each can, then filled two smaller ration cans with water from his canteen and placed them on the burners. When the water came to a boil, he divided a packet of soluble coffee between the two improvised coffee pots. "The Statler people would give a million dollars to get hold of this process," he said. When we had drunk the coffee, he started another batch.

While I was waiting for more coffee, I stood on the mud wall with one of the M.P. officers and looked over the country. A railroad paralleled the highway and we could see a station, with some trees around it, about five miles away. It was a stop between Gafsa and Sened, needed God knows why. "Our guns were out behind there early this morning and Jerry dropped a few shells in among those trees," the officer said. "Then our guns moved forward, way up toward Sened. I think you can go ahead eight or ten miles at least before you have to start to look around. You missed a good show this morning, though. About twenty Stukas came over and a dozen P-40's bounced them and shot down eight. Boy, they were falling all over the place! They'll be back, though," he added cheerily.*

After Norgaard and I had finished our coffee, we climbed back into the jeep and started forward again. Almost immediately the mud-house grove seemed in retrospect a pretty nice place to spend the day. Sened lies in a gap between two bare, east-west ridges. As we moved toward it, we spotted a number of dispersed scout cars and wireless-equipped jeeps, the vehicles characteristic of a reconnaissance troop. "A recon outfit," Norgaard said knowingly. "Aren't they usually fairly well out in front of

---

* Later that day the Stukas did come back with a strong escort of fighters, thirty-one planes in all. Six P-40s from Thélepte attacked them and five of our planes were shot down. They attacked to protect an infantry advance that had been canceled, which is the way things go. I saw the planes still smoking on the hills next day; the pilots, now ashes, had been among the victors of January 15.

everybody?" We drove to within fifty yards of one of the scout cars and climbed out. A couple of soldiers were sitting on the ground with their backs against the wheels of the car, reading books. They had their slit trenches already dug beside them. Norgaard and I walked up to them and asked them what outfit this was. One of the men, a corporal, looked up and said, "Sorry, sir, but you got any identification?" He reminded me of a stage-door man. We showed him our identification cards and he explained that the scout cars, which were, as Norgaard had surmised, a recon outfit, had been all the way around the enemy's position during the previous day and night and had come back to report and await another assignment. "We could have took the place, I guess," he said, probably without much justification.

My companion, like a good Associated Press man, started making the rounds of the scout cars and taking down the names and home towns of the recon soldiers. This is always a fruitful procedure for a press-association man, because he can load up his dispatches with the names, and the papers in the home towns are glad to use them. Every soldier, when he named his home town, said, "And I wish I was there now" or "Boy, how I wish I was there this minute!" The corporal I had spoken to asked me if it was true that Bing Crosby was dead. I said I didn't know. He asked me if Groucho Marx was dead. He said he had heard that they were and that Fred Allen was dead, too. The Army in Tunisia was always full of rumors about well-known people who were supposed to have died. When my companion had written down the names of enough towns like Owensboro, Kentucky, and Central Falls, Rhode Island, we moved on again.

As we drove along, we had a clear view of the ridge north of Sened, and after we had driven a mile or so we saw a number of tanks coming around the western end, just below the crest, and snaking down the southern side of the ridge toward the town. There were occasional puffs of gray smoke on the slope above them, where the enemy was dropping shells. We began to hear our own guns up ahead, quite loud. Then we came upon the ammunition half-tracks of an artillery outfit. The soldiers told us, confidently, that the reconnaissance troop we had just left had been annihilated on the day before and that a tank-destroyer outfit had just lost all its vehicles. This was the tank-destroyer battalion the M.P.'s belonged to. The fact was that the vehicles had been lost in a quagmire in northern Tunisia a month before, but an artilleryman, garbling a conversation with one of the M.P.'s, had brought back the more fascinating report that the tank-busters had been ambushed during the current action. The soldiers said that two batteries out of their battalion were a mile or two ahead of us. The guns were armored 105's, six to a battery.

We drove on across the plain and eventually came upon a tall captain with a Red Cross brassard, standing between two jeeps, both of which were flying Red Cross flags. We stopped to talk to him. The guns we had been told about were now in sight, four hundred yards further on. The captain, whose name was Bradbury, said he was battalion surgeon. Each of the jeeps had two litters slung to its sides, and when dive bombers or German artillery caused a casualty among the gunners, Bradbury would run forward in one of the jeeps and get the wounded man. He stood there looking at the guns like a spaniel watching for a ball to retrieve. "Yesterday I had seventeen," he said, "including several from the infantry that happened to be hit near us. Only three so far today. None in this position so far. We've moved half a dozen times since daybreak." All the shots we heard were going out (boom-scream) and none were coming in (scream-boom), so we weren't worried. I opened a can of Spam and we ate it cold. "Maybe they have pulled their stuff out of Sened already," Norgaard said optimistically. I had been watching the sky all day while he drove, sometimes looking straight up for Stukas and sometimes into the sun for strafers, but nothing had happened, and I began to hope that the P-40's had polished the local Luftwaffe off for the day.

After we had finished the Spam and said so long to Bradbury, Norgaard and I drove on up to the guns and stopped behind them. They were in the open, because there was no cover anywhere around. They had stopped shooting for the moment, probably to change range or target, and we walked up to one gun crew, who were smoking cigarettes beside their piece. As soon as we reached them, an officer shouted over to them from an armored half-track to their rear, telling them to check on our identifications. "I'm sorry, sir," one soldier said, "but after all, how do we know who you are? We got no time for Ayrabs or casual strollers." We showed our identification cards and the soldier, looking at mine, said, "Huh, a *Landsmann!* I'm from New York, too. Fourteent' Street and Avenue A. I wish I was dere now. At a movie, wit' my shoes off."

Then they had to start shooting again. We walked back toward the half-track, which we knew, because of its high radio antenna, was a command vehicle. The officer who had shouted to the gunners was a square-faced, fair-haired major named Burba. He was executive officer of the battalion and had been in command of the two batteries since his C.O., a lieutenant colonel, had been wounded. He was from McAlester, Oklahoma. He was a cool, methodical officer who looked as if he had definite information about everything, so I asked him what his battery was shooting at.

"Enemy guns in a grove of trees back of Sened," he said. "We think their infantry has pulled out of the town already."

I asked him what range he was firing at and he said five thousand yards. "I have one battery here," he said, "and another over about a mile to the right and slightly forward—you can see them over there," and he pointed. "Every fifth shell we fire is a smoke shell, so we can see where we're hitting, and the fire of the two batteries is converging on the grove of trees. When we get all our fire together and just right, we'll come down on them and that will be the end of the battle."

"Where's our infantry?" I asked in a careless tone. I could not see any troops out in front of us.

"There are two battalions in echelon in those two olive groves to the right and forward of the other battery," Burba said, pointing again. "When we've knocked out all resistance, they will go forward and occupy the town. Or maybe the tanks will get there first."

The tanks, as a matter of fact, were in the process of trying to get to the town before the infantry. They were crawling down from the southern side of the ridge, where my colleague and I had already seen them, and moving out in front of the 105's, looking like a file of mechanical toys that a street peddler winds up and sets down on a sidewalk. When they had deployed before us, they turned left and moved on toward the town. They must have been a couple of thousand yards ahead of us when something began kicking up dust and smoke, sometimes in front of them and sometimes behind. "It's those Jerry 88's," Burba said. "They've got the tanks under a crossfire. We'll fix that in a few minutes." The tanks were now coming back toward us, all except one, which remained motionless on the plain. "That's the way the infantry was yesterday," one of Burba's junior officers, who had joined us, said. "They went up toward the firing line in trucks and three or four of the trucks got dive-bombed before the fellows could get away from them. It was a mess. After that they couldn't get anybody back into the trucks for a while. After *we* knock out the opposition, they'll all be heroes."

"That 88 is a great gun," Burba said admiringly, looking at the motionless tank through his binoculars. "Ripped that thing just like a G.I. knife does a tin can. Flat trajectory. High muzzle velocity."

"Pretty long range, hasn't it?" I asked.

"Thirteen thousand five hundred yards," Burba said heartily, as if he were a salesman pushing the German gun to a reluctant prospect.

At this point the six guns in Burba's battery let off as one, and the other battery followed. Then there was a prolonged shrieking noise and something monstrous landed a hundred yards behind us and ricochetted off to our left. It kicked up a lot of dust. It must have been an armor-piercing solid shot, because there was no explosion. "Let's get behind the half-track," Burba said, in the same tone in which he might have said, "Let's get out of this wind." We all moved over behind the vehicle. Something else shrieked past, through the interval between the two guns on the right flank of the battery, it seemed to me, and I couldn't help thinking that while Burba had been explaining to us what we intended to do to the Germans, some equally competent, equally stolid German artillery officer had been outlining his plans of what he intended to do to us.

Norgaard and I had the embarrassing feeling that we were not helping the battery by our presence and that if we got hit we would cause them a lot of extra trouble. We were also embarrassed by the thought that if we left too abruptly, Burba and the others might think we were fair-weather friends. My colleague reminded me that he really had to get back to headquarters at Gafsa by five in order to file a bulletin. I wasn't working for a press association and so I had no bulletin to file, but we had only one jeep between us and I decided that I couldn't expect my companion to wait. I said, "I guess we may as well go, Major. See you some other time." Norgaard said something to the same effect, and we walked away, feeling as sheepish as we ever have in our lives.

We got into our jeep and drove to the rear, past the patient Captain Bradbury. We paused for a moment to say goodbye again. I looked back and saw a column of black smoke rising from one of our gun positions. The enemy had evidently scored a hit.

Each knot of soldiers we passed on the way to the front had seemed a friendly island inviting a prolonged stay. We were not tempted to stop to talk to any of them on the way back. We reached Gafsa, and were about to park our jeep opposite the Hôtel de France, which was serving as American headquarters, when we saw in the street the major general who was in command of the American operation based on Gafsa. We stopped to ask him if the infantry had got to Sened—we had been two hours on the way home—and he said they had and that Sened was now in our hands. "The only damned trouble," he said, "is that the British First Army has called off the whole offensive because there has been some kind of threat in the north. I guess we're going to play it safe and wait for Montgomery." The bigger part of an American armored division which had been held in reserve just outside Gafsa to exploit our initial gains was sent north that night without having fought, and the great projected offensive went into the record as only a raid.

The American forces in the field were under the direct control of Lieutenant General Kenneth Anderson, who was commanding the British First Army at that stage of the campaign. Anderson himself was officially under the command of General Eisenhower, in Algiers. This occasioned considerable confusion of viewpoint among the men in the field, but things got a lot better later when the British Eighth Army, the British First Army, and the American Second Corps were all placed directly, and with equal status, under the command of General Alexander. The aborted offensive cost us a couple of hundred casualties, but we took a hundred and fifty prisoners, which in that period of the campaign seemed a lot. The battle had never developed into a really big affair, but at moments it had seemed about as big as Norgaard or I or anybody we saw between Gafsa and Sened had wanted.

This impression was confirmed when Norgaard and I got ready to turn in after dinner. When we were at Gafsa, we slept on the concrete floor of a small French barracks, which was used as a catch-all hostel for transient officers. In one corner of the barracks, a captain from an American armored-infantry regiment had spread his bedding roll. His outfit had not been involved in the day's action and he had been out in the field in a jeep as an observer of fighting methods. He was a florid, pleasant-faced blond of twenty-seven, and he was reading by the light of a candle he had placed next to one elbow on the floor. We said hello and walked over to talk to him. He was reading Douglas Southall Freeman's "Lee's Lieutenants," which Norgaard had also read, and they got to talking about it. The captain told us that he came from the battlefield region of Virginia, where children save Minié balls instead of Indian arrowheads, and that he knew old Dr. Freeman well. "I own a house at Yellow Tavern, where Jeb Stuart was killed," he said, "and there are some Yankee musket balls in the stair rail. When I was a boy, I used to walk over the battlefields with Dr. Freeman, and he would tell me where the different regiments had stood and where they had charged or retreated and who had been killed and where. I often used to dream of battles when I was a boy. I thought of them like an illustration in a book, all blue and gray and orange and blood-red, and not very noisy." He closed his book and lay down, ready to go to sleep. "My God!" he said. "If I had known they were like this!" I thought of a line in Stendhal's diary: "All my life I have longed to be loved by a woman who was melancholy, thin, and an actress. Now I have been, and I am not happy."

### THE CHEMOUNIS REVISITED

ON the next day, the High Command decided to call off the offensive of which the Sened action was to have been merely the first stage. The Command's decision was supposed to be a secret, but when tank units which had not yet been committed to the fight began pulling out of Gafsa and heading north, the troops remaining there understood what had happened. There was a feeling among the men that as soon as enough tanks had been withdrawn from the region the enemy might come back and counterattack at Sened, but he didn't until a while later, and in the meantime the men who had taken Sened sat tight.

Norgaard and I heard that there were captured enemy guns and tanks at Sened. Since captured material, like prisoners in quantity, was still a novelty at that stage of the North African campaign, we thought we would get into the jeep the Army had lent us and drive out from Gafsa, where we were quartered, to have a look. As soon as we had got out on the naked main road to Sened, both of us were sorry we had left the shade of the palm trees and anti-aircraft guns. The hot, metallic sky, which it hurt your eyes to look into, hung over the road and weighed down on your brain with its implicit Messerschmitts. Every group of tanks or guns you met, parked off the road, seemed an invitation to air attack, and you hurried to get past it. Then, until you reached the next collection of armor, you felt lonely. Signs along the road warned drivers to keep at three-hundred-yard intervals and look out for strafers.

There was no temptation to get off the road and drive across the fields to avoid strafing as we got close to Sened, for the fields had almost certainly been mined by the retreating enemy. Sened was sinister—a wooden *gare* full of wasps' nests; a *buffet*, in a separate building, which two British booby-trap noncoms were busily rigging with their trip wires, as happy as parents decorating a Christmas tree; three or four dwellings, a water tower, and a church, all shattered by shellfire. The fact that the booby-trap men were at work meant that we in our turn were getting ready to abandon the place. You don't booby-trap a place you are going to stay in. We talked to the trappers, both Royal Engineers, one of whom was carrying so many one-pound cakes of TNT under his left arm that they seemed always on the point of wriggling loose. It looks like coarse white laundry soap. When I expressed concern, he said, "Lord love you, sir, it wouldn't explode if it did fall, not without a deetonyter, it wouldn't." The two men wore the fixed, slightly fatuous smile which seems to be a mark of their curious vocation. "We 'ad some nasty ones to tike up before we put ours in," the man with the TNT said. "We've rearranged them so Jerry will 'ave a time with them when 'e comes back. 'E won't be surprised, not 'alf."

There were three torn American medium tanks in a cluster where the main road went by the depot, looking as if they had been punched clean through. Armor-piercing shot from German 88's had gone into them, had bounced around inside like buckshot in a rattle, and then had gone out the other side, leaving the crew to be grilled by the flames as the fuel burned. The charred bodies had been extracted that morning and buried. A soldier's web belt, stiff with blood, lay on the ground outside the hole through which the bodies in one tank had been withdrawn. A couple of soldiers were looking at the belt. One of them was saying, over and over again, "I'll never take no more prisoners! The bastards! I'll never take no more prisoners!" A couple of 88's had lain doggo and caught the tanks with crossfire as they entered the town.

Our artillery was still firing at the ridge of a hill about five miles away. We asked a bearded, wild-looking soldier who was sitting in a parked jeep what the guns were pounding at.

"We got a lot of Germans trapped up there on the mountain," he said.

"How many?" Norgaard wanted to know.

"About a division, I guess," the soldier said.

"I don't see how you could hide a whole division on that hill," Norgaard said calmly.

"They got the mountain all hollowed out and that's where they're hiding," the soldier answered. (A couple of days later, at the American Second Corps headquarters, we asked a G-2 officer what had happened to the Germans trapped on the hill and he said, "Oh, you mean those last nine Heinies? They surrendered.")°

Norgaard and I got back to Gafsa fast. There was an uncomfortable feeling about Sened, a tacit menace that made us feel worse than actually being bombed or shot at.

That night I left the Gafsa region, and I didn't return for six weeks. Meanwhile, the American forces executed, in a rather ragged fashion, a withdrawal from Gafsa and several other towns. We lost almost all of two battalions of armor and two battalions of infantry, and, for the moment at least, all our prestige with the French and Arabs. When the Army recaptured Gafsa, in March, it was in a substantial, intelligent manner, with the entire First Division of infantry. During the operation, I was permitted to tag along with the headquarters of the division. Our troops got back into Gafsa almost without fighting, for the enemy had pulled out before our obviously superior force. The hard fight of the campaign came about a week later, at El Guettar, but that has nothing to do with my memories of Gafsa.

Gafsa was the first town I saw after our side had recaptured it from the enemy, and to me it was, in its small way, a symbol of the fact that this particular breed of bug could be dislodged, like any other. Gafsa is the capital of an administrative district with a population of a hundred and fifty thousand, so the government buildings are far larger than the size of the town itself warrants. Division headquarters, and I with it, moved into the building of the Gendarmerie Nationale, a fine, modern place with sleeping rooms on the upper floors. But the science of booby-trapping has taken a good deal of the fun out of following hot on an enemy's heels. Our engineers had already been through the lower floors of the Gendarmerie looking for booby traps, but they hadn't had time to do the living quarters, in a corner of which I was billeted. It acutely distressed me to turn a doorknob or draw a shutter. Eventually the division engineers decided that the Italians, the last of the enemy to withdraw from Gafsa, had lacked the time, or possibly the skill, to put any booby traps in the buildings. On that first day of my third visit to Gafsa, though, I didn't know what they were going to decide.

Soon after we pulled into town, I went for a walk to see how it had been affected by the occupation, which had lasted four weeks. The sixteenth-century Arab citadel had been partly wrecked by an explosion. Our engineers had used it as a storehouse for explosives during our oc-

---

° This was approximately the place where Mollie, seven weeks later, was to help persuade the Italians to surrender. At the moment of which I now write, he was in Oran, facing charges for leaving his post.

cupancy and, before our withdrawal, had blown it up to keep the enemy from getting the stuff. Our destruction in Gafsa had not, on the whole, been well done. It had been planned, for example, to move a number of locomotives north over the railroad that ran through the town and, after they had gone by, to blow up a railroad bridge to the north, so that we would have the locomotives and the enemy couldn't use the line, but somebody had blown up the bridge first, so the locomotives had to be left in Gafsa. Then, since no preparations had been made to destroy them, they fell into German hands. There was another oversight: the French civilian population of about five hundred had been evacuated by truck, but the native Jews had been left behind.

I met a French-speaking Arab in the market place in front of the old citadel who said he had been some sort of government employee—a police-court interpreter, I think—and had remained through the German occupation. He was frightened, because the houses of all the Frenchmen had been thoroughly pillaged by Arabs and the French notion of justice for Arabs is summary. He was consequently eager to talk and to convince me that his heart, at least, had been with the Allies. Most of the Gafsa Moslems had fled to join their kin in the hills during the German occupation, he said, because they wanted to escape the levies of the Italians and also because a great force of American bombers had come over shortly after the evacuation and flattened a lot of Arab houses. The bombers had killed four hundred Arabs on a breadline in the market place, he said. "The people were much impressed, and those who had gone about talking of the victory of the Germans as certain were discredited," he said, indicating that there are several kinds of propaganda. "They realized that the Americans must have mistaken them for Italian troops," he added adroitly.

I asked him to tell me more about the occupation. "When the Germans and Italians first came here," he said, "they encouraged the people to rob the houses of the French and Jews and some of the more ignorant elements of the population complied with their wishes. The Germans did not stay here long, but went on, leaving an Italian garrison. The Italians were very poor. They pulled up even the young onions out of the gardens in the oasis and ate them as if famished. They broke into Arab houses and stole carpets off the floors and sold them to other Arabs living in the surrounding country, to get a few *sous*. They are a people without shame." The German words *"Araber Geschäft"* had been scrawled in chalk by the Arabs on the doors of a great number of shops, and the Arab told me that this had been done immediately after our evacuation, under instructions given over the Axis Arabic-language radio in Tunis, to protect these Arab establishments from pillage by the incoming Axis troops. "I never listened to that radio, of course," he said, "but so I have heard it related." I said I was surprised that so many Arabs knew even a couple of German words, and he explained that a number of them in Gafsa had been prisoners in Germany during the last war and had learned the

language. It was easy to guess that the town had been full of Arab Axis
agents during our first stay there. Some of them had probably been wearing the G.I. shirts compassionate Yanks had given them.

Presently I walked to the house of the Chemounis, the Tunisian Jewish
family which, on my first visit to Gafsa in January, had entertained Norgaard and me. There had been young Chemouni himself, dressed in a
European business suit, and his old, bearded father, and his attractive
wife, and little, gray-eyed daughter. The house was still standing, but
when I peered in through the open door, it looked as if nobody had lived
there for years. There was nothing left in the place but a few pages of
some Hebrew book scattered on the hard earth floor and a chandelier that
hung crookedly from the roof of the once comfortable room in which
Norgaard and I had drunk sweet wine and eaten olives and sliced pickled
turnips. I wondered whether the family had escaped from Gafsa or been
murdered. I asked a lad who came along the road what had happened to
them and he said that they were all alive and had moved to the old
Jewish quarter of the town, a couple of fetid alleys in which only the
poorest and least Europeanized Jews had lived. The boy, who was Jewish
himself, guided me to the house where the Chemounis were now. A
scarecrow of a young man, wearing a beret and a long blue robe, precipitated himself upon me, sobbing and trying to kiss me. I knew it was
Chemouni, though I could hardly recognize him. "They have stolen even
my trousers," he said, pressing his face against the front of my field
jacket.

Other Jews—many who, like my friend, had a few weeks before been
outwardly European and were now indistinguishable from the most Ori-
ental of Jews—flocked about me with their stories of the occupation. The
Germans had come to the houses of the leading Jews on the first night
and had taken worth-while things like money, jewelry, and stocks of
raw wool, but had not touched their furniture and clothing. They then
had left town, but not before they had invited the Arabs to help themselves to the leavings. As it turned out, there had been a wild competition
between Arabs and Italians to gut the Jewish houses. The Italian commandant of the place had ordered all the Jews into a few houses in the
old quarter and had put them on a ration even smaller than that accorded
the Arabs, which had been minuscule. No Jews had been killed, but two
young ones had come close to going before a firing squad because an
Arab accused them of having betrayed an Axis parachutist to the Americans in December. The two had saved their lives by escaping to the
desert. The Caïd of Gafsa, the town's chief Moslem official, had remained
on the job through the occupation, and so had the spahis, the French-
trained native police. The Caïd had fled with the Italians, fearing that the
returning French would shoot him, but the spahis were still at their posts,
once more under the orders of their French superiors. They were recover-
ing stolen Jewish and French property from Arab houses, but what they

found was now either completely ruined or almost valueless. The Caïd had left a large house containing, as part of the harem, a private movie theatre supplied with an extensive assortment of pornographic films.

Israel had been despoiled again, but it had apparently managed to hoard a few hens and roosters against the day of its deliverance. Near where I was standing, the *shochet*, the ritual slaughterer, an old man with a matted beard, was killing these chickens for family feasts of celebration, holding the blade in his lips between strokes while he smoothed back the neck feathers of the chicken whose throat he was going to slit next. A couple of big Jewish soldiers from the Bronx, with hands huge enough to palm a basketball and great feet that could kick a football sixty yards, placed their arms comfortingly on the shoulders of ancient, tiny matriarchs with whom, because the Tunisian Jews speak neither English nor Yiddish, they had no means of communication except signs. The Bronx Jews and the Tunisian Jews looked as different as a Percheron and an Eohippus.

"The Arabs are very bad," Chemouni said to me. "They have always been bad."

"How long has your family lived in Gafsa?" I asked him.

"I think for two thousand years," he said.

Chemouni's little girl, who spoke French as easily as any child in the Parc Monceau, looked at me with large, frightened, gray eyes. I asked Chemouni if his daughter would go to live in France after we had won the war. He said no, of course not; she would marry and live in Gafsa.

### GAFSA REVISITED

The girl did not stay in Gafsa, nor did my Monsieur Chemouni. When I returned there in the spring of 1956, I learned that both were in Israel, but Chemouni's brother remained—a military tailor for the French garrison.

The "dissidence" in Algeria had brought new trade to Gafsa, this Chemouni explained. There was the biggest French garrison ever, both of ground and air troops, to stop the traffic in munitions across technically neutral Tunisia, which had just regained its independence, to technically French Algeria, which was in full rebellion.

The French still maintained troops in Tunisia—they were withdrawn in subsequent months, except from the naval base of Bizerte. While they were not officially allowed to attack the gun-runners on Tunisian soil, they could follow them and break up their operations as soon as they crossed the line. Airplanes and helicopters were particularly useful for this job. Meanwhile guerillas, all for official purposes Algerians, operated on both sides of the border against the French, while Tunisian troops supposedly operated against the guerillas to preserve Tunisian neutrality.

The French military said that some of the guerillas were themselves

Tunisians, and that the army of the new neutral state merely cooperated with them. The situation was somewhat clarified when the French pulled out and moved across the line into Algeria, where they set up electric barriers along the frontier to keep the gun-runners out. When that happened the military-tailoring business must have fallen off drastically.

The tailor Chemouni told me that much of his work consisted in removing badges of rank from uniforms, because the military believed that the snipers, whether in fact Tunisian or Algerian, picked targets according to grade. Since the snipers had presumably served in the French Army themselves, they presumably recognized the insignia.

There had been a great change since 1943. Tunisians had taken over the civil administration, and French civilians no longer lived among the Moslems in the old town, around the fort and baths. They had removed to the military quarter, around the railroad station on the other side of the oasis, where they felt safer at night. There had been an incident on the road near town a week or two before, when guerillas of some sort had burned a truck and a bus, and cut the throats of the truck-driver, an Italian, and of a European couple traveling in the bus. The husband was a White Russian, employed at a phosphate mine.

Because of this I had had to pay a taxi driver in Tunis extra fare to drive me down to Gafsa, a hundred and fifty miles or so, but we had had a tranquil journey. We had paused only briefly, however, at the old airfield in Thélepte. It felt lonely there; we got the wind up.

The Hotel de France was out of business in Gafsa; its only successors were two very dirty *pensions* near the depot. A young French fighter pilot who talked to me after dinner at one of them thought I was a spy for an American oil company. After I reassured him, he told me that we had been mad to come by road—the country was in a state of anarchy. This was, of course, normal.

At Tunis, the Armée de l'Air had offered to send me in a military plane because they could not guarantee the safety of the roads. The young man at Gafsa seemed overwrought—the dissidents, he said, had taken to shooting at planes with rifles when the planes strafed them. This made him nervous. I did not think he compared well with Rozanoff.

My taxi-driver, a naturalized French citizen of Sicilian birth, spent the night with a friend down the road, a Frenchman who continued to run the municipal electric plant, and whose throat nobody had cut, perhaps because that would have cut the current along with it.

The remaining Jews continued to live in the old town, as they had for a great many centuries before Mohammed was born. I visited another Chemouni there, chief, I was told, of the name. He was a swollen old man with dropsical legs, a merchant who kept a general store, and who lived in a second-floor flat with an electric refrigerator, an index of great wealth. He treated me to sweet liqueur, and said business could be better, but he wasn't thinking of moving, just yet.

There was an old Tunisian proverb, he said: "The worst of those we know is better than the best of those we don't know." So he was going to stay on a while.

Next day my driver, who was named Daniel Portanova, and I drove over to the coast of the Gulf of Gabès, and returned to Tunis by the shore road, uneventfully. I haven't been back to Gafsa since.

Those first few months of intimate, warm, confused war in northwest Africa were made for ad lib fighters like Mollie and Major Cochran. But the campaign reached the age of reason with a lecture which I attended without great expectations.

The first meeting of General Omar Nelson Bradley with the international public, as represented by British and American newspaper and radio correspondents, occurred on the crest of a brush-covered hill at a place called Béja, in northern Tunisia, on April 22, 1943. The American phase of the Allied offensive against the Axis forces in Africa was about to begin. Bradley, who was fifty years old, held the temporary wartime rank of major general, and had no combat record in the First World War and no idiosyncrasies that could be expanded into a legend, had been named to succeed Lieutenant General George S. Patton as commander of the American II Corps, which was the whole American ground force engaged in the African fighting. Since even Patton, for all his pistol-slapping and advance publicity, had failed to make the II Corps work as an offensive unit, correspondents took his replacement by an unknown to mean that the Americans would have a minor role in the final battle against the Axis on the African continent. Press briefings at Patton's headquarters, conducted by an intelligence officer, had been like formal audiences, with all present required to buckle the chin straps of their tin hats, in token of instant readiness to face the moderately distant foe. Before the offensive began, the press-relations officer at Béja had announced with some little embarrassment (the P.R.O. had been commissioned straight out of the publicity department of a movie company, so he was naturally mindful of military dignity) that the new man had decided that he would brief the correspondents in person, and, as there were at least thirty of them and only one of him, he would come to the press camp for this purpose. The new man arrived in a jeep, carrying a map under his arm and attended by his aide, a captain of almost juvenile appearance, who carried an easel and a pointer. The General wore a tin hat—not buckled under the chin, probably because his reconnaissances sometimes took him into shelling and he didn't want his head jerked off. He also wore a canvas field jacket, G.I. pants, and canvas leggings, thus qualifying as the least dressed-up commander of an American army in the field since Zachary Taylor, who wore a straw hat. He had a long jaw and a high, notably convex forehead, and he was wearing spectacles. After the Green Hornet, with his ruddy, truculent face and his beefy, leather-sheathed calves, the new general, lanky and diffidently amiable, seemed a man of milk.

The aide set up the easel in press headquarters; then the General hung the map, took the pointer, and, in a high, not loud voice, as Missourian as the Truman voice that later became familiar to radio listeners, began to demonstrate how the II Corps intended to progress in an eleven-day drive to Mateur, the key to Bizerte, through enemy positions that had stopped the best troops of the British First Army for five months. Some people think a general should have a voice like a recorded bugle call played over a loudspeaker. But the Bradley delivery is really an asset—hesitant, slightly rustic, compelling the hearer to listen hard for the next phrase and at the same time convincing him of the General's candor. At Béja, he laid down his schedule with no more panache than a teacher outlining the curriculum for the new semester. The Americans, he said, had been moved from the south-central to the extreme northwest arc of the Allied semicircle facing the Axis redoubt—because, the correspondents had suspected up to this point, they were to make merely a holding attack, in country so rugged that they could switch quickly to the defensive if the Germans came at them. Meanwhile, the British First and Eighth Armies were to crash through at more promising points on the Axis perimeter. When a correspondent who had been with the British in this zone through the bitter months of frustration asked how the inexperienced 9th Division was going to get Green and Bald Hills, two notoriously nasty positions that had stopped the Guards, General Bradley said that that was up to General Manton Eddy, the division commander, but that he didn't expect any undue delay. All parts of the inquiring correspondent visible above his battle dress turned purple.

Only two American infantry divisions, the 1st and the 9th, appeared on the General's map. The absence of the corps's other infantry outfit, the 34th Division, was interpreted by some to mean that it was being held in defensive reserve and by others that it had been sent home as useless. Either supposition, if confirmed, would bear out the notion that the American attack was not too banefully intended. There was, however, a gap half as wide as a divisional front between the 9th and the 1st. "What are you going to have in there, sir?" a knowing fellow asked. The new general looked at him with a gratified, pedagogical smile, as at a pupil who had asked a bright question. "I'm going to patrol that with a troop of motorized cavalry," he said. (A couple of days later, when General Eddy expressed his own disquiet about the gap, Bradley told him reassuringly, "If they come through there, Bill Kean and I will go in with a couple of BARs." BARs are Browning automatic rifles. Kean, who later commanded the 25th Division in Korea, was then the II Corps's chief of staff.) The new general didn't have much more to say. It was a historic début, although nobody knew it at the time. Had any programs been printed, they would sell at a big premium today.

Bradley had been in Tunisia two months without a command when he took over the II Corps. General George Catlett Marshall, then Chief of Staff of the Army, had, General Marshall later said, sent Bradley there "to be Eisenhower's legs and wisdom." He spent most of his time at the front, returning to Algiers to tell the Commander-in-Chief what was going on. General Eisenhower was not only several hundred miles away; he was—nominally, at least—in command of the British First and Eighth Armies and the French XIX Corps, in addition to the Americans, and was also supreme political arbiter of North Africa, which left him only limited time for tactical details. This had been Bradley's first experience in a real war, and he had been looking at it closely—going up into forward observation posts, and talking to company and platoon leaders and to riflemen to check on what he had learned and taught in the previous thirty-two years. So he was bringing to his first recital what a music critic unafraid of clichés would call a ripened technique and a mature understanding of the content of the music. Into the gap in his offensive alignment, when the time came, he slipped the fresh 34th Division, and, pushing it forward in depth on a rather narrow front, he sent it against Hill 609, the highest eminence of the first range he had to fight across. The 1st had already reached the flanks of 609 and could put artillery fire on it to help the attackers. So employed, the 34th, which so far in this campaign had known only defeat and was considered a liability, took 609 and came out believing itself a division *d'élite*, which was most of what it needed to be one. This made the new general's military gifts manifest to his first audience, and they have never had cause to change their opinion of him. Many generals, in the course of history, have taken a hill at the cost of a division, and as many have lost a division without taking a hill. Bradley took a key hill and gained a division. His troops reached each of their objectives almost exactly in accordance with the schedule he had laid down. "There was one time when Matt Eddy was a few hours behind, up on the left flank," General Bradley said a couple of years later, during the campaign in western France, "but I told him to step on it."

Bradley explained that small bit of virtuosity seven years later, over a drink.

"All hills, with narrow draws between them—a country just laid out for defense," he said of northern Tunisia. "They'd get up in the hills, and when you went down in the draws to get around them, they'd put fire on you." He had thought he knew what to do about the hills, he said—go straight up them, as you would when hunting wild goats in the mountains of Hawaii. It had also occurred to him that the German 88, though its flat trajectory made it wonderful for shooting across valleys at vehicles in the open, would not be much good at firing over hills at close range to hit hidden soldiers on the reverse slopes. "I remember that gap between the Ninth and the First," he said. "What I was thinking was that if the suckers did come in over those hills, they wouldn't have any good road they could get far on, and we could round 'em up before they got far into our rear. It was about nine miles from where they were over to the Djebel Abiod road, and by the time they had climbed down there we could have armor to meet them."

The Chairman sipped at his drink and looked across at the staircase as if he could see the Djebel Abiod road, in the shadow of hills covered with purple wild flowers and separated by narrow black gorges in which dwarf cows found water. Then he smiled. "I wanted that gap for the Thirty-fourth," he said. "Alexander [General, now Viscount, Alexander, the field commander of the joint Allied forces in Africa] and Bedell Smith [Eisenhower's Chief of Staff] had wanted to send the Thirty-fourth home for retraining, they thought it was so bad. It had its tail down between its legs. I said, 'Leave it to me and I'll guarantee that it carries its first important objective, if I have to give it every gun in the Corps.' It's good for troops to feel they have an important objective. You may have to move them up and move them back once or twice when they're green, just to give them the habit of fighting, but if you do it too often they get the feeling they're being thrown away. That treatment had spoiled the Thirty-fourth. So I didn't want it in at the start, when they might think they were getting more of the same. Then I put them at 609. You remember it. It was almost a cliff. But the Thirty-fourth went up it. The suckers got down in the crevices when we put fire on it, and then after our fellows had passed over they came out and took them in the rear. But our fellows cleaned them up. After that, the Thirty-fourth had its tail over the dashboard. You couldn't hold it."

The Thirty-fourth was the division components of which had been so messed around with in the fighting between Sened and Maknassy, while other components had subsequently been set out on hills near Kasserine like goats set out to lure a tiger. Then, when the tiger, in the form of German armor, came, the American armored division that had been cast in the role of big-game hunter lost its nerve and let the Germans scoop up the infantry goats, along with about 100 of our tanks. The residue of the Thirty-fourth was left with a goat mentality, which it imparted to the replacements. Old Dr. Bradley's psychotherapy fixed it up. Confusion, though normal, is not inevitable.

# PART III

ENTR'ACTE

I WAS LUCKY enough to get back to New York at the end of the African campaign, as I have told in the first piece in the book, and had five months at home before I came to the wars again, this time as a passenger on a Norwegian fruit ship that was considered fast enough to run without escort—seventeen knots. She certainly was that time, although I heard she copped it later. You were always hearing that ships you had just been on were sunk, and sometimes it was true. This reefer was of 3,000 tons, very clean and yacht-like, and she landed me in the Adelphi Hotel at Liverpool on November 6, 1943, my fourth and last eastward crossing during the war. My notion was to get to England early in order to be sure of a good spot in the invasion. I did not want to get caught up in some ancillary theatre and then not be able to transfer out in time for the main event, and as the lone correspondent of *The New Yorker* I had to fight my own campaign against red tape and the stuffy lay bureaucrats of the large press organizations, who wanted to make the battle an exclusive feature for their employers, like *Gasoline Alley* or Arthur Krock. When not engaged in this sordid guerilla, I tried various activities to kill time. "Run, Run, Run, Run," arose out of one of them, or out of two of them if you like. It was such an unsettling experience that I didn't write about it at the time; it was hardly a news story, being about something that happened when I wasn't there and then didn't happen when I was. I wrote it in the fall of 1945, at home, but it is all true, except that I made the chief character a more obvious fraud than I am, by lending him some of the characteristics of correspondents I disliked.

# Run, Run, Run, Run

WHEN Allardyce Meecham heard that the boys were dead, he felt that he should have flown with them. Meecham was a war correspondent, but he had not yet had a chance to see much of the war. He had come to England in February, 1944, straight from the Hotel Algonquin, where he had had only four or five days to wear his uniform in the lobby, and he did not feel natural wearing it even after a fortnight in London. His nearest approach to action so far had been a visit to an American bomber station in Essex, where he had arranged to go on a bombing mission with a Marauder crew. Now he felt guilty because he had not gone. If he had he would have been dead, too, and that had not been part of his plan, but he felt somehow that this was an ignoble consideration. At the field, a squadron intelligence officer named Kobold had told him the mediums had been having very small losses, an average of one in two hundred sorties. "I wanted to fly one mission and write a story about it, and pretend to myself that I was a big man," Meecham thought self-accusingly, "but if I had expected they would be killed I wouldn't have gone with them." This may or may not have been true. There was no way now of proving it. But Meecham never gave himself the benefit of the doubt because he was afraid that if he did it once he would take advantage of the precedent. "What could you have done, anyway," he asked himself, "if you had known they were going to be killed? Would you have made some excuse and left? Or would you have tried to get them not to go? They would have wanted to know how you could be sure. They would have said you were crazy. They would have gone anyway." But he continued to feel as if he had done something wrong. Meecham had left the airfield because he had tired of hanging about waiting for flying weather. Three days' missions had been washed out and there was no sign it would open up, and he had a date with a British woman officer in London for Friday evening.

This was Sunday. Meecham was standing at the bar of his hotel in Piccadilly, and next to him was Kobold, the intelligence officer he had met at the bomber base. Kobold had come into London on a weekend pass, and he had just told Meecham the bad news. "I wasn't frightened," Meecham thought. "I really wasn't. I told them I was coming back to fly with them next week. They expected to be there. They had flown forty missions. They didn't think the weather would clear off during the weekend. They said I would be a sucker to stay." The weather had cleared on Friday afternoon, after he had left. Saturday morning the bomber crew had been killed. At what precise minute, Meecham wondered, but he felt almost sure he knew. It was March, and dawn came medium late. They would not have been fairly on their way before eight. Over Beauvais, in the north of France, at nine, nine-thirty, maybe. Perhaps at the moment he had picked up the telephone by his bed to order breakfast. "Two teas, sausage and tomato. Darling, do you want sausage and tomato or sausage and mushroom? There's bacon, but it's usually like eating a candle." That must have been the minute. "Two sausage and tomato, then. And lots of toast. Thank you."

"They had all their bombs aboard," Kobold was saying. He was an oldish lieutenant who felt that he should have been a captain months ago. "One big hell of a cloud of smoke, and then parts of the plane falling out of it. No chutes—no time for them. The other boys brought back wonderful pictures of it. Poor bastards." The intelligence officer talked loudly, a little truculently, because he wanted a couple of B-17 pilots at the other end of the bar to hear him. The heavy-bomber people sometimes talked as if they had all the losses; the lieutenant wanted to impress this pair. He never flew on operations himself.

Meecham stood just six feet in shoes, but because of his thin, long legs and short, beanlike torso he seemed longer than that when he stood up and shorter than that when he sat down. He had a white face, wide at the cheekbones and covered with faint, rusty blotches, and carroty hair that for the last five years had just failed to cover the top of his head. People seeing him at a bar thought of him as tall and red-headed, but others, who had looked at him seated at a restaurant table, remembered him as bald and middle-sized. His eyelashes were almost white. In New York he was a dramatic critic, but as the war entered its fifth year and all his acquaintances—book reviewers, editorial writers, political columnists, racing handicappers, and publishers' assistants—became war correspondents and went overseas, he had felt lonely. There must be something in the war that none of these people were fine enough to perceive, he had told his wife, who had a responsible job in the promotion department of a women's magazine and always referred to herself as a "gal." She had agreed with him. She was a good gal. "Besides," she had said, "I think it would be a professional disadvantage for a dramatic critic after the war not to have been a war correspondent. No one would want to hear you lecture." She was having an affair with a Rumanian fashion photographer, who worked her for assignments. Meecham had been disappointed that even his own wife misread his motives. But, fighting down this disap-

pointment, he had gone to his managing editor and asked to be sent to
Europe. The editor had sent him because he rather thought there would
be a lull before the invasion of the Continent. Meecham would spell one
of the paper's regular correspondents accredited to the Army, who would
come home for a short vacation before the big show began. "But, of
course, if it should start suddenly, you'll be there," the editor had said.
"Yes, sir," Meecham had said in a voice from which he had tried to
exclude excitement. He had felt exalted as he walked over to Abercrombie
& Fitch to be measured for his uniform. But, as he now reflected, he had
not thought that he really might be killed. "I wanted something for nothing," he thought unmercifully. He was on the point of admiring how hard
on himself he could be, and then he remembered that that would consti-
tute self-approval, so he stopped.

Meecham remembered the interior of the Nissen hut he had slept in at
the Marauder field. There had been cots and a table and a stove, hooks on
the walls to hang clothes on, and even coat hangers, but to him it had
been a Spartan place, where he had been more conscious of the war than
in his room in London, which contained a good deal of inlaid furniture
and a double bed with a yellow damask cover. There were electric-light
bulbs in the hut, but they were not shaded, and you had to go outdoors to
get to the latrine. There were six cots in the hut. A Marauder carries a
complement of three officers and three enlisted men; the hut accommo-
dated the officers of two planes. One set of three had gone to town on
pass; men who flew together took their passes at the same time. This gave
Meecham his choice of three cots. The boys of the other Marauder crew
had just come back from forty-eight hours in London. Meecham found
them in the hut when Kobold brought him there in the evening. He had
stayed at the officers' club drinking gin and Italian vermouth with the C.O.
and a couple of non-flying intelligence officers until the bar closed, at ten
o'clock. Then Kobold had guided him to the hut. It would have been hard
to find in the blackout if he had been alone. Kobold had introduced
Meecham to the three crewmates. One of them, a large, hairy, blond
young man, was in bed already. He was Captain Barry, the pilot. Barry
was smoking a last cigarette before going to sleep. One bare, powerful
arm lay outside the blankets as he puffed. A B-26, romantically known as
a Marauder, is not an easy plane to fly, and old pilots get big forearms
and biceps. Barry reached out a big hand to shake Meecham's. "Make
yourself at home," he said. Brownlea, the co-pilot, a wiry young man with
a crew haircut, sat at the table with his back to the stove, reading what
Meecham observed wonderingly was a book by Robert Briffault, an author Meecham associated vaguely with Granville Hicks and Ouida. "I
hope you don't mind loud noises," Brownlea said. "Barry is about to go to
sleep. Luckily they have radar here or somebody would have shot him

down before this. When he snores he sounds exactly like a four-motor job. He has the Air Force sack medal with so many clusters it looks like a bunch of grapes." "Brownlea is an intellectual," Barry said. "He is a wizard intellectual, they would say in the R.A.F. He is very cheesed with life. He thinks life is a ruddy pantomime. Someday when he is at the controls he will be thinking of an ideology and he will prang the crate. A wizard prang." Elkan, the bombardier-navigator, was sitting on a cot, looking over a set of shiny photographer's prints; he had interrupted the examination only long enough to nod at Meecham when Kobold introduced them. He was a thin young man who in civilian clothes could have been mistaken for a high-school junior. He could not weigh more than a hundred and fifteen pounds and he had a long, pointed nose and large ears. He was still wearing the Class A uniform blouse and pinks in which he had come back from London, and the garrison cap was still on his head. The left breast of his blouse was pretty well loaded with ribbons—even Meecham could recognize the Silver Star, the Distinguished Flying Cross, the Air Medal nutmegged with oak-leaf clusters, the E.T.O. ribbon dotted with stars, and a couple of the innocuous red-and-yellow ones that make good background even though they don't mean anything much.

Kobold went away and Meecham settled down on a cot. "I'm glad to have you here, sir," Brownlea said to Meecham. "Barry and Elkan are good joes, but Elkan is emotional and Barry is inclined to pure escapism. I have been wanting a chance to talk to someone who has really been around a lot."

Meecham was ashamed to tell him that his travels, until this trip, had been limited to a tourist-class vacation in France when he was in college and four trips to the Central City, Colorado, annual dramatic festivals, so he said nothing.

"Don't give Brownlea any encouragement, sir," Elkan said, "or he will read you the first ten chapters of his book."

"I wouldn't think of it," Brownlea said. "Anyway, they're only in a kind of outline form. I really don't know anything about writing. What I want to know is what you think of the Russians."

Meecham considered himself an untrammelled liberal—during the Spanish Civil War he had attended several cocktail parties for the benefit of the Loyalists—but he had heard talk at home about the Fascist mind of the Air Corps, so he was careful in answering. He liked these boys so much already that he didn't want to alarm or antagonize them. He said merely, "I know the Russians are our Allies. I mean, I believe they're sincere, and they're certainly fighting hard."

"Is that all?" Brownlea said. "Why, they're absolutely wonderful. They're the only hope I see for civilization. Surely, sir, you don't think capitalist society can survive all this? Say, have you ever read this man Briffault?"

"Brownie got a brushoff from a society dame at a bottle club in London," Barry said. "She said she was going to spend a penny and she never came back. He's been a militant proletarian ever since."

Meecham said that, of course, the rôle Russia would be called upon to play in the future should not be underestimated.

"Well, I don't worry much about that," Barry said, "although I still have a card in the typographical union, so it burns my ass when I read in the *Reader's Digest* that organized labor is to blame for about everything that gets screwed up. I worked my way through the University of California that way, setting type at night on a paper in Oakland. Where the hell does the *Reader's Digest* think I am, and where is the bird who is writing that stuff? Sitting on his can, I bet. But being from the Coast, I mean, I don't think very much about this war. I'd like to be out smacking those Japs around. I haven't got anything too much against the Germans, except Hitler is a son of a bitch."

"I have," Elkan said. "I'm a Jew, and they've been killing millions of Jews who didn't do a goddam thing to them. I hate the bastards. I like to think of what the bombs will do to them when we make our run."

"You see?" Brownlea said. "Pure emotion. Barry and Elkan don't know anything about the economic bases of imperialism. They reduce everything to personal relationships."

"She said she had to spend a penny," Barry said to nobody in particular. "Brownie offered to lend her a shilling. She gave him a look that said, 'Anybody that dumb . . .' And the brush."

Elkan said, "To change the subject, which of these pictures do you like the best?"

"Are they of a broad?" Barry asked.

"No, you wolf—me," Elkan answered severely. "I went down to see the Tower of London yesterday, and then I walked around and had some pictures taken at a photographer's. I want to pick out the best one and have some copies made from it to send home. I want to send them to my mother and my girl and people like that." Meecham had already learned that Elkan's parents lived in Bayonne, New Jersey, where his father had a dry-cleaning store. He had gone two years to Rutgers but hadn't had enough money to continue, and for a year or so before he enlisted he had helped in the store. He hadn't as much assurance as some of the bigger, louder boys, who gave the impression that the whole Air Force came from Texas, but the fellows in his squadron had a lot of respect for him. Barry, Brownlea, and Meecham began passing the photographer's proofs from one to another. Meecham could see that the two pilots were considering them very seriously. In all but one of the proofs, Elkan had the visor of his cap pulled well down and was scowling and puffing out his chest. The photographer had got a good, clear picture of the ribbons. But the thin, triangular face and the frail, bony neck still looked like a little boy's. Only one of the proofs showed Elkan smiling. The wide smile made him look younger and more ingenuous than ever, but the picture was the only one of the lot that wasn't absurd. All three of the consultants agreed it was the best.

"That's the only one that looks like the real Ernie," Barry said.

"That's the one your mother would like to have," said Brownlea.

And Meecham said, "That's the best." He could sense that Ernie was disappointed and that if he had not been there the little bombardier-navigator might have tried to argue with the others.

But Elkan accepted the reinforced verdict. "Christ," he said sadly, "I guess I'll never look like a hero." Meecham could see that he was worrying about his girl back home.

They had talked a while longer and then turned in. Meecham had felt unexpectedly ashamed because his body looked so white and old compared to theirs. He was forty-three and the last exercise he could remember had been a fight with the juvenile of a show he had panned in 1937, but the bartender and the home-and-garden editor had stopped it after the first swing, when the juvenile's pince-nez fell on the floor.

There had been no mission the next morning, on account of the weather. Meecham had got up at seven and gone dutifully to mess, but the boys had chosen to sleep until nearly noon.

"It must be awfully slow for you here, sir," Barry had said the next time Meecham saw him. "I suppose you wanted to go over with us and see some fun."

"It isn't dull at all," Meecham had said, and meant it. "It's very interesting." He had not added, "It's all new to me," because he felt a childish reluctance to let the boys know he was so green. He hadn't really thought of flying a mission on his first visit to the field, either. But Barry looked so competent and unworried that Meecham had found himself saying, "I sure would like to go with you. Do you think the C.O. would let me?"

Barry had grinned and said, "Sure. We've flew lots of correspondents in our ship. It breaks the monotony." And they had shaken hands on it.*

Meecham had slept in the hut a second and third night and each had been followed by a day of bad weather. Even in this brief time he had begun to think of himself as a member of the crew of the Typographical Error, the name Barry had given his B-26. He had gone through the preliminary processes of a Marauder mission, which at that time he had thought piquant rather than grim. The squadron intelligence officer had told him what to do if he had to bail out over France. He was to hide his parachute and then take cover and lie still until somebody found him. The French underground people would be pretty sure to find him, the intelligence officer said, and they would smuggle him across France and

* Harold Ross, the great editor of *The New Yorker*, said when he read this in manuscript that Barry, a college man and a linotyper, would not have said, "flew." My only answer was that the prototype of Barry in real life *had* said "flew." Since I was pretending to write fiction, this was not a valid argument, but I had my way. I can see now that "we've flew" looks unconvincing. But I hear the pseudonymous Barry's voice in my head sometimes, and he still says it.

into a neutral country, although it might take months. The prospect had sounded alluring as the intelligence officer described it, and Meecham had been unable to stop daydreaming about adventures with admiring and sympathetic Frenchwomen. The one thing the officer had not said anything about was what to do if you were dead. So Meecham had not thought about it.

On the third bad morning he had begun to feel bored and had remembered the date with the woman officer in London. There was a train at noon and he had decided to leave by it. When he began packing his bag the boys were still in bed, and when he finished he went around to each cot and shook hands before he started for the jeep that was to take him to the railway station. Meecham could remember Barry's strong grip and Elkan's slender hand and Brownlea grinning and waving his clenched left fist. Brownlea's father, Meecham had learned, was president of a savings bank in Boston.

Remembering, Meecham felt that the date with them was more binding than if they had survived and that he could never be pleased with himself if he did not fly a mission now. But there was no exhilaration in the thought. He returned to Essex three days later. He found it easy to arrange, at Ninth Air Force Headquarters, for permission to go along on a bombardment. "The story has been done a lot of times before," a public-relations officer warned him. "There's nothing much to it." Meecham explained that he just wanted to see what it was like. He didn't say anything about the crew of the Typographical Error. It seemed to him for a moment, after they had said he could go, that he was doing a causeless thing. It isn't being brave, he told himself, because the mathematical chance of getting hurt is no greater now than it was last week, and then it was very small. Barry and his ship just had bad luck. And there won't be any story in it either. But he was afraid, and that was precisely what he could not afford to admit to himself. Nobody at the field seemed astonished that he wanted to do it. The boys at the officers' club made him welcome with gin and Italian vermouth, and he was introduced to the officers he was now assigned to fly with. Their ship was named the Roll Me Over,* and they were nice boys enough, Meecham thought, but it was like a widower's marriage; he could not get as interested in them as in the dead crew. Schifferdecker, the pilot, was a squat, broad-shouldered boy who had played football at Cornell, where he had taken a course in hotel manage-

---

* From that great song:
    "Roll me over, in the clover,
    Roll me over, lay me down, and do it again—"
which was the pre-invasion "Battle Hymn of the Republic." It was frequently asserted, during World War II, that "this is not a singing war." It was—people always sing when they are frightened—but the songs did not lend themselves to community performance.

ment. He kept telling Meecham that after the war the British would have to build modern hotels all over England if they expected any Americans ever to come back there. Thurman, the co-pilot, a tall, handsome young man from someplace in Wisconsin, did not have much to say for himself. He had a girl in a show in London, his crewmates said, and he considered every hour he had to spend at the field time wasted. "Missions are the only chance he has to catch up on his sleep," Schifferdecker said. Muldowney, the bombardier-navigator, was a pale, gray-eyed young man who looked like a very youthful Franchot Tone and knew it, and who had played in a dance band in St. Paul before enlisting in the Air Corps. "It's a good deal, having a correspondent along," he told Meecham. "We'll be in a soft spot, right in the center of one of the middle elements, where nothing ever happens. Those flak gunners loose off at the first ships, and then, when the first elements drop their bombs, the gunners run like hell. We'll have a breeze. Same thing for fighters. We haven't been getting much fighter opposition. The Heinies keep most of that in Germany to use against the heavy bombers. But what we have been getting usually lays for the rear element, on the way home, hoping to knock off stragglers. We lost a ship that way yesterday. The boys in the middle have a soft touch." Muldowney had a wide, white grin. "An easy one is always all right with me," he went on. "I've had twenty-eight missions so far, and every easy one means that much better a chance to finish the fifty."

There was no cot for Meecham in the hutment where the Roll Me Overs slept, so he spent the night in a hut in another part of the field, about half a mile from the mess hall. The men in the hut with him were armament and engineering officers. Only two were in bed when Meecham got there. The rest were up most of the night preparing planes for the takeoff. They got in so late that they had just begun to snore when an orderly turned on the lights before dawn next morning. They stayed in bed, the blankets over their heads, while Meecham and the two men who had been in bed early began to dress. Meecham hated to get up early in the morning for any reason at all, and on this particular day he felt worse than usual. He dressed fast, for him, but he was not yet familiar with lace boots, and he had to fumble around in his musette bag to find toothpaste and a towel. Then he felt colicky and went out to look for a latrine. By the time he returned the two other men had gone to the mess hall, and he began to fear that he would lose his way in the dark. The buildings were, of course, blacked out, so he would have no lighted windows to guide him. It would sound like an implausible excuse for missing the raid. He went out of the hut and saw the silhouette of a jeep moving up the road past the hut. There were at least a dozen men on it, some sitting on the hood. He yelled, "Going up to mess?" Someone shouted to him to jump on. Awkwardly he ran along beside the slowly moving jeep, not knowing quite how to get aboard without knocking some other rider off his perch. The jeep stopped and somebody said, "Come along, Pop. You can sit in the back." One of the youngsters in the back seat scrambled out and found a few inches of space on a mudguard, and half a dozen hands grabbed Meecham and hoisted him into the place just vacated. He rode along to the mess hall oblivious of everything except his humiliation. At table he found Schifferdecker and Thurman. Muldowney came along a couple of minutes later, carrying a shiny brown quilted flying suit which he had drawn for Meecham. The breakfast was poor—an omelet badly made of powdered egg and bacon that was all rind and grease. The fruit juice was all gone and the coffee tasted metallic. He wondered if the breakfast was really that bad or if he was frightened. "This is pisspoor chow," Thurman said, and Meecham was reassured. The men in the mess hall straggled out in little groups, crewmates and fellows who knew each other, and climbed into weapons carriers for the ride out to the dispersal building for the briefing. Meecham, of course, rode with the Roll Me Overs.

The briefing reminded him of a lecture in a compulsory course at college. The hall was filled with fellows in flying gear who talked to each other and did not seem too attentive. The intelligence officer stood on a dais at one end of the hall and waved a pointer at various spots on a large map that was projected on a screen behind him. Meecham learned later that all the fliers had been to these particular targets several times and that the lecture had about the same interest for them as an explanation of how to reach New Rochelle. "Our primary target today will be the Montdidier airfield," the officer said. "There is a battery of six mediums on the approach to the Montdidier field. Six mediums." Somebody whistled. "All of you can go now except the bombardiers. Bombardiers stay a minute after the others leave."

Meecham went out with Schifferdecker and Thurman and three sergeants who had joined them in the briefing hall. The sergeants were the rest of the Roll Me Over's crew—radio-gunner, flight engineer, and tail gunner. They were named Mickiewicz, Klopstock, and Leopardi. Muldowney had to stay to get his detailed bombing map. When he came out they all got into a weapons carrier with perhaps twenty other fliers. The carrier rolled along on the cinder path that circled the field, stopping at each plane to let off the men who were going to fly in it. So Meecham found himself eventually standing under the shadow of the Roll Me Over. It was daylight now, but the sky was still pink with the embers of dawn. In the truck the boys had been singing a song of which Meecham had been able to distinguish only the first line, "How's your love life?"° He put on the flying suit over his G.I. pants, his sweater, and his combat jacket. Muldowney was brisk and happy, although cold. He rubbed his gloved hands together furiously and stamped about in his flying boots. Schifferdecker was serious and conscientious, conferring with the ser

---

° This was not a classic, like "Roll Me Over," and I never heard it again. It sounded like something they would get off the other side of a hit record in the officers' lounge.

geants. Thurman leaned against the fuselage and Meecham noticed that he looked sleepy. He wondered if Thurman could have got down to London on a late train and back in time to fly. Meecham nodded toward the ship and asked Muldowney if it was all right to get aboard. Muldowney said sure, and went ahead to show the way. This was a moment Meecham had anticipated with distaste, because he didn't know how to get into a B-26 and had a feeling it might call for some display of acrobacy. It was not so hard as he had feared. There were two metal stirrups no higher than those on an English saddle, and when you got one foot up you reached up with your hands and caught two metal handles in the interior of the plane. Then you swung yourself up and in. He could see that it would be easy to get out when they returned—he would only have to swing himself out by the handles and drop. Somehow this was a major satisfaction. Muldowney motioned him into a compartment behind the nose of the plane. There was no need to kneel or crawl. "There's a hell of a lot of room in these things," Muldowney said. "More than in a Fort. You just sit over there at the side on that pile of chutes." The others came aboard one by one. Schifferdecker and Thurman went past Meecham and into the pilots' compartment, in the nose. The sergeants joined Meecham and Muldowney in the compartment behind the pilots' because Schifferdecker would want their weight up forward for the takeoff. "This is a place for the navigator to work," Muldowney told Meecham, "but there isn't any real navigating to do when we follow the leader in a big formation like today. Of course, if we got crippled or had to beat it off by ourselves for any reason, it would be different. I just wander around the ship when we get going, sometimes here and sometimes in the bomb bay. We're carrying frag bombs today, by the way. Thirty one-hundred-pound frag bombs. We drop them on the runway and dispersal area to take care of planes and personnel. Sometimes we carry a couple of big ones, but today frags." The motors were turning over. Other planes taxied by them on their way to the runway. Then the Roll Me Over began to roll, too. The motors made such a noise that conversation became impractical, although it was still possible to understand a shouted monosyllable. The compartment in which Meecham rode was comfortable, but there was only a view straight out to either side. There was nothing to see in either direction except other B-26s. The plane was swaying and slipping about and he could see Thurman turn and swear. Schifferdecker was running the ship. The pilots sat next to each other. The backs of their seats were armor-plated, as a protection against pieces of flak. Meecham could see there was room for a man to crouch behind them, and he looked forward enviously because there was more to see from the nose of the plane. Thurman, as if reading his thoughts, waved to him to come forward, and he did, scrunching his torso and hams down behind Thurman's seat, while his legs extended over behind Schifferdecker's.

Now the sky was as blue as the Bay of Naples on the wall of a spaghetti joint, and it was full of B-26s. They flew in "loose fives," their favorite formation. Meecham started to count all those in sight; he made it sixty-seven, including the planes on the Roll Me Over's wings, but more appeared constantly and he stopped counting. He deduced that the B-26s were just circling while the groups assembled and that the serious part of the expedition had not begun yet. Then the course began to seem to him more purposeful. Almost before he was sure of this, Thurman was plucking at his elbow, waving an arm downward. They were over the coast, heading out over the Channel, which looked not blue but had, at its English edge, the color of a puddle of rain water glistening in sunlight. Then it became lead color. Meecham noticed for the first time that the motors were saying words. They were saying words, groaning, rather, "No, no, no, no." He had ridden in planes before but he had never recognized the words. When they got over the French coast, he thought, "I should be curious. I haven't seen France in twenty years." He looked and it seemed quite like England. He leaned close to Thurman's ear and shouted, "How long to over target?" Thurman howled back, "Twenty minutes." Meecham went back to the pile of parachutes in the navigator's cabin and Muldowney appeared, probably from the bomb bay, and seemed to be saying something about "fighters." Meecham returned to his place behind the pilots and looked down. He saw a midget plane far below them. It was a Spitfire, but he did not know it; he could not tell Allied fighters from Germans. All the attention began to embarrass Meecham. He felt that Muldowney was treating him like a grandfather on a Sunday auto ride. Muldowney reached through the doorway to the pilots' compartment and tapped Meecham on the shoulder. He wanted to show him something dead ahead, a series of specks in the sky. Then Muldowney grinned and started back to the bomb bay. The specks were not fighters, Meecham saw as the plane drew up on them, but puffs of black smoke. They multiplied, as he watched, and hung in the air, little black balls of grime. He knew what they were from his sporadic attendance at newsreel theatres. The planes of the forward elements were flying through them now. The flak was at very nearly the right altitude, and Meecham began to hear a new sound over the motors—a sharp "Pak!" like a champagne cork popping and then "S-s-s" like half the wine in the bottle fizzing out. The "Pak!" was the shell bursting, and the fizz was the flight of the fragments. Once Thurman threw up a hand in front of his face and flattened himself against the back of his seat, but nothing happened. Meecham wondered if it had been a close one or if Thurman was just jumpy from too much tomcatting. The co-pilot was waving his hand now and Meecham, following his gesture, could see the bombs falling away from the planes up ahead of them, like chewing-gum nuggets out of a vending machine. Then there were no more puffs in the sky. He felt Muldowney's hand on his shoulder again. The boy had been away only an instant, it seemed. Muldowney was laughing and waving his hands palm upward. Thurman took off his earphones and put them on Meecham, so Meecham could listen to the intercom. Schifferdecker said to Meecham through the intercom, "How'd you like it?" Meecham tried to smile, and for all he knew succeeded. Then Schifferdecker made Thurman take the ship. Meecham understood from that that they were on the way home. He gave Thurman the earphones again. The motors said now, "Run, run, run, run." He said to himself, "I am not making this up, that is what they are saying." He listened again and they were indeed saying, "Run, run," instead of "No, no." Meecham looked at the air speed indicator and it said "330," which pleased him. Then he went back to Muldowney's compartment and relaxed on the parachutes. Muldowney was grinning and waving his hands and shouting into Meecham's ear, and finally Meecham could understand what he was saying: "I told you that flak would stop as soon as the first planes got their bombs away!" Meecham succeeded in asking whether *he* had got his bombs away and Muldowney joined a thumb and forefinger in a circle to show he had put his bombs right on the bull's-eye. Sergeant Mickiewicz, a bulky blond with a red face, appeared in the compartment and grinned at Meecham. Nothing happened on the way back, but it seemed five times as long as it had going out.

When they got out of the plane, Schifferdecker started swearing. "The goddam wash nearly made me airsick," he said. "Those goddam cowboys in the ships on our wings must think they're driving taxicabs. Whoever checked them out in a bomber ought to have his head examined. What a ratfuck!" He explained that a ratfuck was "a rat race, but all bollixed up."

Thurman said, "If they don't keep us too long at the goddam interrogation I can catch the twelve-o'clock train to London."

Muldowney said, "Twenty-nine down and twenty-one to go. I hope they send us a correspondent on every trip! I wonder if any of those leading planes got flak in them."

Meecham felt unreasonably exalted. After all, he told himself reprovingly, he had only escaped from a danger that he had got himself into. And not a great danger, either, he thought. I didn't see one plane shot down. Still, he couldn't help thinking, pretty good for a dramatic critic. He had forgotten Barry and Elkan and Brownlea.

Meecham was still in the midst of his euphoria when he boarded the London train at Chelmsford in midafternoon. He had not been in as much haste to get away as Thurman, and had remained to eat a pretty good lunch of pork chops and canned pineapple at the field. The train was crowded, and although he had a first-class ticket, he had to stand in the corridor outside a compartment filled with American enlisted men who had got on further up the line. When they saw his war-correspondent shoulder flash they tapped on the glass and asked him in. They were all

Fortress men who, it appeared, had been on dozens of twelve-hour missions over Germany, from almost all of which they had returned with
their ships aflame and three engines out. Meecham was ashamed to tell
them he had been only as far as France that morning. By the time the
train arrived at Liverpool Street station his exuberance was waning. Coming out into Broad Street, he felt hungry again. He had had what for
him was a phenomenally long day. He stopped in at a place called Gow's,
a combination fishmonger's and restaurant, and ordered a dozen oysters
at the counter. He ordered a second dozen, but the man behind the
counter said that the Ministry of Food did not allow them to sell more
than eight bob worth to a customer and he had had it. Meecham felt a
certain resentment; he had half a mind to tell the man where he had been
that morning. That would show him. But perhaps the man had a son in
the R.A.F., so he would not be impressed. Or three R.A.F. sons, all killed
in the Battle of Britain, so he would be pained by any reference to flying.
The thought recalled Barry and Brownlea and Elkan for the first time that
day. Meecham wondered why it had seemed essential that, because of
them, he go on a mission after they were dead. He paid for his oysters
and went out into the street to look for a taxi. He hoped his girl was in
town and had no date for the evening. After all, this ought to impress
her.

Another time-killing expedient of mine was to try to construct from
information what life in occupied France must be, and in this I had great
assistance from friends in the British Political Warfare Board and with the
Free French Government in London, who supplied me with hundreds of
clandestine newspapers published in France and smuggled out by their
agents. The next piece is one of a series I wrote that winter under the
same generic title—the newspapers reminded me that another kind of
war was going on across the Channel while we waited for spring. Looking
at this sample now, I think it should help the people who have grown up
since to understand a lot about current French attitudes.

# Notes from the Kidnap House—1944

THE secret newspapers of France do not give French people much news
of the outside world. That is left to the British radio and the Algiers radio,
which do not have the paper and distribution problems of the journals in
enemy-occupied territory. Since most of the resistance newspapers are no
larger than a sheet of typewriter paper and have only four pages, they

concentrate on local news and editorial comment. The three largest groups of publications—those in each group are loosely affiliated—are Communist, Socialist, and Mur, this last name being short for Mouvements Unis de Résistance. Mur is an organization of "new men," men who are not connected with the old political parties, and is strongly de Gaullist. The masthead of all Mur papers carries the slogan "One chief, de Gaulle; one struggle, for our liberties." Mur is for "social as well as political democracy," by which it means the nationalization of banks and probably of heavy industry, ruthless punishment of the rich men and Vichy politicians who collaborated openly or tacitly, and the guidance of France by a "new élite" of men who have made their way up through the resistance movements. The editorials in its papers maintain that "the shame of Vichy does not excuse the shortcomings of preceding governments." Some editorials in the Mur papers oppose the presence in Algiers of men like Pierre Cot, Vincent Auriol, and other pre-Vichy government figures, although conceding that in the interest of unity they must be tolerated for a brief while. Mur is nationalistic, occasionally to the point of xenophobia, whereas the Socialist and the Communist newspaper groups place more emphasis on the class struggle and less on the personal leadership of de Gaulle and new élites. Yet these, too, endorse de Gaulle and the Algiers government, and Mur endorses in some degree the class struggle. The difference lies in the importance each faction gives the different aspects of the fight. The Socialists, the largest single party in France before the armistice, defend most of their party record, and the heroic attitude of Léon Blum since his arrest, especially at the Riom trial, has added weight to this defense. Blum, like Edouard Herriot, has become a martyr in his own lifetime. *Populaire*, Blum's old newspaper, has seven regional editions, all clandestine, and reaches at least a million readers. Its preoccupation with the party record sometimes makes it seem to look backward too much. Recently it published a noble but nostalgic appeal to President Roosevelt to vindicate the New Deal by disregarding the demands of American capitalists. The editorialist, in his hideout, apparently had not heard that the term "New Deal" is now in the same limbo as "Popular Front." In almost every issue, *Populaire* runs, under the heading of "Our Martyrs," a list of Socialist resistants shot by the Gestapo or murdered by the Vichy militia, as if to emphasize the fact that the Socialists have at last become a party of action. The Communist press, headed by the several editions of *L'Humanité* and comprising a number of newspapers for various vocational groups of intellectuals and workers, benefits not only from the present prestige of Russia but from the name that Communist resistants have won for courage and austerity.

There are dozens of other resistance papers, of political shades more difficult to classify, ranging from *L'Aurore*, the organ of conservative Republican resistance, to a little sheet called *Le Soviet*, which carries at its masthead the line "Long live Trotsky and Lenin! Down with Stalin, grave-digger of the Third International!" All, however, agree on at least two points. *The first of these is the French refusal to be patronized or treated as a decadent nation, especially by the English-speaking nations, whom the French blame for rebuilding Germany between the two great wars, before leaving France to fend for herself in 1939. The resistants look forward to liberation not as a favor but as the first small installment due them on a debt of blood.* Smuts'* speech last November served to intensify this feeling, which crystalized in the streamer headline of one clandestine paper, *Libération*: "Pétain, Badoglio, Smuts Examples of Intelligence of Marshalls." "Great Britain three years ago carried all the hopes of our people; these are things one does not forget, in spite of the Smutses," an editorialist, in hiding from the Gestapo, wrote in *Libération*. *"France decadent? Really? Well, if all France were in ruins, if there survived of all her decimated people only a few women and old men, the representative of France, whoever he might be, would have the right to sit with Churchill, Roosevelt, and Stalin and be treated with the most profound respect*, because, if there hadn't been a certain nation called France and a certain battle called Verdun, Monsieur Smuts might now, with a little luck, be a junior native customs official in South Africa. . . . *With or without Smuts, the European resistance movement is going to remake the Continent into a free Europe of free citizens.* Taught by our common experience of slavery, we have more in common with the men of Free Belgium, of Tito or Ribar, than with most Francophile diplomats. Who knows if the greatest service Smuts could render us is not to awaken our compatriots to the true mission of France: to remake Europe and open Africa?" Another clandestine paper, *Franc-Tireur*, says, *"The countries that hoped to save themselves the horrors of war by neutrality and those who could organize for victory out of the reach of the enemy while for nine months we held the line—haven't they also their responsibilities? Didn't they count too much on France and her Army, on the military qualities of her people, to conquer a force they had allowed to develop?* This war, in which we were the sacrificed advance guard, has been waged against a racial dictatorship which intended to hold the world underfoot. It is unthinkable that it should end in another dictatorship, nationalistic or plutocratic. France, even defeated, remains great enough and has enough claims to gratitude not to merit the treatment of a vassal or a servant." This feeling was also revealed in a statement Daladier made to the German police who a year ago came to the prison of Bourrassol to remove him to the Reich. "I congratulate myself," he said, "for having declared war in 1939. A year later you would have won the war. Today I have the pleasure of telling you that you are irretrievably lost."

*The second point of universal agreement is that France remains intrinsically great. These two basic sentiments make the resistance press*

---

* I forget what Smuts said, but they didn't like it. I almost forget who Smuts was. That was before South Africa made the headlines.

*hypersensitive to any hint of infringement on French sovereignty. A re-
cent report from Washington that General Eisenhower would choose the
Frenchmen with whom the Allies would treat meant to many resistants
that the Americans would attempt to choose the rulers of France. Since,
in the minds of French workingmen, America has always stood for big
business and since the de Gaullists feel that the State Department has
always worked against them,* there is an almost universal fear that the
English-speaking powers will try to impose a Kolchak government in
striped pants, headed by a shifty *type* like Georges Bonnet. Bonnet was
not allowed to participate officially in the Vichy regime because of his
association with the Jewish bank of Lazard Frères, and therefore he could
now be presented as being free of the Vichy taint. Camile Chautemps,
who has been in Washington long enough to be able to disclaim any
connection with the "later excesses" of the Vichy regime, is another bogey
of the resistance men. The recollection of the high favor Bonnet and his
friends enjoyed, back in the Munich days, with men still prominent in the
British government, such as Halifax, Hoare, and Simon, does not dispose
resistants to look forward to receiving British support against the tendency they think they see in American policy. An extreme statement of
the frame of mind that has resulted from the refusal of the Allied governments to commit themselves is the following, in *Combat: "We think it
would be criminal and absurd to have complete confidence in foreign
military staffs, in foreign military representatives, or in officers of the
French Army of the colonial type to set up a republic and let the citizens
of France express themselves.* To say everything—if a choice has to be
made one day between 'terrorism' and AMG, our choice is made. Of
ourselves we are sure, of 'practical men' we are not."

More interesting to me than the editorial opinion of these journalists—
who, since they live in constant danger of being captured, tortured to
make them give information about their colleagues (usually by having
their fingernails torn out), and then shot, lack the calm detachment of,
say, Arthur Krock—are the pictures of French life presented, at least by
implication, in such publications as *Bulletin des Chemins de Fer*, the
clandestine organ of the railroad workers. Railroad men have perhaps
the hardest rôle in the resistance movement. A factory saboteur faces the
danger of detection and arrest, but when a railroad worker wrecks a train
he may not survive to be arrested. Furthermore, trains and freight yards
are constant targets of bombing attacks; a railroader takes the same risks
as the German troops among whom he finds himself. There are no air-raid
shelters in freight trains as there are in factories. Moreover, railroaders
furnish much of the information about troop and ammunition movements
that leads to air attacks, and thus they call down the lightning on themselves. These dangers are superimposed upon conditions which are diffi-

cult enough in themselves—"overwork, long hours, pathetic remnants of rolling stock left by the Boche, coal dust that hardly burns in place of the good fuel of other days"—and upon the psychological strain of having to work for the Germans. "I know your suffering at feeling yourselves unarmed executioners of your countrymen when you drive trains toward Germany heavy with conscripted French workmen," one writer in *Bulletin* tells his comrades. (Many times, it may be noted, train crews have managed to stop somewhere and give the deportees a chance to escape through the windows of the cars.) "I know how you feel when you drive toward Germany freight trains loaded with all the substance that the Boche has drained from our rich land," the writer continues, "but you must endure, because you alone can on the great day, you eight hundred thousand rail workers, prevent the German from applying his strategy, paralyze his troop movements, isolate his units, immobilize his supplies, break his power, and precipitate his defeat."

The remainder of the same issue of *Bulletin* is more matter-of-fact. There is a prescription for getting rid of a fellow-employee who appears to be spying on resistance activities (accidentally drop a packing case on his toes), a list of the past month's railroad wrecks, and a note on a low *type*, an assistant stationmaster at the Perrache station, in Lyons, who curries favor with the German police. This *type* was present when political prisoners in a train passing through were throwing notes to friends on the platform. He saw a man on the platform cover a note with his foot. "The swine pointed the man out to a cop," *Bulletin* records. "He will not be overlooked." There is also the story of the wrecking of three civilian express passenger trains, with a heavy loss of life. These wrecks were the work not of any resistance group, readers are informed, but of *agents provocateurs* trying to twist public opinion against patriots. Patriot saboteurs do not molest trains of no military importance, especially passenger trains.

Another publication I always like to find in a packet that a friend in the underground movement now and then brings to my flat in London is *La Terre*, which calls itself "the organ of peasant resistance." Farmers, as a group, have always had the temperament and the facilities for resisting official pressure. Readers of *La Terre* are continually enjoined to delay threshing, to hide their harvests until they can be turned over to the *Maquis*, or at least to sell their crops privately to other Frenchmen, since any food delivered to Vichy authorities will be siphoned off to the Germans and sent out of the country. The government has inspectors to check up on agricultural production and delivery. Some of the inspectors, of course, are "reasonable," shutting their eyes to all discrepancies, since they are at heart as anti-Boche as anybody else. Others, not "reasonable," are mobbed or ambushed and beaten up with farm implements. In a Breton village, my latest *La Terre* informs me, three hundred people gathered around an inspector who had complained of the light weight of some pigs delivered by a farmer, and chased him into the mayor's office, from which the gendarmes had to rescue him. In another village, also in Brittany, an officious gendarme tried to make the farm wives stop baking, because the farmers are supposed to deliver all their flour to the government. Enraged women dumped him into a horse trough. In the Yonne department, farmers hide requisitioned horses and cows; in Loir-et-Cher, the farmers deliver no eggs, insisting that the hens stopped laying in 1940. In Seine-et-Oise, the peasants have formed committees to demand high grain prices. Everywhere the peasants unite to hunt informers, just as farmers in Iowa, not long ago, used to chase process servers. *La Terre* holds up the example of the scorched earth set by the Russian peasants. Incidentally, "Le Père Milon," de Maupassant's story of a Norman peasant who spent his nights killing German soldiers during the 1871 occupation, has been republished, according to *La Terre*, as a resistance pamphlet.

There are labor papers of all political shades. One, *Les Informations Sociales*, analyzes for French workers, in the tone of the *New Republic*, the Beveridge Plan and the differences between the C.I.O. and the A.F.L. *Les Informations* describes itself as "the bulletin of information for militant unionists." In addition to publishing informative articles, it has reprinted, without comment, Stalin's decree dissolving the Third International. It reports feelingly the arrest and deportation to Germany of Léon Jouhaux, president of the Confédération Général du Travail, for a time a fellow-prisoner of Herriot in the fortress of Bourrassol, and it denounces several prewar labor leaders who had accepted posts in fake labor unions set up by Vichy and are now trying to hedge against the defeat of Germany. It gives a long list of leaders of miners' unions sentenced for starting a strike against the Germans and it praises miners for bearing so much of labor's struggle against the enemy.

*C.G.T.*, clandestine journal of the now submerged but still powerful Confédération, argues the necessity of beginning at once to rebuild a world labor movement and cites an index of prices which have made life almost impossible for French workmen in the last few years. In October, 1942, bread was up, over prewar prices, a hundred and forty per cent, potatoes two hundred per cent, wine two hundred and thirty per cent, and shoes three hundred and twenty-five per cent. *Mouvement Ouvrier Français*, another labor publication, says that the working class is the main object of German attack: the employers continue to eat well, even though they must pay high prices, but workers have the choice of producing goods for the conqueror at starvation wages in France or of being deported to Germany, where, on rations almost as scanty, they will be killed by Allied bombers. *Combat*, the most widely circulated Mur paper, notes, apropos of the deaths of French workmen in air raids in the Reich, that the French censor forbids the phrase "Died in Germany" in the death notices that relatives insert in French papers, although the German papers, with their usual maudlin bad taste, carry long accounts of ceremonies held over the graves of French workers killed in the Reich. Germans put pansies on the graves of Frenchmen they have brought to Germany for forced labor, a proof, *Combat* says, of the well-known Boche sensibility.

One of the leading publications in the resistance press is *Cahiers du Témoignage Chrétien*, an excellently printed monthly which sets forth the Catholic arguments in favor of resistance. One issue, discussing whether collaboration is permissible for a Christian, decides that "collaboration with Nazism, perverse in itself, is against the interests and soul of France. Conclusion: *non possumus.*" *Cahiers*, which reaches a large portion of the clergy and Catholic intellectuals, presents religious arguments against racism and anti-Semitism. It is interesting to observe the parallel reactions to Nazism in publications of sections of the clandestine press representing widely divergent groups. *Lettres Françaises*, the underground organ of French writers, charges that "a high proportion of pederasts among the collaborationists is to be expected, for to be against one's own country is against nature." The same sort of thought on the depravity of collaboration occurs in one of the regional clandestine publications, *Combat du Languedoc*. "That the Boche tortures and massacres accords with his business of being a Boche, but that a Frenchman sells other Frenchmen to the enemy, that is the ultimate depth of abjection. On the day of liberation, patriots . . . will sweep away the obscure rabble of informers for the Gestapo. Not even the memory of their crimes must survive in free France."

The regional publications have the strongest and most acrid odor of conflict. One issue of *Combat du Languedoc*, for example, contains a long blacklist of the traitors in surrounding towns and departments. There is in one town an ex-Republican priest who now informs against other clergymen who harbor Jews and *Maquis*; in another there is a Negro doctor, "forgetful of Nazi doctrines," who spies, and "a woman who sent her husband to forced labor and remained with a German soldier." There is a man who took money to betray the place where patriots had hidden the Strasbourg Cathedral's bells, removed to southwest France in 1939. Another man listed was a gunrunner for the Spanish Republicans in the civil war who has now turned coat and informs against refugees escaping across the Pyrenees. There is the president of a chamber of commerce who toasted a German victory, the Germanophile prefect kept by the widow of a former president of the Republic, the French colonel who sent his son to a Schutzstaffel cadet camp. Collaborators are named in print, even down to a man who was seen to tear a Lorraine cross from the neck of a young girl. From another regional publication I cite this excerpt: "Clermont-Ferrand—Our comrade ———— was arrested at sixteen-thirty, October 26th. He was brought to the morgue at two o'clock the next afternoon. His face was swollen almost beyond recognition; his neck bore marks of strangulation. All his fingernails had been torn out. One foot was swollen, enormous. He had two bullet holes in his temple. The execution- ers are known. They will not be tortured. They will be shot like dogs."

"*La Voix du Nord*," the oldest and most powerful regional underground publication in the north of France, which has been occupied by the Germans since 1940, begins the latest issue I have received with a eulogy of Cardinal Lienart, Archbishop of Lille, who in a sermon defended the refusal of labor to work for Germans. This, in strongly Catholic Flanders, is news of the greatest importance. *Le Patriote de l'Oise*, another re- gional paper, thanks the Bishop of Beauvais for his steadfastness, and *La France Unie*, published in Brittany, praises the leading Catholic preacher of Rennes for his sermons on resistance; he has, the paper says, proved that deportation contradicts the doctrines of Christ. The first two of these publications have a strong Communist tinge, which indicates that the Germans and Laval have brought the French church and the French Communist Party into agreement for the first time in history. *La Voix du Nord* cites as a less appetizing example the local Catholic official of Secours National, a Pétain version of *Winterhilfe*, who takes, for his nephews and nieces, the best shoes and clothes donated to this charity. His sister, *La Voix* declares, then distributes the remainder to the needy, but only to the needy who attend mass regularly. Another local petty grafter it names is a police adjutant who stops people carrying small parcels of food in the streets and confiscates them unless the people can prove that they have been bought legally but who himself levies an illegal tribute of a pound of butter every week from each farm wife. It notifies people living on the coast that Germans billeted in coastal villages have been provided with civilian clothing in which to escape if a surprise landing is made by the Allies. *La Voix* urges its readers to memorize the faces of these Germans, so that they will be able to point them out to Allied troops.

*Le Patriote de l'Oise*, which appears to be Communist, tells of police raids on "our de Gaullist friends" in the district in which it is published. It warns of the presence of Vichy state police in the town of Creil and advises readers to "leave cafés when these *types* enter." *La Voix* tells how gendarmes surrounded a house in which they knew a Communist was hiding, in a village in Flanders; it was his own house, in the town of his birth, and it was a public secret that he had returned there. The man tried to escape by an attic window and the gendarmes shot him off the roof. "We know them," *La Voix* concludes simply. Until some assurance to the contrary is received, many writers in the resistance papers seem to fear that the Allies are coming to rescue the gendarmes.

# PART IV

## AND SO
## TO VICTORY

## *For Bunny Rigg*

WE DID get to France, as you must know if you have seen the Cinemepic called *The Longest Day*, in which with swashbuckling magnificence tricked out with little homely touches a glittering team Eisenhowered by Darryl Zanuck storms the Hun-infested shores, and with John Wayne and Robert Mitchum alternately carrying the ball sweeps on, over the hills, to the unforgettable refrain of a theme song that I keep getting mixed up with

"Ballocks, and the same to you,"

which has been bowdlerized into the "River Kwai March." The original words fit in perfectly with the Wayne-Zanuck-Mitchum version.

Everybody, of course, had his own D-Day.

# Cross-Channel Trip

THREE days after the first Allied landing in France, I was in the wardroom of an LCIL (Landing Craft, Infantry, Large) that was bobbing in the lee of the French cruiser Montcalm off the Normandy coast. The word "large" in landing-craft designation is purely relative; the wardroom of the one I was on is seven by seven feet and contains two officers' bunks and a table with four places at it. She carries a complement of four officers, but since one of them must always be on watch there is room for a guest at the wardroom table, which is how I fitted in. The Montcalm was loosing salvos, each of which rocked our ship; she was firing at a German pocket of resistance a couple of miles from the shoreline. The suave voice of a B.B.C. announcer came over the wardroom radio: "Next in our series of impressions from the front will be a recording of an artillery barrage." The French ship loosed off again, drowning out the recording. It was this same announcer, I think—I'm not sure, because all B.B.C. announcers sound alike—who said, a little while later, "We are now in a position to say the landings came off with surprising ease. The Air Force and the big guns of the Navy smashed coastal defenses, and the Army occupied them." Lieutenant Henry Rigg, United States Coast Guard Reserve, the skipper of our landing craft, looked at Long, her engineering officer, and they both began to laugh. Kavanaugh, the ship's communications officer, said, "Now what do you think of that?" I called briefly upon God. Aboard the LCIL, D Day hadn't seemed like that to us. There is nothing like a broadcasting studio in London to give a chap perspective.

I went aboard our LCIL on Thursday evening, June 1st. The little ship was one of a long double file that lay along the dock in a certain British port.* She was fast to the dock, with another LCIL lashed to her on the other side. An LCIL is a hundred and fifty-five feet long and about three hundred dead-weight tons. A destroyer is a big ship indeed by comparison; an LST (Landing Ship, Tanks) looms over an LCIL like a monster. The LCIL has a flat bottom and draws only five feet of water, so she can go right up on a beach. Her hull is a box for carrying men; she can sleep two hundred soldiers belowdecks or can carry five hundred on a short

* Weymouth.

ferrying trip, when men stand both below and topside. An LCIL has a stern anchor which she drops just before she goes aground and two forward ramps which she runs out as she touches bottom. As troops go down the ramps, the ship naturally lightens, and she rises a few inches in the water; she then winches herself off by the stern anchor, in much the same way a monkey pulls himself back on a limb by his tail. Troop space is about all there is to an LCIL, except for a compact engine room and a few indispensable sundries like navigation instruments and anti-aircraft guns. LCILs are the smallest ocean-crossing landing craft, and all those now in the European theatre arrived under their own power. The crews probably would have found it more comfortable sailing on the Santa María. Most LCILs are operated by the Navy, but several score of them have Coast Guard crews. Ours was one of the latter. The name "Coast Guard" has always reminded me of little cutters plying out to ocean liners from the barge office at the Battery in New York, and the association gave me a definite pleasure. Before boarding the landing craft, I had been briefed, along with twenty other correspondents, on the flagship of Rear Admiral John L. Hall, Jr., who commanded the task force of which our craft formed a minute part, so I knew where we were going and approximately when. Since that morning I had been sealed off from the civilian world, in the marshalling area, and when I went aboard our landing craft I knew that I would not be permitted even to set foot on the dock except in the company of a commissioned officer.

It was warm and the air felt soporific when I arrived. The scene somehow reminded me more of the Sheepshead Bay channel, with its fishing boats, than of the jumping-off place for an invasion. A young naval officer who had brought me ashore from the flagship took me over the gangplank of the landing craft and introduced me to Lieutenant Rigg. Rigg, familiarly known as Bunny, was a big man, thirty-three years old, with clear, light-blue eyes and a fleshy, good-tempered face. He was a yacht broker in civilian life and often wrote articles about boats. Rigg welcomed me aboard as if we were going for a cruise to Block Island, and invited me into the wardroom to have a cup of coffee. There was standing room only, because Rigg's three junior officers and a Navy commander were already drinking coffee at the table. The junior officers—Long, Kavanaugh. and Williams—were all lieutenants (j.g.). Long, a small, jolly man with an upturned nose, was a Coast Guard regular with twenty years' service, mostly as a chief petty officer. He came from Baltimore. Kavanaugh, tall and straight-featured, was from Crary, North Dakota, and Williams, a very polite, blond boy, came from White Deer, Texas. Kavanaugh and Williams were both in their extremely early twenties. The three-striper, a handsome, slender man with prematurely white hair and black eyebrows, was introduced to me by Rigg as the C.O. of a naval beach battalion which would go in to organize boat traffic on a stretch of beach as soon as the first waves of infantry had taken it over.[*] He was going to travel to the invasion coast aboard our landing craft, and since he disliked life ashore in the marshalling area, he had come aboard ship early. The commander, who had a drawl hard to match north of Georgia, was in fact a Washingtonian. He was an Annapolis man, he soon told me, but had left the Navy for several years to practice law in the District of Columbia and then returned to it for the war. His battalion was divided for the crossing among six LCILs, which would go in in pairs on adjacent beaches, so naturally he had much more detailed dope on the coming operation than normally would come to, say, the skipper of a landing craft, and this was to make conversations in the tiny wardroom more interesting than they otherwise would have been.

Even before I had finished my second cup of coffee, I realized that I had been assigned to a prize LCIL; our ship was to beach at H Hour plus sixty-five, which means one hour and five minutes after the first assault soldier gets ashore. "This ship and No. X will be the first LCILs on the beach," Rigg said complacently. "The first men will go in in small boats, because of mines and underwater obstacles, and Navy demolition men with them will blow us a lane through element C—that's sunken concrete and iron obstacles. They will also sweep the lane of mines, we hope. We just have to stay in the lane."

"These things move pretty fast and they make a fairly small target bow on," Long added cheerfully.

The others had eaten, but I had not, so Williams went out to tell the cook to get me up some chow. While it was being prepared, I went out on deck to look around.

Our landing craft, built in 1942, is one of the first class of LCILs, which have a rectangular superstructure and a narrow strip of open deck on each side of it.[**] Painted on one side of the superstructure I noted a neat Italian flag, with the legend "Italy" underneath so that there would be no mistake, and beside the flag a blue shield with white vertical stripes and the word "Sicily." There was also a swastika and the outline of an airplane, which could only mean that the ship had shot down a German plane in a landing either in Sicily or Italy. Under Britain's double summer time, it was still light, and there were several groups of sailors on deck, most of them rubbing "impregnating grease" into shoes to make them impervious to mustard gas. There had been a great last-minute furore about the possibility that the Germans might use gas against the invasion, and everybody had been fitted with impregnated gear and two kinds of

[*] This officer's name could not be used then, either because he commanded a unit in the invasion, or because he was wounded in the course of this operation. He was Eugene Carusi, again an attorney in Washington.
[**] It was the LCIL-88.

protective ointment. Our ship's rails were topped with rows of drying shoes.

"This is the first time I ever tried to get a pair of shoes pregnant, sir," one of the sailors called out sociably as I was watching him.

"No doubt you tried it on about everything else, I guess," another sailor yelled as he, too, worked on his shoes.

I could see I would not be troubled by any of that formality which has occasionally oppressed me aboard flagships. Most of the sailors had their names stencilled in white on the backs of their jumpers, so there was no need for introductions. One sailor I encountered was in the middle of a complaint about a shore officer who had "eaten him out" because of the way he was dressed on the dock, and he continued after I arrived. "They treat us like children," he said. "You'd think we was the pea-jacket navy instead of the ambiguous farce." The first term is one that landing-craft sailors apply to those on big ships, who keep so dry that they can afford to dress the part. "The ambiguous farce" is their pet name for the amphibious forces. A chief petty officer, who wore a khaki cap with his blue coveralls, said, "You don't want to mind them, sir. This isn't a regular ship and doesn't ever pretend to be. But it's a good working ship. You ought to see our engine room."

A little sailor with a Levantine face asked me where I came from. When I told him New York, he said, "Me too—Hundred twenty-second and First." The name stencilled on his back was Landini. "I made up a song about this deal," he said, breaking into a kind of Off to Buffalo. "I'm going over to France and I'm making in my pants."

Through the open door of the galley I could watch the cook, a fattish man with wavy hair and a narrow mustache, getting my supper ready. His name was Fassy, and he was the commissary steward. He appeared to have a prejudice against utensils; he slapped frankfurters and beans down on the hot stove top, rolled them around, and flipped them onto the plate with a spatula. I thought the routine looked familiar and I found out later that in his civilian days Fassy had worked in Shanty restaurants in New York.

While I was standing there, a young seaman stencilled Sitnitsky popped his head into the galley to ask for some soap powder so he could wash his clothes. Fassy poured some out of a vast carton into a pail of hot water the boy held. " 'Not recommended for delicate fabrics,' " the steward read for the infantry to gather up on their way through to positions inland.

Since the frankfurters and beans were ready, I returned to the wardroom. There the board of strategy was again in session. The beach we were headed for was near the American line, only a mile or two from Porten-Bessin, where the British area began. Eighteen years before I had walked along the tops of the same cliffs the Americans would be fighting under. In those days I had thought of it as holiday country, not sufficiently spectacular to attract *le grand tourisme* but beautiful in a reasonable, Norman way. This illogically made the whole operation seem less sinister to me. Two pillboxes showed plainly on photographs we had, and, in addition, there were two houses that looked suspiciously like shells built around other pillboxes. Our intelligence people had furnished us with extraordinarily detailed charts of gradients in the beach and correlated tide tables. The charts later proved to be extraordinarily accurate, too.

"What worries me about landing is the bomb holes the Air Forces may leave in the beach before we hit," the commander was saying when I entered. "The chart may show three feet of water, but the men may step into a ten-foot hole anywhere. I'd rather the Air Forces left the beach alone and just let the naval guns knock out the beach defenses. They're accurate."

The general plan, I knew, was for planes and big guns of the fleet to put on an intensive bombardment before the landing. A couple of weeks earlier I had heard a Marine colonel on the planning staff tell how the guns would hammer the pillboxes, leaving only a few stunned defenders for the infantry to gather up on their way through to positions inland.

"We're lucky," the commander said. "This beach looks like a soft one."

His opinion, in conjunction with frankfurters and beans, made me happy.

We didn't get our passengers aboard until Saturday. On Friday I spent my time in alternate stretches of talk with the men on deck and the officers in the wardroom. Back in Sicily, the ship had been unable to get off after grounding at Licata, a boatswain's mate named Pendleton told me. "She got hit so bad we had to leave her," he said, "and for three days we had to live in foxholes just like infantrymen. Didn't feel safe a minute. We was sure glad to get back on the ship. Guess she had all her bad luck that trip."

Pendleton, a large, fair-haired fellow who was known to his shipmates as the Little Admiral, came from Neodesha, Kansas. "They never heard of the Coast Guard out there," he said. "Nobody but me. I knew I would have to go in some kind of service and I was reading in a Kansas City paper one day that the Coast Guard would send a station wagon to your house to get you if it was within a day's drive of their recruiting station. So I wrote 'em. Never did like to walk."

Sitnitsky was washing underclothes at a sink aft of the galley once when I came upon him. When he saw me, he said, "The fois' ting I'm gonna do when I get home is buy my mudder a washing machine. I never realize what the old lady was up against."

Our neighbor LCIL, tied alongside us, got her soldier passengers late

Friday night. The tide was low and the plank leading down to our ship from the dock was at a steep angle as men came aboard grumbling and filed across our deck to the other LCIL. "Didjever see a goddam gangplank in the right place?" one man called over his shoulder as he eased himself down with his load. I could identify a part of a mortar on his back, in addition to a full pack. "All aboard for the second Oran," another soldier yelled, and a third man, passing by the emblems painted on the bridge, as he crossed our ship, yelled, "Sicily! *They* been there, too." So I knew these men were part of the First Division, which landed at Oran in Africa in 1942 and later fought in Sicily. I think I would have known anyway by the beefing. The First Division is always beefing about something, which adds to its effectiveness as a fighting unit.

The next day the soldiers were spread all over the LCIL next door, most of them reading paper-cover, armed-services editions of books. They were just going on one more trip, and they didn't seem excited about it. I overheard a bit of technical conversation when I leaned over the rail to visit with a few of them. "Me, I like a bar [Browning automatic rifle]," a sergeant was saying to a private. "You can punch a lot of tickets with one of them."

The private, a rangy middleweight with a small, close-cropped head and a rectangular profile, said, "I'm going into this one with a pickaxe and a block of TNT. It's an interesting assignment. I'm going to work on each pillbox individually," he added, carefully pronouncing each syllable.

When I spoke to them, the sergeant said, "Huh! A correspondent! Why don't they give the First Division some credit?"

"I guess you don't read much if you say that, Sarge," a tall blond boy with a Southern accent said. "There's a whole book of funnies called 'Terry Allen and the First Division at El Guettar.' "

All three men were part of an infantry regiment. The soldier who was going to work on pillboxes asked if I was from New York, and said that he was from the Bensonhurst section of Brooklyn. "I am only sorry my brother-in-law is not here," he said. "My brother-in-law is an M.P. He is six inches bigger than me. He gets an assignment in New York. I would like to see him here. He would be apprehensive." He went on to say that the company he was with had been captured near the end of the African campaign, when, after being cut off by the Germans, it had expended all its ammunition. He had been a prisoner in Tunis for a few hours, until the British arrived and set him free. "There are some nice broads in Tunis," he said. "I had a hell of a time." He nodded toward the book he was holding. "These little books are a great thing," he said. "They take you away. I remember when my battalion was cut off on top of a hill at El Guettar, I read a whole book in one day. It was called 'Knight Without Armor.' This one I am reading now is called 'Candide.' It is kind of unusual, but I like it. I think the fellow who wrote it, Voltaire, used the same gag too often, though. The characters are always getting killed and then turning out not to have been killed after all, and they tell their friends what happened to them in the meantime. I like the character in it called Pangloss."*

Fassy was lounging near the rail and I called him over to meet a brother Brooklynite. "Brooklyn is a beautiful place to live in," Fassy said. "I have bush Number Three at Prospect Park."

"I used to have bush Number Four," the soldier said.

"You remind me of a fellow named Sidney Wetzelbaum," Fassy said. "Are you by any chance related?"

I left them talking.

Our own passengers came aboard later in the day. There were two groups—a platoon of the commander's beach battalion and a platoon of amphibious engineers. The beach-battalion men were sailors dressed like soldiers, except that they wore black jerseys under their field jackets; among them were a medical unit and a hydrographic unit. The engineers included an M.P. detachment, a chemical-warfare unit, and some demolition men. A beach battalion is a part of the Navy that goes ashore; amphibious engineers are a part of the Army that seldom has its feet dry. Together they form a link between the land and sea forces. These two detachments had rehearsed together in landing exercises, during which they had travelled aboard our LCIL. Unlike the Coastguardsmen or the infantry on the next boat, they had never been in the real thing before and were not so offhand about it. Among them were a fair number of men in their thirties. I noticed one chief petty officer with the Navy crowd who looked about fifty. It was hard to realize that these older men had important and potentially dangerous assignments which called for a good deal of specialized skill; they seemed to me more out of place than the infantry kids. Some sailors carried carbines and most of the engineers had rifles packed in oilskin cases. There were about a hundred and forty men in all. The old chief, Joe Smith, who was the first of the lot I got to know, said he had been on battleships in the last war and had been recalled from the fleet reserves at the beginning of this. He took considerable comfort from the fact that several aged battleships would lay down a barrage for us before we went in. You could see that he was glad to be aboard a ship again, even if it was a small one and he would be on it for only a couple of days. He was a stout, red-faced, merry man whose home town was Spring Lake, New Jersey. "I'm a tomato squeezer," he told me. "Just a country boy."

Cases of rations had been stacked against the superstructure for the passengers' use. The galley wasn't big enough to provide complete hot meals for them but it did provide coffee, and their own cook warmed up

* He and I were having a Voltairean reunion right there. I had been at El Guettar too, and had never heard what happened to the battalion.

canned stew and corned beef for them for one meal. The rest of the time they seemed simply to rummage among the cans until they found something they liked and then ate it. They ate pretty steadily, because there wasn't much else for them to do.

Our landing craft had four sleeping compartments belowdecks. The two forward ones, which were given over to passengers, contained about eighty bunks apiece. Most of the crew slept in the third compartment, amidships, and a number of petty officers and noncoms slept in the fourth, the smallest one, aft. I had been sleeping in this last one myself since coming aboard, because there was only one extra bunk for an officer and the commander had that. Four officers who came aboard with the troops joined me in this compartment. There were two sittings at the wardroom table for meals, but we managed to wedge eight men in there at one time for a poker game.

There was no sign of a move Saturday night, and on Sunday morning everybody aboard began asking when we were going to shove off. The morning sun was strong and the crew mingled with the beach-battalion men and the soldiers on deck. It was the same on board every other LCIL in the long double row. The port didn't look like Sheepshead Bay now, for every narrow boat was covered with men in drab-green field jackets, many of them wearing tin hats, because the easiest way not to lose a tin hat in a crowd is to wear it. The small ships and helmets pointed up the analogy to a crusade and made the term seem less threadbare than it usually does. We were waiting for weather, as many times the crusaders, too, had waited, but nobody thought of praying for it, not even the chaplain who came aboard in mid-morning to conduct services. He was a captain attached to the amphibious engineers, a husky man I had noticed throwing a football around on the dock the previous day. He took his text from Romans: "If God be for us, who can be against us?" He didn't seem to want the men to get the idea that we were depending entirely on faith, however. "Give us that dynamic, that drive, which, coupled with our matchless super-modern weapons, will ensure victory," he prayed. After that, he read aloud General Eisenhower's message to the Allied Expeditionary Force.

After the services, printed copies of Eisenhower's message were distributed to all hands on board. Members of our ship's crew went about getting autographs of their shipmates on their "Eisenhowers," which they apparently intended to keep as souvenirs of the invasion. Among the fellows who came to me for my signature was the ship's coxswain, a long-legged, serious-looking young man, from a little town in Mississippi, who had talked to me several times before because he wanted to be a newspaperman after the war. He had had one year at Tulane, in New Orleans, before joining up with the Coast Guard, and he hoped he could finish up later. The coxswain, I knew, would be the first man out of the ship when she grounded, even though he was a member of the crew. It was his task to run a guideline ashore in front of the disembarking soldiers. Then, when he had arrived in water only a foot or two deep, he would pull on the line and bring an anchor floating in after him, the anchor being a light one tied in a life jacket. He would then fix the anchor—without the life jacket, of course—and return to the ship. This procedure had been worked out after a number of soldiers had been drowned on landing exercises by stepping into unexpected depressions in the beach after they had left the landing craft. Soldiers, loaded down with gear, had simply disappeared. With a guideline to hold onto, they could have struggled past bad spots. I asked the boy what he was going to wear when he went into the water with the line and he said just swimming trunks and a tin hat. He said he was a fair swimmer.

The rumor got about that we would sail that evening, but late in the afternoon the skipper told me we weren't going to. I learned that the first elements of the invasion fleet, the slowest ones, had gone out but had met rough weather in the Channel and had returned, because they couldn't have arrived at their destination in time. Admiral Hall had told correspondents that there would be three successive days when tide conditions on the Norman beaches would be right and that if we missed them the expedition might have to be put off, so I knew that we now had one strike on us, with only two more chances.

That evening, in the wardroom, we had a long session of a wild, distant derivative of poker called "high low rollem." Some young officers who had come aboard with the troops introduced it. We used what they called "funny money" for chips—five-franc notes printed in America and issued to the troops for use after they got ashore. It was the first time I had seen these notes, which reminded me of old-time cigar-store coupons. There was nothing on them to indicate who authorized them or would pay off on them—just *"Emis en France"* on one side and on the other side the tricolor and *"Liberté, Egalité, Fraternité."* In the game were three beach-battalion officers, a medical lieutenant (j.g.) named Davey, from Philadelphia, and two ensigns—a big, ham-handed college football player from Danbury, Connecticut, named Vaghi, and a blocky, placid youngster from Chicago named Reich. The commander of the engineer detachment, the only Army officer aboard, was a first lieutenant named Miller, a sallow, apparently nervous boy who had started to grow an ambitious black beard.

Next morning the first copy of the *Stars and Stripes* to arrive on board gave us something new to talk about. It carried the story of the premature invasion report by the Associated Press in America. In an atmosphere heavy with unavowed anxiety, the story hit a sour note. "Maybe they let out more than *Stars and Stripes* says," somebody in the wardroom said. "Maybe they not only announced the invasion but told where we had landed. I mean, where we *planned* to land. Maybe the whole deal will be called off now." The commander, who had spent so much time pondering element C, said, "Add obstacles—element A.P." A report got about among the more pessimistic crew members that the Germans had been tipped off and would be ready for us. The Allied high command evidently did not read the *Stars and Stripes*, however, for Rigg, after going ashore for a brief conference, returned with the information that we were shoving off at five o'clock. I said to myself, in the great cliché of the second World War, "This is it," and so, I suppose, did every other man in our fleet of little ships when he heard the news.

# *II*

PEACE or war, the boat trip across the English Channel always begins with the passengers in the same mood: everybody hopes he won't get seasick. On the whole, this is a favorable morale factor at the outset of an invasion. A soldier cannot fret about possible attacks by the Luftwaffe or E-boats while he is preoccupied with himself, and the vague fear of secret weapons on the far shore is balanced by the fervent desire to get the far shore under his feet. Few of the hundred and forty passengers on the LCIL I was on were actively sick the night before D Day, but they were all busy thinking about it. The four officers and twenty-nine men of the United States Coast Guard who made up her complement were not even queasy, but they had work to do, which was just as good. The rough weather, about which the papers have talked so much since D Day and which in fact interfered with the landing, was not the kind that tosses about transatlantic liners or even Channel packets; it was just a bit too rough for the smaller types of landing craft we employed. An LCIL, as its name implies, is not one of the smallest, but it's small enough, and aboard our flat-bottomed, three-hundred-ton job the Channel didn't seem especially bad that night. There was a ground swell for an hour after we left port, but then the going became better than I had anticipated. LCTs (Landing Craft, Tanks), built like open troughs a hundred feet long, to carry armored vehicles, had a much worse time, particularly since, being slow, they had had to start hours before us. Fifty-foot LCMs (Landing Craft, Mechanized) and fifty-foot and thirty-six-foot LCVPs (Landing Craft, Vehicles and Personnel), swarms of which crossed the Channel under their own power, had still more trouble. The setting out of our group of LCILs was unimpressive—just a double file of ships, each a hundred and fifty-five feet long, bound for a rendezvous with a great many other ships at three in the morning ten or fifteen miles off a spot on the coast of lower Normandy. Most of the troops travelled in large transports, from which the smaller craft transferred them to shore. The LCILs carried specially packaged units for early delivery on the Continent doorstep.

Rigg turned in early that evening because he wanted to be fresh for a hard day's work by the time we arrived at the rendezvous, which was to take place in what was known as the transport area. So did the commander of the naval beach battalion who was riding with us. I stood on deck for a while. As soon as I felt sleepy, I went down into the small compartment in which I had a bunk and went to sleep—with my clothes on, naturally. There didn't seem to be anything else to do. That was at about eight. I woke three hours later and saw a fellow next to me being sick in a paper bag and I went up to the galley and had a cup of coffee. Then I went back to my bunk and slept until a change in motion and in the noise of the motors woke me again.

The ship was wallowing slowly now, and I judged that we had arrived at the transport area and were loafing about. I looked at my wristwatch and saw that we were on time. It was about three. So we hadn't been torpedoed by an E-boat. A good thing. Drowsily, I wondered a little at the fact that the enemy had made no attempt to intercept the fleet and hoped there would be good air cover, because I felt sure that the Luftwaffe couldn't possibly pass up the biggest target of history. My opinion of the Luftwaffe was still strongly influenced by what I remembered from June, 1940, in France, and even from January and February, 1943, in Tunisia. I decided to stay in my bunk until daylight, dozed, woke again, and then decided I couldn't make it. I went up on deck in the gray predawn light sometime before five. I drew myself a cup of coffee from an electric urn in the galley and stood by the door drinking it and looking at the big ships around us. They made me feel proletarian. They would stay out in the Channel and send in their troops in small craft, while working-class vessels like us went right up on the beach. I pictured them inhabited by officers in dress blues and shiny brass buttons, all scented like the World's Most Distinguished After-Shave Club.* The admiral's command ship lay nearby. I imagined it to be gaffed with ingenious gimmicks that would record the developments of the operation. I could imagine a terse report coming in of the annihilation of a flotilla of LCILs, including us, and hear some Annapolis man saying, "After all, that sort of thing is to be expected." Then I felt that everything was going to be all right, because it always had been. A boatswain's mate, second class, named Barrett, from Rich Square, North Carolina, stopped next to me to drink his coffee and said, "I bet Findley a pound that we'd be hit this time. We most always is. Even money."

We wouldn't start to move, I knew, until about six-thirty, the time

* An allusion to an advertisement then widely familiar, but which I now forget.

when the very first man was scheduled to walk onto the beach. Then we would leave the transport area so that we could beach and perform our particular chore—landing one platoon of the naval beach battalion and a platoon of Army amphibious engineers—at seven-thirty-five. A preliminary bombardment of the beach defenses by the Navy was due to begin at dawn. "Ought to be hearing the guns soon," I said to Barrett, and climbed the ladder to the upper deck. Rigg was on the bridge drinking coffee, and with him was Long, the ship's engineering officer. It grew lighter and the guns began between us and the shore. The sound made us all cheerful and Long said, "I'd hate to be in under that." Before dawn the transports had begun putting men into small craft that headed for the line of departure, a line nearer shore from which the first assault wave would be launched.

Time didn't drag now. We got under way sooner than I had somehow expected. The first troops were on the beaches. The battleship Arkansas and the French cruisers Montcalm and Georges Leygues were pounding away on our starboard as we moved in. They were firing over the heads of troops, at targets farther inland. Clouds of yellow cordite smoke billowed up. There was something leonine in their tint as well as in the roar that followed, after that lapse of time which never fails to disconcert me. We went on past the big ships, like a little boy with the paternal blessing. In this region the Germans evidently had no long-range coastal guns, like the ones near Calais, for the warships' fire was not returned. This made me feel good. The absence of resistance always increases my confidence. The commander of the naval beach battalion had now come on deck, accoutred like a soldier, in greenish coveralls and tin hat. I said to him cheerfully, "Well, it looks as though the biggest difficulty you're going to have is getting your feet in cold water."

He stood there for a minute and said, "What are you thinking of?"

I said, "I don't know why, but I'm thinking of the garden restaurant behind the Museum of Modern Art in New York."* He laughed, and I gave him a pair of binoculars I had, because I knew he didn't have any and that he had important use for them.

Our passengers—the beach-battalion platoon and the amphibious engineers—were now forming two single lines on the main deck, each group facing the ramp by which it would leave the ship. Vaghi and Reich, beach-battalion ensigns, were lining up their men on the port side and Miller, an Army lieutenant with a new beard, was arranging his men on the starboard side. I wished the commander good luck and went up on the bridge, which was small and crowded but afforded the best view.

An LCIL has two ramps, one on each side of her bow, which she lowers and thrusts out ahead of her when she beaches. Each ramp is handled by means of a winch worked by two men; the two winches stand

---

* I liked a woman who lived across the street from there.

side by side deep in an open-well deck just aft of the bow. If the ramps don't work, the whole operation is fouled up, so an LCIL skipper always assigns reliable men to operate them. Two seamen named Findley and Lechich were on the port winch, and two whom I knew as Rocky and Bill were on the other. Williams, the ship's executive officer, was down in the well deck with the four of them.

We had been in sight of shore for a long while, and now I could recognize our strip of beach from our intelligence photographs. There was the house with the tower on top of the cliff on our starboard as we went in. We had been warned that preliminary bombardment might remove it, so we should not count too much upon it as a landmark; however, there it was and it gave me the pleasure of recognition. A path was to have been blasted and swept for us through element C (underwater concrete and iron obstacles) and mines, and the entrance to it was to have been marked with colored buoys. The buoys were there, so evidently the operation was going all right. Our LCIL made a turn and headed for the opening like a halfback going into a hole in the line. I don't know whether Rigg suddenly became solicitous for my safety or whether he simply didn't want me underfoot on the bridge, where two officers and two signalmen had trouble getting around even without me. He said, "Mr. Liebling will take his station on the upper deck during action." This was formal language from the young man I had learned to call Bunny, especially since the action did not seem violent as yet, but I climbed down the short ladder from the bridge to the deck, a move which put the wheelhouse between me and the bow. The upper deck was also the station for a pharmacist's mate named Kallam, who was our reserve first-aid man. A landing craft carries no doctor, the theory being that a pharmacist's mate will make temporary repairs until the patient can be transferred to a larger ship. We had two men with this rating aboard. The other, a fellow named Barry, was up in the bow. Kallam was a sallow, long-faced North Carolinian who once told me he had gone into the peacetime Navy as a youth and had never been good for anything else since. This was his first action, except for a couple of landings in Nicaragua around 1930.

The shore curved out toward us on the port side of the ship and when I looked out in that direction I could see a lot of smoke from what appeared to be shells bursting on the beach. There was also an LCT, grounded and burning. "Looks as if there's opposition," I said to Kallam, without much originality. At about the same time something splashed in the water off our starboard quarter, sending up a high spray. We were moving in fast now. I could visualize, from the plan I had seen so often in the last few days, the straight, narrow lane in which we had to stay. "On a straight line—like a rope ferry," I thought. The view on both sides changed rapidly. The LCT which had been on our port bow was now on our port quarter, and another LCT, also grounded, was now visible. A number of men, who had evidently just left her, were in the water, some up to their necks and others up to their armpits, and they didn't look as if they were trying to get ashore. Tracer bullets were skipping around them and they seemed perplexed. What I hate most about tracers is that every time you see one, you know there are four more bullets that you don't see, because only one tracer to five bullets is loaded in a machine-gun belt. Just about then, it seems in retrospect, I felt the ship ground.

I looked down at the main deck, and the beach-battalion men were already moving ahead, so I knew that the ramps must be down. I could hear Long shouting, "Move along now! Move along!," as if he were unloading an excursion boat at Coney Island. But the men needed no urging; they were moving without a sign of flinching. You didn't have to look far for tracers now, and Kallam and I flattened our backs against the pilot house and pulled in our stomachs, as if to give a possible bullet an extra couple of inches clearance. Something tickled the back of my neck. I slapped at it and discovered that I had most of the ship's rigging draped around my neck and shoulders, like a character in an old slapstick movie about a spaghetti factory. The rigging had been cut away by bullets. As Kallam and I looked toward the stern, we could see a tableau that was like a recruiting poster. There was a twenty-millimetre rapid-firing gun on the upper deck. Since it couldn't bear forward because of the pilot house and since there was nothing to shoot at on either side, it was pointed straight up at the sky in readiness for a possible dive-bombing attack. It had a crew of three men, and they were kneeling about it, one on each side and one behind the gun barrel, all looking up at the sky in an extremely earnest manner, and getting all the protection they could out of the gunshield. As a background to the men's heads, an American flag at the ship's stern streamed across the field of vision. It was a new flag, which Rigg had ordered hoisted for the first time for the invasion, and its colors were brilliant in the sun. To make the poster motif perfect. one of the three men was a Negro, William Jackson, from New Orleans, a wardroom steward, who, like everybody else on the LCIL, had multiple duties.

The last passenger was off the ship now, and I could hear the stern anchor cable rattling on the drum as it came up. An LCIL drops a stern anchor just before it grounds, and pays out fifty to a hundred fathoms of chain cable as it slowly slides the last couple of ship's lengths toward shore. To get under way again, it takes up the cable, pulling itself afloat. I had not known until that minute how eager I was to hear the sound of the cable that follows the order "Take in on stern anchor." Almost as the cable began to come in, something hit the ship with the solid clunk of metal against metal—not as hard as a collision or a bomb blast; just "clink." Long yelled down, "Pharmacist's mate go forward. Somebody's hurt." Kallam scrambled down the ladder to the main deck with his kit. Then Long yelled to a man at the stern anchor winch, "Give it hell!" An LCIL has to pull itself out and get the anchor up before it can use its motors, because otherwise the propeller might foul in the cable. The little engine which supplies power for the winch is built by a farm-machinery company in Waukesha, Wisconsin, and every drop of gasoline that went into the one on our ship was filtered through chamois skin first. That engine is the ship's insurance policy. A sailor now came running up the stairway from the cabin. He grabbed me and shouted, "Two casualties in bow!" I passed this information on to the bridge for whatever good it might do; both pharmacist's mates were forward already and there was really nothing else to be done. Our craft had now swung clear, the anchor was up, and the engines went into play. She turned about and shot forward like a destroyer. The chief machinist's mate said afterward that the engines did seven hundred revolutions a minute instead of the six hundred that was normal top speed. Shells were kicking up waterspouts around us as we went; the water they raised looked black. Rigg said afterward, "Funny thing. When I was going in, I had my whole attention fixed on two mines attached to sunken concrete blocks on either side of the place where we went in. I knew they hadn't been cleared away—just a path between them. They were spider mines, those things with a lot of loose cables. Touch one cable and you detonate the mine. When I was going out, I was so excited that I forgot all about the damn mines and didn't think of them until I was two miles past them."

A sailor came by and Shorty, one of the men in the gun crew, said to him, "Who was it?" The sailor said, "Rocky and Bill. They're all tore up. A shell got the winch and ramps and all." I went forward to the well deck, which was sticky with a mixture of blood and condensed milk. Soldiers had left cases of rations lying all about the ship, and a fragment of the shell that hit the boys had torn into a carton of cans of milk. Rocky and Bill had been moved belowdecks into one of the large forward compartments. Rocky was dead beyond possible doubt, somebody told me, but the pharmacist's mates had given Bill blood plasma and thought he might still be alive. I remembered Bill, a big, baby-faced kid from the District of Columbia, built like a wrestler. He was about twenty, and the other boys used to kid him about a girl he was always writing letters to.* A third wounded man, a soldier dressed in khaki, lay on a stretcher on deck breathing hard through his mouth. His face looked like a dirty drumhead; his skin was white and drawn tight over his high cheekbones. He wasn't making much noise. There was a shooting-gallery smell over every-

* Every letter began: "Well, Hazel, here I am again."

thing, and when we passed close under the Arkansas and she let off a salvo, a couple of our men who had their backs to her quivered and had to be reassured. Long and Kavanaugh, the communications officer, were already going about the ship trying to get things ticking again, but they had little success at first.

Halfway out to the transport area, another LCIL hailed us and asked us to take a wounded man aboard. They had got him from some smaller craft, but they had to complete a mission before they could go back to the big ships. We went alongside and took him over the rail. He was wrapped in khaki blankets and strapped into a wire basket litter. After we had sheered away, a man aboard the other LCIL yelled at us to come back so that he could hand over a half-empty bottle of plasma with a long rubber tube attached. "This goes with him," he said. We went alongside again and he handed the bottle to one of our fellows. It was trouble for nothing, because the man by then had stopped breathing.

We made our way out to a transport called the Dorothea Dix that had a hospital ward fitted out. We went alongside and Rigg yelled that we had four casualties aboard. A young naval doctor climbed down the scramble net hanging on the Dix's side and came aboard. After he had looked at our soldier, he called for a breeches buoy and the soldier was hoisted up sitting in that. He had been hit in one shoulder and one leg, and the doctor said he had a good chance. The three others had to be sent up in wire baskets, vertically, like Indian papooses. A couple of Negroes on the upper deck of the Dix dropped a line which our men made fast to the top of one basket after another. Then the man would be jerked up in the air by the Negroes as if he were going to heaven. Now that we carried no passengers and were lighter, the sea seemed rough. We bobbed under the towering transport and the wounded men swung wildly on the end of the line, a few times almost striking against the ship. A Coastguardsman reached up for the bottom of one basket so that he could steady it on its way up. At least a quart of blood ran down on him, covering his tin hat, his upturned face, and his blue overalls. He stood motionless for an instant, as if he didn't know what had happened, seeing the world through a film of red, because he wore eyeglasses and blood had covered the lenses.* The basket, swaying eccentrically, went up the side. After a couple of seconds, the Coastguardsman turned and ran to a sink aft of the galley, where he turned on the water and began washing himself. A couple of minutes after the last litter had been hoisted aboard, an officer on the Dix leaned over her rail and shouted down, "Medical officer in charge says two of these men are dead! He says you should take them back to the beach and bury them." Out there, fifteen miles off shore, they

---

* This was me. It seemed more reserved at the time to do it this way—a news story in which the writer said *he* was bathed in blood would have made me distrust it, if I had been a reader.

evidently thought that this was just another landing exercise. A sailor on deck said, "The son of a bitch ought to see that beach."

Rigg explained to the officer that it would be impossible to return to the beach and ordered the men to cast off the lines, and we went away from the Dix. Now that the dead and wounded were gone, I saw Kallam sneak to the far rail and be sicker than I have ever seen a man at sea. We passed close by the command ship and signalled that we had completed our mission. We received a signal, "Wait for orders," and for the rest of the day we loafed, while we tried to reconstruct what had happened to us. Almost everybody on the ship had a headache.

"What hurts me worst," Lechich said, "is thinking what happened to those poor guys we landed. That beach was hot with Jerries. And they didn't have nothing to fight with—only carbines and rifles. They weren't even supposed to be combat troops."

"I don't think any of them could be alive now," another man said.

As the hours went by and we weren't ordered to do anything, it became evident that our bit of beach wasn't doing well, for we had expected, after delivering our first load on shore, to be employed in ferrying other troops from transports to the beach, which the beach-battalion boys and engineers would in the meantime have been helping to clear. Other LCILs of our flotilla were also lying idle. We saw one of them being towed, and then we saw her capsize. Three others, we heard, were lying up on one strip of beach, burned. Landing craft are reckoned expendable. Rigg came down from the bridge and, seeing me, said, "The beach is closed to LCILs now. Only small boats going in. Wish they'd thought of that earlier. We lost three good men."

"Which three?" I asked. "I know about Rocky and Bill."

"The coxswain is gone," Bunny said. I remembered the coxswain, the earnest young fellow who wanted to be a newspaperman, and who, dressed in swimming trunks, was going to go overboard ahead of everyone else and run a guideline into shore.

"Couldn't he get back?" I asked.

"He couldn't get anywhere," Rigg answered. "He had just stepped off the ramp when he disintegrated. He must have stepped right into an H. E. shell. Cox was a good lad. We'd recommended him for officers' school." Rigg walked away for the inevitable cup of coffee, shaking his big tawny head. I knew he had a headache, too.

A while afterward, I asked Rigg what he had been thinking as we neared the coast and he said he had been angry because the men we were going to put ashore hadn't had any coffee. "The poor guys had stayed in the sack as late as they could instead," he said. "Going ashore without any coffee!"

*   *   *

Long was having a look at the damage the shell had done to our ship, and I joined him in tracing its course. It had entered the starboard bow well above the waterline, about the level of the ship's number, then had hit the forward anchor winch, had been deflected toward the stern of the boat, had torn through the bulkhead and up through the cover of the escape hatch, then had smashed the ramp winch and Rocky and Bill. It had been a seventy-five-millimetre anti-tank shell with a solid-armor-piercing head, which had broken into several pieces after it hit the ramp winch. The boys kept finding chunks of it around, but enough of it stayed in one piece to show what it had been. "They had us crisscrossed with guns in all those pillboxes that were supposed to have been knocked off," Long said. "Something must have gone wrong. We gave them a perfect landing, though," he added with professional pride. "I promised the commander we would land him dry ass and we did." Long has been in the Coast Guard twenty years and nothing surprises him; he has survived prohibition, Miami and Fire Island hurricanes, and three landings. He is a cheerful soul who has an original theory about fear. "I always tell my boys that fear is a passion like any other passion," he had once told me. "Now, if you see a beautiful dame walking down the street, you feel passion but you control it, don't you? Well, if you begin to get frightened, which is natural, just control yourself also, I tell them." Long said that he had seen the commander start off from the ship at a good clip, run well until he got up near the first line of sand dunes, then stagger. "The commander was at the head of the line about to leave the ship when young Vaghi, that big ensign, came up and must have asked him for the honor of going first," Long said. "They went off that way, Vaghi out ahead, running as if he was running out on a field with a football under his arm. Miller led the soldiers off the other ramp, and he stepped out like a little gentleman, too." The space where the starboard ramp had once been gave the same effect as an empty sleeve or eye socket.

It was Frankel, a signalman who had been on the bridge, who told me sometime that afternoon about how the wounded soldier came to be on board. Frankel, whose family lives on East Eighteenth Street in Brooklyn, was a slender, restless fellow who used to be a cutter in the garment centre. He played in dance bands before he got his garment-union card, he once told me, and on the ship he occasionally played hot licks on the bugle slung on the bridge. "A shell hit just as we were beginning to pull out," Frankel said, "and we had begun to raise the ramps. It cut all but about one strand of the cable that was holding the starboard ramp and the ramp was wobbling in the air when I saw a guy holding on to the end of it. I guess a lot of us saw him at the same time. He was just clutching the ramp with his left arm, because he had been shot in the other shoulder. I'll never forget his eyes. They seemed to say, 'Don't leave me behind.' He must have been hit just as he stepped off the ramp leaving the ship. It was this soldier. So Ryan and Landini went out and got him. Ryan worked along the rail inside the ramp and Landini worked along the outside edge of the ramp and they got him and carried him back into the ship. There was plenty of stuff flying around, too, and the ramp came away almost as soon as they got back. That's one guy saved, anyway." Ryan was a seaman cook who helped Fassy, the commissary steward, in the galley, and Landini was the little First Avenue Italian who had made up a special song for himself—"I'm going over to France and I'm making in my pants."

Along about noon, an LCVP, a troughlike fifty-footer, hailed us and asked if we could take care of five soldiers. Rigg said we could. The craft came alongside and passed over five drenched and shivering tank soldiers who had been found floating on a rubber raft. They were the crew of a tank that had been going in on a very small craft and they had been swamped by a wave.* The tank had gone to the bottom and the soldiers had just managed to make it to the raft. The pharmacist's mates covered them with piles of blankets and put them to bed in one of our large compartments. By evening they were in the galley drinking coffee with the rest of us. They were to stay on the ship for nearly a week, as it turned out, because nobody would tell us what to do with them. They got to be pretty amphibious themselves. The sergeant in command was a fellow from Cleveland named Angelatti. He was especially happy about being saved, apparently because he liked his wife. He would keep repeating, "Gee, to think it's my second anniversary—I guess it's my lucky day!" But when he heard about what we thought had happened to the men we put ashore, he grew gloomy. The tanks had been headed for that beach and should have helped knock out the pillboxes. It hadn't been the tankmen's fault that the waves had swamped them, but the sergeant said disconsolately, "If we hadn't fucked up, maybe those other guys wouldn't have been killed." He had a soldier's heart.

# III

ON the morning of D Day-plus-one, the LCIL was like a ship with a hangover. Her deck was littered with cartons of tinned rations left behind by the land fighters she had carried to the Norman shore. There was a gap where the starboard ramp had been and there were various holes in the hull and hatches to mark the path of the anti-tank shell that had hit her while she had been on the beach. Everybody aboard was nursing a

* These were amphibious tanks, with inflated canvas "jackets," and they were self-propelled. The censor allowed no reference to them, since they were a novelty. Of 32 headed for our beach, 28 flooded out. Only the weather was to blame.

headache. The big fellows running the show had found nothing for us to do since our one run to the beach, which we had reached at 7:35 A.M. on D Day. The reason we hadn't been sent in again was that the German resistance was so strong that now the troops were being taken in only on smaller craft, which offered smaller targets. So we hung around in the Channel, waiting for orders and talking over the things that had happened to us. The men in the engine room, which was so clean that it looked like the model dairy exhibit at the World's Fair—all white paint and aluminum trim—had sweated it out at their posts during the excitement on deck and the engine-room log had been punctiliously kept. On the morning of D-plus-one, Cope, the chief machinist's mate, a tall, quiet chap from Philadelphia, told somebody that from the order "Drop stern anchor" to the order "Take in on stern anchor," which included all the time we had spent aground, exactly four minutes had elapsed. Most of us on deck would have put it at half an hour. During those four minutes all the hundred and forty passengers we carried had run off the ramps into three feet of water, three members of our Coast Guard complement of thirty-three had been killed, and two others had rescued a wounded soldier clinging to the end of the starboard ramp, which had been almost shot away and which fell away completely a few seconds later. The experience had left us without appetite. I remember, on the afternoon of D Day, sitting on a ration case on the pitching deck and being tempted by the rosy picture on the label of a roast-beef can. I opened it, but I could only pick at the jellied juice, which reminded me too much of the blood I had seen that morning, and I threw the tin over the rail.

By D-plus-one we were beginning to eat again. That morning I was on the upper deck talking to Barrett, a seaman from North Carolina, when we saw a German mine go off. It threw a column of water high into the air and sank a ship near it, a transport called the Susan B. Anthony. German planes had been fiddling around above our anchorage during the night, without bombing us; evidently they had been dropping mines. We had seen three of the planes shot down. Barrett looked at the waterspout and said, "If we ever hit a mine like that, we'll go up in the air like a arrow."

Susan B. put her nose in the air and slipped backward calmly, like a lady lowering herself into an armchair. In twenty minutes she was gone. It looked as if all her crew got off. Barrett had bet a pound, even money, that we would be hit during the action. I asked him if he had collected the bet and he said, "Sure. As long as we got hit whether I take the money or not, I might as well take it." In the wardroom, Kavanaugh, the communications officer, talked to me about Bill, one of the Coast Guard boys who had been hit. Long told me about a patch he had devised that would expand in water and would close up any underwater holes in the hull, and seemed rather to regret that he had had no chance to try it out. Lieutenant Rigg kept repeating a tag line he had picked up from Sid Fields, a

comedian in a London revue: "What a performance! What a performance!" But the most frequent subject of conversation among both officers and men was the fate of the fellows we had put on the beach, usually
referred to collectively as "those poor bastards." We had left them splash-
ing through shallow water, with tracer bullets flying around them and
only a nearly level, coverless beach immediately in front of them and with
a beach pillbox and more of the enemy on a cliff inshore blazing away
with everything they had. We had decided that hardly any of our men
could have survived.

Late that afternoon our landing craft got an order to help unload
soldiers from a big troopship several miles off the French shore. We were
to carry the men almost as far as the beach and then transfer them to
Higgins boats. One of our ramps was gone and the other one was not
usable, and it would have been superfluous cruelty to drop a soldier with
a full pack into five feet of water, our minimum draught. We gathered
from the order that the Germans were no longer shooting on the beach;
this, at least, represented progress.

The soldiers who lined the decks of the transport, all eager to get
ashore at once, belonged to the Second Division; they wore a white star
and an Indian head on their shoulder flashes. A scramble net hung down
the port side of the vessel, and soldiers with full equipment strapped to
their backs climbed down it one by one and stepped backward onto our
landing craft. As each man made the step, two seamen grabbed him and
helped him aboard. It often took as much time to unload the soldiers from
a big ship as it did for the ship itself to get from Britain to the Norman
coast, and it seemed to me that a small expenditure on gangplanks of
various lengths and furnished with grapples, like the ones used in boarding operations in ancient naval battles, would have sped these transfers
more than a comparable outlay for any other device could possibly have
done.

While we were loading the men, a thirty-six-foot craft approached us
on the other side. There were two other thirty-six-footers there side by
side already. The newest thirty-six-footer got alongside the outer one of
the pair of earlier arrivals and the crew boosted up a man who had been
standing in the stern of the boat and helped him on to the other craft. The
man made his way unsteadily across both of the intervening thirty-six-
footers to us, and men on the boats passed his gear, consisting of a
typewriter and a gas mask, along after him. He was in a field jacket and
long khaki trousers without leggings. The clothes were obviously fresh out
of a quartermaster's stores. He wore the war correspondent's green shoulder patch on his field jacket. His face and form indicated that he had led
a long and comfortable life, and his eyes betrayed astonishment that he
should be there at all, but he was smiling. Some of our Coastguardsmen
helped him over our rail. He said that he was Richard Stokes of the St.
Louis *Post-Dispatch*, that he had been a Washington correspondent and

a music critic for many years, that he had wanted to go overseas when we got into the war, and that he had finally induced his paper to send him over. He had got airplane passage to Britain, where he had arrived two weeks before, and had been sent to the invasion coast on a Liberty ship that was to land men on D-plus-one. "It seems just wonderful to be here," Stokes said. "I can hardly believe it." He had been very much disappointed when he found out that because of the violence of the German resistance, the Liberty ship was not going to land her passengers for a couple of days. The ship's captain had said to him, "There's another crowd going ashore. Why don't you go with them?" Then the skipper had hailed a boat for him. "And here I am," said Stokes. "It's too good to be true." He was sixty-one years old, and the world seemed marvellous to him. He said he had never been in a battle and he wanted to see what it was like.

We got all our soldiers—about four hundred of them—aboard and started in toward the same stretch of shore we had left in such haste thirty-six hours before. The way in looked familiar and yet devoid of the character it had once had for us, like the scene of an old assignation revisited. The house with the tower on top of the cliff was now gone, I noticed. The naval bombardment, although tardy, had been thorough. Scattered along the shore were the wrecked and burned-out landing craft that had been less lucky than ours. Several of our men told me they had seen the LCT that had been burning off our port quarter on D Day pull out, still aflame, and extinguish the fire as she put to sea, but plenty of others remained. Small craft came out to us from the shore that had so recently been hostile, and soldiers started climbing into them, a less complicated process than the transfer from the troopship because the highest points of the small craft were nearly on a level with our main deck. I could see occasional puffs of smoke well up on the beach. They looked as if they might be the bursts of German shells coming from behind the cliff, and I felt protective toward Stokes. "Mr. Stokes," I said, "it seems to be pretty rough in there." He didn't even have a blanket to sleep on, and he didn't have the slightest idea whom he was going to look for when he got in; he was just going ahead like a good city reporter on an ordinary assignment. He watched two boats load up with soldiers and then, as a third came alongside—I remember that the name painted inside her ramp was "Impatient Virgin"—he said, "Mr. Liebling, I have made up my mind," and went down and scrambled aboard, assisted by everybody who could get a hand on him. He got ashore all right and did some fine stories. A couple of weeks afterward he told me, "I couldn't stand being within sight of the promised land and then coming back."

There was nothing for us to do during the daylight hours of D-plus-two, but toward eight o'clock in the evening we got an order to go out to

another troopship and unload more Second Division soldiers, who were to
be taken to a beach next to the one where we had landed on D Day. The
ship was an American Export liner. Several other LCILs were also assigned to the job of emptying her. I was on our bridge with Rigg when we
came under her towering side, and the smell of fresh bread, which her
cooks had evidently been baking, drove all other thoughts from our minds.
Rigg hailed a young deck officer who was looking down at us and asked
him if he could spare some bread. The officer said sure, and a few minutes
later a steward pushed six long loaves across to our bridge from a port-
hole at approximately our level. They were an inestimable treasure to us.
Everything is relative in an amphibious operation; to the four-man crews
who operate the thirty-six-foot LCVPs, which are open to the weather and
have no cooking facilities, an LCIL seems a floating palace. They would
often come alongside us and beg tinned fruit, which they would receive
with the same doglike gratitude we felt toward the merchantman for our
bread.

The soldiers came aboard us along a single narrow plank, which was
put over from the port side of the troopship to our rail, sloping at an
angle of forty-five degrees. We pitched continuously in the rough water,
and the soldiers, burdened with rifles and about fifty pounds of equipment apiece, slid rather than ran down the plank. Our crew had arranged
a pile of ration cases at the rail, right where the gangplank was fastened,
and the soldiers stepped from the end of the plank to the top case and
then jumped down. We made two trips between the merchantman and
the small boats that night, and only one soldier fell, and was lost, between
the ships during the whole operation. That, I suppose, was a good percentage, but it still seemed to me an unnecessary loss. On our first trip from
ship to shore, while we were unloading soldiers into small boats a couple
of hundred yards off the beach, there was an air raid. The soldiers standing on our narrow deck, with their backs to the deckhouse walls, had
never been under real fire before, but they remained impassive amid the
cascade of Bofors shells that rose from hundreds of ships. Much of the
barrage had a low trajectory and almost scraped the paint off our bridge.
On one ship some gunners who knew their business would hit a plane,
and then, as it fell, less intelligent gun crews would start after it and
follow it down, forgetting that when a plane hits the water it is at the
waterline. An anti-aircraft shell travelling upward at an angle of not more
than twenty degrees wounded Commander Carusi sleeping in a dugout
on the side of a cliff ashore a couple of nights later.*

A beach-battalion sailor came out to us on one of the first small boats
from the shore. He was a big, smiling fellow we had brought from En-

* Carusi says that he was lying outside the dugout awaiting evacuation next morning,
when one medical corpsman said to another, "No use taking that white-haired old
sonofabitch. He won't make it." It made Gene so sore he *ordered* them to take him.
They got him back to England and he survived.

gland on our first trip to the invasion coast, one of "those poor bastards" we had all assumed were dead. The cooks hauled him into the galley for sandwiches and coffee, and within a couple of minutes officers as well as men were crowding about him. Nearly everybody we asked him about turned out to be alive—the commander of the beach battalion; Miller, the Army lieutenant; little Dr. Davey; Vaghi and Reich, the poker-playing ensigns; Smith, the beach battalion's veteran chief petty officer; and others whom we had got to know on the ship. They had had a rough time, the sailor said. They had lain for five hours in holes they had scooped in the sand when they went ashore, while one or two American tanks which had landed shot at pillboxes and the pillboxes shot back. Then some infantrymen who had landed in small boats at H Hour worked their way up the beach and took the German positions, releasing our friends from the position in which they were pinned down. They were living on the side of a hill now and getting on with their work of organizing traffic between ship and shore. It was very pleasant news for us aboard the landing craft. We worked all night unloading soldiers, but the Coast Guard crew didn't mind; they were in a good mood.

Early the next day, D-plus-three, I thumbed a ride ashore to go visiting. I hailed a passing assault craft, a rocket-firing speedboat, which took me part of the way and then transferred me to an LCVP that was headed inshore. The LCVP ran up onto the beach, dropped her bow ramp, and I walked onto French soil without even wetting my feet. This was the moment I had looked forward to for four years minus nine days, since the day I had crossed the Spanish frontier at Irún after the fall of France. Then the words of de Gaulle—"France has lost a battle but not the war"—were ringing in my ears, for I had just heard his first radio speech from London, but I had not dared hope that the wheel would turn almost full circle so soon. There was the noise of cannonading a couple of miles or so beyond the cliffs, where the First Division was pushing on from the fingerhold it had made good on D Day, but on the beach everything was calm. Troops and sailors of the amphibious forces had cleared away much of the wreckage, so that landing craft coming in would not foul their hulls or anchor chains; metal road strips led up from the water's edge to the road parallel with the shore. Men were going about their work as if there were no enemy within a hundred miles, and this was understandable, because no German planes ever arrived to molest them as they unloaded vehicles and munitions for the troops up ahead. To men who had been in other campaigns, when a solitary jeep couldn't pass down a road without three Messerschmitts' having a pass at it, this lack of interference seemed eerie, but it was true all the same. During the first week after the invasion began, I didn't see one German plane by daylight. Almost in front of me, as I stepped off the boat, were the ruins of the concrete blockhouse that had fired at us as we ran in on D Day. The concrete had been masked by a simulated house, but the disguise had been shot away and the place gaped white and roofless. I had more a sense of coming home to the United States Army than to France, for the first M.P. of whom I inquired the way to the command post of the beach battalion said he didn't know. This is S.O.P., or standard operating procedure, because a soldier figures that if he tells you he knows, he will, at best, have trouble directing you, and if the directions turn out to be wrong you may come back and complain. He has nothing to lose by denying knowledge.

I walked along the beach and met a beach-battalion sailor. He was equally unknowledgeable until I convinced him that I was a friend of the commander. Then he led me two hundred yards up a cliff to the place I had asked about. The commander was not there, but a Lieutenant Commander Watts* and a Lieutenant Reardon, both New Yorkers, were. They had gone ashore on another landing craft, but I had met them both while we were in port in Britain awaiting sailing orders. They had landed five hundred yards up the beach from us and had, of course, got the same reception we got. The command post was installed in a row of burrows in the face of the cliff from which the Germans had fired down on the incoming boats and the beach on D Day; now it was we who overlooked the beach. In the side of another cliff, which was almost at a right angle to this one, the Germans had had two sunken concrete pillboxes enfilading the beach, and I realized that the crossfire had centred on our landing craft and the others nearby. Meeting these men reminded me of what the First Division soldier had said to me a few days earlier about "Candide": "Voltaire used the same gag too often. The characters are always getting killed and then turning out not to have been killed at all, and they tell their friends what happened to them in the meantime."

Watts said that after they had left their landing craft, they had run forward like hell and then had thrown themselves down on the beach because there was nothing else to do. The forepart of the beach was covered with large, round pebbles about the size, I imagine, of the one David used on Goliath, and when the German machine-gun bullets skittered among them the stones became a secondary form of ammunition themselves and went flying among the men. "We had infantry up ahead of us, but at first they were pinned down too," Watts said. "A couple of tanks had landed and one of them knocked out a seventy-five up on the side of the hill, but in a short while the Germans either replaced it or got it going again. Then, after a couple of hours, two destroyers came and worked close in to shore, although there were plenty of mines still in there, and really plastered the pillboxes. The infantry went up the hill in the face of machine-gun fire and drove the Germans out of the trench

* Henry B. Watts, Jr., now chairman of the Board of Governors of the New York Stock Exchange.

system they had on the crown of the hill. I'll show it to you in a couple of minutes. It's a regular young Maginot Line. By nightfall we felt fairly safe. We found out later from prisoners that the Three Hundred and Fifty-second German Field Division had been holding anti-invasion exercises here the day before we attacked. They had been scheduled to go back to their barracks D Day morning, but when scouts told them about the big fleet on the way in, they decided to stay and give us a good time. They did." It wasn't until a week later, in London, that I found out that because of this untoward circumstance our beach and those on either side of it had been the toughest spots encountered in the landings, and that the losses there had not been at all typical of the operation.

I was delighted to discover Smith, the old chief petty officer, reclining in a nearby slit trench. He was looking very fit. He was forty-seven, and I had wondered how he would do in the scramble to the beach. He had not only made it but had gathered a large new repertory of anecdotes on the way. "A guy in front of me got it through the throat," Smitty said. "Another guy in front of me got it through the heart. I run on. I heard a shell coming and I threw myself face down. There was an Army colonel on one side of me, a Navy captain on the other. The shell hit. I was all right. I looked up and the captain and the colonel was gone, blown to pieces. I grabbed for my tommy gun, which I had dropped next to me. It had been twisted into a complete circle. I was disarmed, so I just laid there."

While I was listening to Smitty, Reardon, talking over a field telephone, had located the commander somewhere on top of the cliff, along the German trench system, which had been taken over by the amphibious engineers as billets. Watts and I decided to walk up and find him. We made our way along the face of the cliff, on a narrow path that led past clusters of slit trenches in which soldiers were sleeping, and got up to the crest at a point where some Negro soldiers had made their bivouac in a thicket. We followed another path through a tangled, scrubby wood. The Germans had left numbers of wooden skull-and-crossbones signs on the tree trunks. These signs said *"Achtung Minen"* and *"Attention aux Mines."* Whether they indicated that we had taken the enemy by surprise and that he had not had time to remove the signs put up for the protection of his own and civilian personnel, or whether the signs were put there for psychological purposes, like dummy guns, was a question for the engineers to determine. Watts and I took care to stay in the path.

We found the commander, who was in good form. He said he had lost only a couple of the forty-five beach-battalion men who had been on the landing craft with us but that in the battalion as a whole the casualties had been fairly heavy. "Not nearly what I thought they would be when I left that boat, though," he said.

*   *   *

The trench system was a fine monument to the infantrymen of the First Division who had taken it. I couldn't help thinking, as I looked it over, that the German soldiers of 1939–41 would not have been driven from it in one day, even by heroes, and the thought encouraged me. Maybe they were beginning to understand that they were beaten. There were no indications that the position had been under artillery fire and I could see only one trace of the use of a flamethrower. As I reconstructed the action, our fellows must have climbed the hill and outflanked the position, and the Germans, rather than fight it out in their holes, had cleared out to avoid being cut off. They had probably stayed in and continued firing just as long as they still had a chance to kill without taking losses. As the French say, they had not insisted. The trenches were deep, narrow, and so convoluted that an attacking force at any point could be fired on from several directions. Important knots in the system, like the command post and mortar emplacements, were of concrete. The command post was sunk at least twenty-five feet into the ground and was faced with brick on the inside. The garrison had slept in underground bombproofs, with timbered ceilings and wooden floors. In one of them, probably the officers' quarters, there was rustic furniture, a magnificent French radio, and flowers, still fresh, in vases. On the walls were cheap French prints of the innocuous sort one used to see in speakeasies: the little boy and the little girl, and the coyly equivocal captions.

An engineer sergeant who showed us through the place said that the Americans had found hairnets and hairpins in this bombproof. I could imagine an *Oberstleutnant* and his mistress, perhaps the daughter of a French collaborationist, living uneventfully here and waiting for something in which the *Oberstleutnant* had unconsciously ceased to believe, something that he wished so strongly would never happen that he had convinced himself it would happen, if anywhere, on some distant part of the coast. I thought of the Frenchmen I had known in 1939, waiting in a similar mood in the Maginot Line. The sergeant, a straight-featured Jewish fellow in his late thirties, said, "Those infantrymen were like angels. I tell you, I laid there on the beach and prayed for them while they went up that hill with nothing—with bayonets and hand grenades. They did it with nothing. It was a miracle." That made me feel good, because the infantry regiment involved had long been my favorite outfit.* The commander was sardonic about one thing. "You remember how I used to worry about how my men would fall into bomb holes and drown on the way in because the Air Forces had laid down such a terrific bombardment?" he asked. "Well, I defy you to find one bomb hole on this whole beach for a mile each way."

The commander and Watts accompanied me back to the shore. On the

---

* 16th Regiment, First Division.

way, we stopped at a field hospital that had been set up under canvas. There I talked to some Italian prisoners who were digging shelter trenches. They were fine, rugged specimens, as they should have been, because since the Italian surrender they had undoubtedly had plenty of exercise swinging pickaxes for the Todt organization. Their regiment of bridge-building engineers had been disarmed by the Germans in Greece and the men had been given the choice of enrolling in Fascist combat units or in labor service, they told me. They had all chosen labor service. They seemed to expect to be commended for their choice. They had built many of the trenches in the district. "We wouldn't fight for Hitler," they assured me. I thought that the point had been pretty well proved. Now they were digging for us. They said that all Germans were cowards.

We went down to the shore, and the commander, who, being beach-master, was in charge of all traffic alongshore, hailed a Duck for me. The Duck put me on an LCVP, which took me back to my ship. On the way out, I realized that I had not seen a single French civilian the entire time ashore.

When I came aboard our landing craft, Long, the engineering officer, grinned at me.

"Did you notice a slight list, sometimes on one side, sometimes on the other, the last two days?" he asked.

I said, "You mean the one you said must be on account of the crew's all turning over in their sleep at the same time?"

"Yes," he said. "Well, today we found an open seam down in the stern. She started to list that night the big bomb dropped next to us, but you were sleeping too sound to get up. So maybe we'll go back to port. She has no ramps, the forward anchor winch is sheared in half, and she may as well go into the yard for a couple of days."

The morning of D-plus-four, Rigg signalled the command ship for permission to put back to Britain. As soon as the signalman blinked out the message, every man on board knew there was a chance we would go back, and even fellows who had expressed a low opinion of Weymouth looked extremely happy. While we were waiting for an answer to our request, an LCIL that acted as a group leader, a kind of straw boss among the little ships, passed near us, and the lieutenant on her bridge ordered us over to help tow a barge of ammunition. We were to be paired with another LCIL on this job. The barge, a two-hundred-and-fifty-tonner, was loaded with TNT, and the idea was for one LCIL to make fast on each side of her and shove her in to shore. The Diesel motors of an LCIL, although they can move their craft along at a fair speed, haven't the towing power of a tug. The two LCILs bounced about in the choppy sea for quite a while as we tried to get towing lines aboard the big barge that would hold. Even after we finally got started, every now and then the lines would snap and we would bounce against the side of the barge, as we put more lines aboard her, with a crash that disquieted us, even though we had been told many times that the explosive was packed so carefully that no jouncing would possibly set it off. We were very happy when the barge grounded on the beach according to plan and we could cast off and leave her. Just before we had finished, the group leader came along again and an officer on her bridge shouted over to us through a megaphone, "Report to control-ship shuttle service!" This meant that we were going back to Britain; control ships organize cross-Channel convoys. We were not sorry to go.

By Sunday, D-plus-five, when we at last got started, the water had smoothed out so much that the Channel was like the Hyde Park Serpentine. The flat-bottomed LCIL will bounce about in the slightest sea, but today our craft moved along like a swanboat. The water was full of ration cartons, life jackets, and shell cases, and on the way over we picked up one corpse, of a soldier wearing a life jacket, which indicated that he had never got ashore. Since German planes were dropping mines every night, the lookout was instructed to keep a sharp watch for suspicious objects in the water, and this was almost the only thing it was necessary to think about as we loafed along. A seaman from Florida named Hurwitz was lookout on the bow in the early morning. "Suspicious object off port bow!" he would bawl, and then "Suspicious object off starboard quarter!" Most of the suspicious objects turned out to be shell cases. Finally, Hurwitz yelled "Bridge! The water is just full of suspicious objects!"

The main interest aboard now was whether we would get to port before the pubs closed, at ten o'clock in the evening. Long was getting unheard-of speed out of his motors and it seemed that we would make the pubs easily. Then we happened upon a British LCT that was all alone and was having engine trouble. She asked us to stand by in case her motors conked out altogether. We proceeded at four knots. When the British skipper signalled to us, "Doing my utmost, can make no more," which meant that our chance of beer had gone glimmering, Rigg made a gesture that for delicacy and regard for international relations must have few parallels in naval history. He ordered a signal that may someday be in schoolbooks along with Nelson's "England expects every man to do his duty." "Never mind," he signalled the crippled LCT. "We would have been too late for pub-closing time anyway."

I have left the story of *our* Longest Day—I did not stop to see Wayne and Mitchum lead their charge—in the form in which I wrote it and saw it through censorship and sent it on by wireless from London in parts, as fast as I could after getting ashore. The writing, naturally, took more than one day. While I was writing it the first of the doodlebugs, or V-1's, arrived in the London sky, and continued to pass overhead during the labor of composition.

They caused considerable confusion the first night because they came intermittently for hours, instead of in groups like normal bombers, and so the air raid sirens, controlled by radar, kept sounding alerts and all clears. The things though unmanned had motors. I had no right to pull aside my blackout curtain to see what was happening, and I did not want to interrupt my work to go down to the street—I had a twinge of gout, anyway—so I passed the night in a state of baffled curiosity and fell asleep toward morning. I was awakened by the waitress who brought my breakfast at the set hour, a big Irish girl, who had come to London to work for the good wartime wages. British girls of her age were subject to draft. She drew the curtains, and when I asked her what the hell had been going on, she said, without heat:

"It's them pilotless airplanes. I do hope they won't be a success."


I have left it that way because it is on the whole more accurate than I could make it today. A situation later assumes meanings that it did not have at the time, and you write them into it in retrospect and fool yourself. I have, however, reinserted a few details barred by the censor, like the loss of the Susan B. Anthony, the nature of the flooded tanks and Gene Carusi's name and what happened to him. I have been inconsistent even in this. I find I have not named the men killed; the coxswain was Moran, the men at the winch Rocky Simone and Bill Frere. Bill was the man whose blood got on me, although I had seen shreds, too, of what I afterward learned had been Moran, and I was impressed, when I reflected on Frere's name, to think that I had been drenched in a "brother's" blood. Afterward I re-reflected and have settled for coincidence.

Also, the instant of that day that recurs to me most often has been that when I sat with the roast-beef tin in my hand—the label said it had been packed in Uruguay—and couldn't eat, a most unusual difficulty for me. The meat in the opened tin had a jellied look, and the stuff sloshing on the forward deck, as the LCI-88 rolled, had a jellied look too—the shell had torn open dozens of the cans of rations the soldiers had left aboard, and the liquid on the deck was a mixture of blood and condensed milk, with Campbell's soup. It was an insult.

The rules of the censor also barred reporting that we had seen the LCI-85, another of our group, capsize and sink, riddled and abandoned, and there were other casualties we did not ourselves know at the time. Of the ten LCI's, including the 88, of LCI-flotilla 110, that went in at that hour, four were sunk, and all of the rest, I think, were hit. Those lost were, besides the 85, the 91, 92 and 93, all hit *before* they discharged their passengers, a high proportion of whom were killed. When it was all over, the planners decided that LCI's were too high and vulnerable for the work.

Altogether H plus 65 on Easy Red Beach, Omaha, was an even bloodier mess than we knew at the time, and I am glad we didn't. Anybody who thinks there was a theme song should have his head examined.

# PART V

## DIRECTION: PARIS

I CROSSED over into France again aboard a Landing Ship, Tanks, on June 24th. The Channel was criss-crossed by convoys, traveling without incident, and on Omaha there were new roads, and traffic M.P.'s to show you the way out. The five briefer stories that follow, all despatches, chronicle my advance on Paris, leaving out a few devious detours that I did not think would interest Harold Ross and Bill Shawn, my editors at *The New Yorker*. One was to Rennes, the first large French city we liberated after the breakout. I remembered Rennes from the pre-war past—1926—as a city whose warm ways belied its austere appearance, and early reports had the population, of both sexes, lavishing its gratitude on Americans. I had a particular memory of an establishment there called *La Feria* (the Fair) that had impressed me, in 1926, by its provincial elegance, as if a ring of the doorbell admitted you to the world of Maupassant's Maison Tellier. I remembered also that Rennes was the seat of an Archbishop, the primate of Brittany, who should be able to communicate a sharp insight into the relations between the devout Bretons and the Occupant during the invasion, a subject that suddenly interested me. I visited the Archbishop first, a splendid gentleman named Roques, who had been noble in the resistance, and who was promoted to Cardinal within a short time, along with two or three other resistance Archbishops, while a number of senior Pétainist Cardinals temporarily withdrew from public life. The Church never runs short of suitable spokesmen in a new situation. The Archbishop had taught, either French literature in Germany or German literature in France, I now forget which, for many years as a priest, and had a deep understanding of the German soul, which he found poorly cooked, like a runny *oeuf en gelee,* and so, likely to disintegrate at a slight shock, such as the vibration of a loud vulgar voice with an Austrian accent.

I proceeded later—not directly, for I have a sense of fitness—from the Archbishop's palace to La Feria, to which a cop was kind enough to direct me. It now stood alone, untouched, in a great expanse of bombing rubble around the railroad yards, which had received constant attention from our planes. I found only the Madame, who had been the *sous-maîtresse* in 1926, and two *pensionnaires* in residence, since the Boche had moved out, and La Feria's future under the new order was unclear. The decor had been modernized in a nasty way just before the war began. Madame was touched by my fidelity and long memory, but especially by my sense of what was proper in calling on the Archbishop first. She was, like all *Bretonnes*, pious, and told me she found it paid.

"Do you know," she said, "of all the buildings in the quarter of the railroad station, only the Cathedral and La Feria were spared by the bombardments."

# Letters from France

FOR a year before the Allied landings here, Germans occupied a large, moated, Norman farmhouse near which I now live. Sixty of them were billeted in it, sleeping in great, pine-panelled living rooms on mattresses they had stolen from a nearby summer hotel and in the fetid warmth which is a German soldier's ideal of comfort. This atmosphere is customarily maintained by keeping all windows and doors closed tight. The owners of the farmhouse, who moved into the kitchen wing when their guests took over, listened regularly to the B.B.C. broadcasts and always harbored from two to six young men who were evading forced labor in Germany. In the evening, Madame H.,* the matriarch who rules the family, clipped certain items bearing on the war from the German-controlled French newspapers, or, when there was nothing worth clipping, reread old items in the collection she was gathering. A couple of nights ago, while I was drinking warm milk in the kitchen, which, because Americans are billeted in the house now, is still the family living room, Madame showed me her clippings. The first one was dated August 17, 1941. Each of them had to do either with a proclamation by a German *Kommandantur* or with a Vichy official threatening reprisal for some act of sabotage committed in northwestern France or with an announcement of the execution of hostages, invariably described as "Jews and Communists."

Madame H., who had no direct contact with the resistance movement and knew nothing first-hand about the victims named in the newspapers, felt certain from the first that they were on the only decent side. Collaborationist cant never deceived her for a moment, and yet she is of the type most susceptible to Pétainolatry—rich, intensely Catholic, and in considerable fear of "Reds." Her son, a blond, broad-headed chap with a decided limp, was a prisoner of war in Germany for three years. He had served in Alsace in a French engineering regiment and right after his capture was set to work with other prisoners digging up French mines. A

* Hamel was the name.

mine exploded, killing six of his comrades and shattering one of his feet.
Even after that, he was sent into forced labor, first in Alsace and then in
Germany. Officials of the local *Kommandantur* approached Madame H.
some time after the armistice with an offer to have her son sent home if
she would persuade him to be an informer against farmers who were
withholding cattle and fats from the Germans. She said she would prefer
not to have her son home. Eventually the Germans released him anyway,
along with a few thousand other crippled or tubercular prisoners, when,
in 1943, Vichy put on a great drive to induce young Frenchmen to volunteer for labor in Germany to "relieve" prisoners of war who had been
there since 1940. These incapacitated prisoners were supposed to be the
advance guard of a great mass of returning Frenchmen; actually, they
were the only ones ever released. Young H., as he will be known in the
countryside as long as his mother lives, although he is now over forty,
came home with a great admiration for the Alsatians, who, he says, are
the most patriotic French he ever met, and with an almost patronizing
view of Germans. "A German is either a bandit or a decent fellow," he
says. "There are no in-between Germans. The bandits run the rest. I have
seen the Germans in air raids, and individually they are shameless cowards, but fantastic discipline keeps them going." He says there was
enough food, but it was all starchy, and that few German workmen, even
at the time he left the country, seemed to believe that Germany could win
the war, whereas most French prisoners were confident even in the worst
days that Germany would lose.

When H. returned to Normandy and saw what the German Army had
become by then, he grew optimistic, too, like most of the Normans who
had stayed home. The athletes in uniform who had invaded western
France in 1940 had given place to a mixed lot of Georgians, Russians,
Poles, and adolescent and middle-aged Germans, and the motorized equipment that had amazed the French in the blitzkrieg days had been shipped
away to active fronts and been supplanted in great part by horse-drawn
vehicles. The soldiers of the polyglot regiments seemed resigned to defeat
and stuffed themselves in quiet desperation, consuming Norman butter
and milk as if they were trying to eat enough to last them through the
black years they saw ahead of them. The arrogance of the invaders had
given way to the alternate fits of meekness and ill manners of the garrison
troops. The Germans were so short of motor vehicles that they com-
mandeered farmers' carriages for their officers and sometimes drafted
farmers to drive them. A substantial farmer, a neighbor of Madame H.,
tells about the time he drove a German major to a railroad station three
miles from the officer's billet; he managed to take an hour getting to the
station, pretending first that he didn't know the way and then that the
horse had gone lame. The German missed his train and was furious about
it, but the Norman pretended not to understand anything he said. This
was the sort of thing that kept the Germans miserable; they had the

feeling that they were constantly being tricked and laughed at. The German authorities knew that they were getting only a fraction of the cattle and dairy produce available, but they couldn't confiscate the herds without putting a stop to production, since they had no agricultural personnel of their own to put on the farms.

Few of the country people in Normandy expected a landing there. The majority, in fact, thought that there would be no landing at all but that the Allies would wear Germany down by bombing. They were perhaps persuaded to this way of thinking by a hope that their land would not be fought upon. But the landings, when they came, delighted them. The discomfiture of the Germans was particularly pleasing, and peasants, offering their best bottled cider to Americans, suddenly burst into laughter as they remember how the supermen scuttled off. During the first days of the invasion, there was a bit of foolish talk in British newspapers, and probably also in American papers, which I have not seen, about the Normans' lack of enthusiasm, stories evidently written by correspondents who acquired their ideas of Frenchmen from music-hall turns and comic drawings. One might as well expect public demonstrations of emotion in Contoocook, New Hampshire, or in Burrillville, Rhode Island, as in Normandy, where the people are more like New Englanders than they are like, for instance, Charles Boyer. Young men of the resistance groups did invaluable service both before and after the landing; they drew us plans of German fortifications before we landed and then went through the German lines repeatedly during the fighting in order to get information about enemy movements. Not one report of a French civilian's sniping at Allied troops has been authenticated, and relations between our soldiers and the country people are excellent everywhere, now that the inevitable misunderstandings of the early days have passed.

A common cause of misunderstanding was the farmers' habit of loitering about fields which had been requisitioned for Allied tank parks. One Armored Forces colonel was thinking of having the *maire* of a certain village shot as an obvious spy when a French-speaking American officer interrogated the *maire* and found that he was just waiting around for a chance to milk his cows. "There may perhaps be a war and you may perhaps be beating Boches," said the *maire*, with traditional Norman scepticism, raising his voice occasionally as the sound of guns threatened to drown his words, "but what I am sure of is that my horned beasts must be milked." Even the farmers who were happiest to see the Allied tanks arrive are now beginning to ask wistfully when they are going to get their pastures back again.

The French sometimes misinterpreted American actions, too. There was, for example, the *maire* of a small *commune* just outside Cherbourg who came into Army Civil Affairs headquarters there five days after we took the city and complained to a French liaison officer that American troops had put him out of the *mairie* and that now he had no place in which to carry on the affairs of the *commune*. The French liaison officer, Captain Gérard Lambert, an energetic Gaulliste, replied emphatically, "But that is against all the policy set on high levels! They have no right to commandeer a French Government building unless for extreme military necessity," and he and the *maire* immediately drove off to the *mairie*. There were no American troops there, but a sign on the door said, "Keep Out—U. S. Military Police." As Captain Lambert and the *maire*, who must have been around seventy-five, climbed the stairs to the first floor, the captain said, "This is curious. Why did they order you out?"

The old man answered indignantly, "Because they said there were mines in the cellar."

The captain said with dignity, "You are an idiot."

"However, my captain," the old man said, "it is not certain there are mines in the cellar." So he did remain.

All sorts of difficulties were referred to our Civil Affairs officers during the first few days following the liberation of any city. The manager of the Cherbourg branch of the Banque de France requested Lieutenant Colonel Frank Howley, Cherbourg Civil Affairs Chief, to have a guard posted over a certain heap of rubble in Valognes, a town which had been almost completely flattened by artillery fire. The bank manager explained that he had sent a hundred million francs to the Valognes branch for safekeeping, because he had expected the bombardment of Cherbourg. A shell had demolished the Valognes branch and two adjoining buildings had collapsed on top of it, so the hundred million francs were now buried under all three. The manager seemed to fear that some casual looter might shove the ruins out of the way and unearth the money, a feat which, actually, a steam shovel will probably accomplish in about two weeks.

Cherbourg, the nearest thing to a big city we have yet captured, was the first testing ground in France for the Allies' Army Civil Affairs Branch. When the Americans took over, on June 27th, the city had no water, electricity, gas, transportation, or government. The Vichy *sous-préfet* had fled and so had twenty-five thousand of Cherbourg's civilian population of forty thousand. The Civil Affairs team, headed by Colonel Howley, an American, and including both British and American officers, moved in before the street sniping had ended, and immediately started in on the job of resuscitation. The Civil Affairs men's task, as Howley saw it, was to get the city government functioning normally again. The Civil Affairs Branch had no enlisted personnel it could put to work policing the streets or making repairs. Cherbourg had had a fairly modern water system; water was pumped from the little Divette River to a purifying plant, from which it was distributed through mains. Bombs had broken the pipeline from the river to the plant. Major John C. Diggs, a former sanitary engineer for the State of Indiana, is Public-Works Officer in the Howley team. He got together the staff of the Cherbourg water system, who told him that the Germans had taken away all the reserve pipe. He got piping from the Army Engineers, the French installed it with their own work-men, and on July 1st the city had water again. "All they needed was a little encouragement," Major Diggs told me. "I've seen several floods and hurricanes in Indiana and the effect on local governments is always the same—they're a bit stunned, like a man suffering from battle shock. A little shove gets them going again." When it was time to turn the water on, a new problem presented itself, one that it is safe to say nobody in Washington or London had foreseen. There were hundreds of empty buildings in Cherbourg, many of them partly wrecked. The hastily de-parting owners had left the taps open. When the water was turned on, thousands of gallons would not only be wasted but would do further damage to the structures. Men with loudspeakers borrowed from the local American Psychological Warfare Unit were sent through the streets to warn people to turn off their taps. This expedient did not, of course, take care of the empty houses, so the British Major Palfrey, Police Officer of the team, the American Lieutenant Colonel Hensel, who is its Civil Defense expert, and the American Lieutenant Davis, who is a former battalion chief in the Columbus, Ohio, fire department, got in touch with the French police, the Défense Passive, and the local fire department, respec-tively, and members of all three services went, just to be sure, to every house in the city and turned off the open taps. Two other officers, Lieu-tenant Robertson and Captain Westervelt, who were utilities and tele-phone men in civilian life, got the electric-power and telephone system restored to service in much the same thorough-going fashion.

On June 29th, M. Coulet, General de Gaulle's Normandy delegate, installed in office, as the new *sous-préfet* of Cherbourg, M. Le Viander, who had been chief engineer of the municipality and active in the resis-tance movement. He had been absent from the city when the invasion came but had made his way to the Allied lines a couple of days after the landings. Police and civil servants fell into line and took orders from the new *sous-préfet*, who was, after all, a colleague who had been in civil service a long time, more readily, in most cases, than they had taken them from his Vichy predecessor. He knew precisely which of his sub-ordinates had collaborated beyond absolute necessity, and he sacked them. They were not numerous. After that, the *sous-préfecture* and the Civil Affairs men worked smoothly together. The same thing had already happened in Bayeux, where M. Coulet had his headquarters and where he had installed another resistance *sous-préfet*. The Civil Affairs team in the much smaller but architecturally more interesting Bayeux is headed by a Britisher and includes both American and British officers.

Coulet, a tall, thin-lipped, smooth-shaven man of slightly sombre elegance, speaks English well. He has no army behind him, but he has the prestige, in a Norman's eyes, of representing the only French government the Normans recognize, the Gouvernement Provisoire, and he proceeds with complete assurance, making contact with the resistance group in each district as soon as the Allied forces enter it, and organizing the district with the assistance he receives from local resistance leaders. It is a program which up to now has worked smoothly and bloodlessly. So far, there have been neither legal nor unofficial executions.—

JULY 20 (BY WIRELESS)

The contrast which existed in the first World War between the front and behind the lines has returned with the present Allied campaign in Normandy. Staff officers drive toward the front along roads upon which the shadow of a strafing plane never falls and, leaving it, return to an area in which traffic and sanitation are as well organized as in Westchester. Nobody worries about the possibility of a flanking movement or a breakthrough by the enemy because our flanks rest on the sea and the enemy has shown no signs of real striking power. Even within a couple of miles of the front there is only slight danger, because the Germans have disclosed little artillery. The arrival of a shell on a road near a command post is something to talk about for the next three days. The last few hundred yards make all the difference; the fighting is a nasty business in which hedgerows, drainage ditches, and apple trees have assumed the same lethal associations as Tunisian *djebels*. This struggle for orchards and pastures is disheartening because it is so repetitious. There is, as Army men say, no observation in this country, which means that you can't see an enemy position until you have taken the one in front of it. Even then you don't know that it really is an enemy position until a machine gun opens fire on you from a hedge or a mortar in the next field ahead starts dropping stuff in the one you have just taken. It is not safe to assume that any corner of any field you are attacking is undefended. The property sense of the Norman is so strong that no bit of useful land is without its surrounding hedge and ditch. The Germans dig in behind the hedges like moles—moles with excellent eyesight—and the pattern of the fields frequently gives them a fine opportunity for crossfire, which happens to be one of their specialties. The business of rooting them out of these fields is both dangerous and tedious, and it is one phase of war in which airpower is of almost no help, because foliage conceals the defenders from strafing planes and because bombing entire fields on speculation is likely to pay extremely small dividends in dead Germans. Our artillery is useful in inducing machine gunners to keep their heads down, but foot soldiers have to make the actual kills.

After each few days of this hedgerow fighting, one of our divisions comes to a small town, which it takes. The towns, except for their names, are as much alike as the orchards: always the main street that is merely a stretch of the motor highway; the austere gray stone church that had survived eight centuries and then been shattered the week before; the trepanned, amputated houses with glassless windows; and, if there is one café still ungutted, the sign upon it that says "Off limits to military personnel." A unit takes a mild pride in the catalogue of the towns it has captured—such as St. Jean de Daye, known to the troops as Saint John D Day, and La Haye de Puits, called Hooey da Pooey—but that's about all. There are usually several dead Germans in the buildings of these towns, snipers left behind by their retreating comrades and killed by incoming Americans. Our soldiers, preoccupied with the possibility of surviving snipers and with the mortar fire that the enemy is sure to drop back into any town he has abandoned, hurry past the bodies with only perfunctory interest. There is more affinity between a wax dummy and a corpse than between a corpse and a live man. Some of the corpses wear fairly good gray-green uniforms, and others wear nondescript rags. The most impressive corpses seldom come from the best regiments; the most effective German troops here are the starveling adolescents of the new Nazi formations. Older, more fully developed men give up sooner. The Russians, Georgians, and Poles who were starved into enlisting in German coastal regiments are naturally the easiest game of all. Unfortunately, we have liquidated most of these "static" troops and are now meeting a higher percentage of Germans. For all their stubbornness in defense, the Germans have not been making any counterattacks in force. This has led to a certain optimism, particularly in the zone beginning a thousand yards to the rear of the line. Some officers are saying that the situation reminds them of Tunisia late in April, 1943, when the Germans, though still hanging on to good defensive positions, were about to collapse rather suddenly.

Many peasants remain in their homes in the battle areas, despite the efforts of both Germans and Americans to move them out. The Germans have been trying to evacuate people and their livestock before them as they retreat, but the peasants hide themselves and their beasts. When American troops start fighting around their farmhouses, our Civil Affairs officers attempt to get the peasants to move back of our lines, for their own protection, but they usually say that they won't go unless they can take their cattle with them, and since they can't take their pasture along with the cattle this is not practical. A crop farmer can leave his land for a time and find it there when he comes back, but herds will stray or starve or sicken or wander into machine-gun fire if left to themselves, and the Normans stick to their cows. Near St. Lô, a refugee camp has been established for people whose homes have been destroyed. It is an unusual refugee camp, because it does not receive any supplies from the Army; the French authorities provide the food and the farmers of the district donate clothing and furniture. The refugees have organized themselves into a self-governing community and have succeeded in making themselves more comfortable than the American soldiers of the local Civil Affairs detachment, who are now taking French lessons from the refugee children. Almost every family has deaths to mourn, but the tragic aspect of the situation is naturally not comprehended by the children, who consider the affair a sort of large-scale picnic and are not disturbed by the racket of the American medium artillery immediately behind their temporary home. The subway-train noise the shells make as they go over the children's heads merely provokes them to imitative whistles. Very old people are similarly unmoved by the war. A well-to-do farmer's widow, crippled with rheumatism, and her *bonne* were the only inhabitants left in the village of St. André de L'Epine after two days of heavy fighting. When our Civil Affairs detachment got there, it evacuated them in an ambulance. The mistress was seventy-seven and the maid seventy-two, and the thing that had made the greatest impression on them was the fact that they hadn't been able to get any milk or vegetables for several days and had had to eat their pet rabbit. Their house had been badly damaged and every other building in the village had been flattened.

The Fourteenth of July apparently found everybody in the liberated zone happy. Tricolors that had not seen the light since the Pétain armistice fluttered over houses and draped window sills everywhere, usually along with homemade American flags and often with signs saying "Vive l'Amérique" or "Merci à Nos Libérateurs." The understanding recently reached between de Gaulle and the United States Government seemed to have removed the last suspicion entertained by the French, and the crowds that gathered for the ceremonies in front of the *mairies* were unaffectedly joyous. As one thick-waisted old farmer, an ex-cuirassier, said, "An armored formation has cut up my best pasture, a promising heifer has gone up with a mine, and a bomb has removed most of the tiles from the roof of my house, but, *Monsieur*, I assure you, I was never so happy in my life." And Mme. Hamel said, as she put on her red-white-and-blue rosette (an extra-large one), "Last year I wore a blue dress, my daughter a white one, and my daughter-in-law a red one, and we walked down the street arm in arm, because it was forbidden to wear the tricolor. Now it is different." However, it would be a mistake to assume, because things have gone so smoothly in the part of France liberated up to now, that there will be no serious problems, especially of relief, in *départements* which are either less self-sufficient or which the Germans have had more time to loot. It is also too soon to be able to say that in the big cities the change of regime will be effected with as little violence as it has in the essentially reasonable, rural Normandy. Still, there is every justification for being satisfied with the way things have gone so far.

There was one ceremony on Bastille Day that had not been foreseen—the burial of Brigadier General Theodore Roosevelt, who had died of a heart attack after surviving more front-line perils than any other general officer in this theatre of operations. Nearly all of Roosevelt's scrapes were of his own seeking; he was as nearly fearless as it is given to man to be. The name "Rough Rider," in white letters on his jeep, was a familiar sight just behind the lines in four campaigns of this war. It had been painted out by the time of the funeral and the vehicle had been returned to the motor pool and anonymity, and there was no other charger to lead behind the scout car that carried this flamboyant little man's body to the grave. Nothing else was missing from the solemnities. The man who used to tell his friends in New York how as a small boy he had put on the shoes of his father, the former President, and walked ecstatically about his bedroom at Sagamore Hill was never a sufficiently acute politician to fill them, but he found his métier in 1940, when he took up his reserve commission in the Army. Old Teddy was a dilettante soldier and a first-class politician; his son was a dilettante politician and a first-class soldier. After serving with the First Division in Africa and Sicily and with the French in Italy, he was assigned to a new unit, as assistant division commander, a couple of months before D Day. It was the Fourth Division, which had never fought before, and, by his own example, he gave it much of the lift that took it across the beaches and all the way to Cherbourg. It is no longer a run-of-the-mill division but one of the best in the Army, and his death has endowed it with a tradition. In the circumstances, it was easy to condone his indiscriminate passion for reciting poems, which he rolled out with the large facility of a juke box full of quarters. He was a man you had to see fight to believe in. *

The taking of St. Lô was the climax of the hedgerow phase of our campaign. St. Lô, at the juncture of several major highways, is a larger version of the rural crossroads that are the prizes of smaller operations. The correspondents, going out every day in jeeps to the St. Lô sector of the front, got to know every turning in the lanes, bordered by the omnipresent hedges, that led to the suburbs where the final attack was to be made. Troops fanned out from these lanes to fight their way through the fields. Each day it was possible for vehicles to get past one or two more turnings in the lanes; one remembered these new turnings by the burned-out halftracks or by groups of dead cows. The jeeps that carried the correspondents breasted a seemingly regular stream of other jeeps

* Roosevelt and I had a date to meet at the Café de la Regence in Paris on the fourteenth. Instead, we kept it as described above.

with litters, each bearing two seriously wounded men, strapped to their hoods. The stream was regular because the casualties in this sort of war, though they vary from field to field, don't vary from day to day. You lose a few more men in one hedge-fenced pasture and one or two less in another; there is never a spate of casualties, but the stream never dries up, either. There were about as many German as American wounded on the litters, but we seemed to see many more German than American dead on the ground, probably because we were advancing over terrain that had been hammered by American artillery, whereas the enemy had employed comparatively little artillery. We also got to know every sizable gap in the ragged seven-to-ten-foot-high hedges along the lanes, for the gaps en-abled enemy snipers and mortar crews to see and to shoot accurately. A rapidly moving jeep raised a cloud of dust that might bring down mortar fire even where there was no gap; a jeep creeping at the ten miles an hour that is prescribed in the area seemed to the occupants to be minutes getting past each gap. When, by the evening of July 18th, the Americans had fought themselves out of the turnings and hedgerows, they rushed into the town of St. Lô with all the joy of a band of claustrophobes released from a maze.

The Germans, as expected, broke out what artillery they had and bom-barded St. Lô as soon as our troops came in, and our tired infantrymen, lying face down in the streets at the foot of the buildings, realized that life is just a succession of frying pans and fires. The correspondents, flat on their faces like the rest, wondered whether the Pulitzer Prize was worth all this trouble. They were further depressed by the magnificent aplomb of the brigadier general* who walked erect down the centre of the street, directing troop movements with a cane. When a sniper's bullet went through his right arm, he transferred the cane to his left hand. That gesture will be hard for us to match in our autobiographies.

AUGUST 4 ( BY WIRELESS )

Riding, last week, down the road that led to Coutances, Avranches, and beyond evoked memories of the tragic June of 1940, when refugees streamed down the one route left open for civilians between Paris and Tours. Last week, as four years ago, the road was choked with vehicles moving as slowly as a trickle of water through dust, but this time, instead of autobuses and pitiful automobiles loaded with civilians, the traffic was halftracks, empty ambulances, tank destroyers, two-and-a-half-ton trucks, the small, tracked carriers ( called weasels ) that take ammunition across country, and, scattered through all the heavy stuff, jeeps. The procession

* Norman D. (Dutch) Cota, then of the 29th Division. He later got one of his own, the 28th. The victor of St. Lô was the C.O. of the 29th—Major-General Charles W. Gerhardt.

was heading toward the Germans instead of away from them. One would never have believed, in peacetime, that the mere act of riding slowly down a road in an uncomfortably crowded vehicle on two separate occasions could produce such antithetical emotions. In 1940, the unfortunates on the road stared apprehensively at the sky every time the procession stopped because of a jam. In 1944, soldiers in trucks grinned every time they heard an airplane motor. The Luftwaffe had lost its terror; the Ninth Air Force was patrolling the skies of France with absolute authority. The men moving forward had a hunch that no serious battle awaited them. It turned out that they were mostly right. There were some sharp local actions, which were less counterattacks than group attempts to escape, but in general the parallel with the end of the Tunisian campaign held good: German resistance, disconcertingly stiff in the earlier phase of the Normandy fighting, crumbled suddenly and swiftly, and American units heading toward their objectives unexpectedly found themselves racing other units that had progressed farther and faster than anyone had anticipated. It was a disturbing experience for the artillery officers, who soon found that there was no place that their shells would not be likely to fall among Americans advancing from other points of the compass.

I watched the air bombardment that preceded the breakthrough from an upstairs window of a Normandy farmhouse. The dwelling looked south, toward the area, five miles away, which was to be bombed. There were three ridges, the first two crowned with poplars, the third with pines, between the farmhouse and the target area. One stream of bombers came in to the left of the farmhouse, turned behind the third ridge, dropped its bombs, and came away to my right; another stream came in over my right, turned, and went off to the left. For two hours the air was filled with the hum of motors, and the concussions of the bombs, even though they were falling five miles away, kept my sleeves fluttering. I was living with a headquarters battery of divisional artillery, and some of the men in it, watching the bombardment from the sloping ground under my window, rolled on the grass with unsportsmanlike glee. Their emotion was crude but understandable. "The more bombs we drop, the less fight there'll be left in them," a soldier said, and, remembering the first bombs on Paris in 1940 and all the bombings I have seen decent people undergo since then, I could not feel ashamed of the men's reaction.

The only residents of the farm who seemed uncomfortable were a great, long-barreled sow and her litter of six shoats, who walked about uneasily, shaking their ears as if the concussions hurt them. At brief intervals, they would lie down in a circle, all their snouts pointing toward centre. Then they would get up again, perhaps because the earth quivering against their bellies frightened them. Puffs of black flak smoke dotted the sky under the first two waves of bombers; one plane came swirling down, on fire and trailing smoke, and crashed behind the second ridge of poplars. White parachutes flashed in the sun as the plane fell. A great cloud of slate-gray smoke rose from behind the trees where it had gone down. Soon after that the flak puffs disappeared; the German gunners either had been killed or, as one artillerist suggested, had simply run out of ammunition. The succeeding waves of planes did their bombing unopposed. It was rather horrifying, at that.

After the bombardment, we waited all afternoon for the order to advance. We had heard that the divisional artillery headquarters and the division's battalion of medium howitzers, which throw their shells about seven miles, were to be moved up that night to positions beyond the line the Germans had held that morning. As it happened, the breakthrough wasn't quite as abrupt as all that. We didn't move until the evening, and then we moved only a couple of miles, to a hollow behind the first ridge of poplars, territory that infantry of another division had won from the enemy a couple of days before. When night fell, neither our own infantry division,* which the Germans have been good enough to refer to as a *corps d'élite*, nor our armor had even gone into battle. The infantry divisions ahead of us** had been expected to move forward hard on the tail of the air bombardment and make an opening through which we and the armor would pass, but they had not advanced appreciably. Discouraging rumors, such as frequently attend the opening of offensives, cropped up in the small, exclusive mess of the divisional artillery that night. One was that the Germans had not been shaken by the bombardment, another that they had been annihilated but that bomb craters had made all the roads impassable. The favorite explanation of the delay, I am afraid, was that the divisions ahead of us had snarled things up as usual.†

Next morning, at seven o'clock, a combat team of infantry from the division I was with went into action. By nine o'clock, the news came that the men had advanced thousands of yards in the first hour, and all day they kept on moving forward, against slight opposition. Parts of two armored divisions, engaged at other points, also made rapid advances. The early discouragement around our headquarters disappeared. The mess even made generous allowances for the shortcomings of other infantry divisions. (It turned out afterward that they had run into an abortive German offensive just beyond the bombed area and had not done badly at all.) The artillery prepared to move up behind the infantry, in order to shoot it out of trouble when it ran up against the inevitable tough going. But the tough going that had developed at some point in every other

* The First, of course.
** Fourth, Ninth and Thirtieth.
† This was unjust. Many of those glorious bombs had fallen short *on* the Thirtieth, which suffered its top day of casualties.

operation the division had participated in, whether in the Mediterranean campaign or in France, did not develop in this curious advance.

"The dough," as officers of divisional artillery call the infantry, flowed forward for five days; the artillery followed, but it was hardly ever called upon to shoot. Whenever the Germans looked as though they might make a stand, some other American unit got behind them. By the fifth evening, the gunners found themselves in the impasse I have already described. It was an artillerist's nightmare: there was no place they *could* shoot without fear of hitting some of our own people. Army Corps headquarters had marked on a map what are called "no fire" lines; these lines completely hemmed our guns in. On that fifth night, the division stretched out toward Coutances like a long finger. There were—theoretically, at least— Germans in front of us and on both flanks, but there was part of an American armored division behind the Germans in front of us and there were other American troops behind the Germans on our right. Still other American troops were supposed to be getting around to the rear of the Germans on our left, too, and all the Germans in the area were trying to get out at once. The chief danger we faced was being trampled to death by escaping supermen while we slept.

Divarty, the familiar term for divisional artillery headquarters, is under ordinary conditions an ideal place to follow the progress of a battle, or at least one division's part in it, because Divarty controls the small spotter planes, usually Piper Cubs, which serve as the division's eyes. The pilots and observers in these craft, known to "the dough" as Maytag Messerschmitts, are not Air Forces men but artillery officers. They report not only on targets and the effect of the division's artillery fire but on all enemy troop and vehicle movements they observe. This information is channelized through Divarty to Division, which is short for division headquarters. When ground observation is available, Divarty has the best of that, too, for the artillery has its observers at points of vantage up in the line with advanced elements of the infantry. These observers have telephone lines to their battalions, and the battalions in turn have direct lines to Divarty. The infantry is served by a parallel but separate telephone network. Communications between the infantry and the artillery go through a division switchboard. The infantry and artillery of a division live like a sensible married couple—in the same house but in separate beds.

There is a detached, academic atmosphere about Divarty that is lacking in the larger, more bustling Division, and artillerists in general view war with the objectivity of men who seldom see their victims. The headquarters battery of Divarty has no guns; it merely has a switchboard, a set of maps, and a lot of telephone wires. Divarty is a small, itinerant brain trust which moves quietly with the front-line troops and calls down upon distant Germans the thunder of the division's battalions of artillery. It sets up its command post in a farmhouse or barn within the division area, lays its wires to the battalions, and blacks out windows and chinks through which light might escape. Then, after nightfall, when the Cubs come down, its higher officers sit around a long row of tables—in an atmosphere that recalls a newspaper copy desk during the slack hours—drinking strong coffee and playing cribbage while they wait for telephone calls. A call comes in, and an executive officer engages in a brief conversation, rings off, then remarks, "Infantry patrols report some sort of Jerry movement at that road junction at 4124. Mediums can reach it." He picks up the telephone again, makes a call, and returns to his cribbage game, and outside, in the night, twelve hundred pounds of high explosive scream toward the dark crossroad twenty-five times, at short, irregular intervals. In this particular engagement, however, we simply ran out of crossroads to shoot at.

## My Dear Little Louise

DURING our breaking-out offensive in Normandy, the division artillery headquarters occupied four command posts in five days. A French family was living in one wing of the first house we used, although most of the roof was gone and a couple of the bedrooms had only three walls, but the farmhouses in which we had our second and third command posts were deserted. The Germans had forced all the inhabitants to leave. In our fourth one, we found civilians again. The Germans, not expecting so quick an advance, had not evacuated people from what they still considered the rear area. In the barnyard of that place, we found a dead Panzer Grenadier of a Schutzstaffel division. His paybook said that he had been born in Essen, and on his body there was a typewritten form which he had filled out but obviously had not had time to hand in to his company commander, asking for what we would call an emergency leave to go home. His reason was "Bombing deaths in family—urgent telegram from wife." He had been hit by a fragment of shell, but it had not torn him up much. A detail of our fellows buried him in back of the barn.

The dead cows were more of a problem. Now that we have moved on to Brittany, one of the things that make us happy is that we are out of dead-cattle country. The war moves more swiftly and it isn't necessary to drop artillery shells on every field and crossroad. Besides, the cattle in Brittany are fewer and more scattered than in Normandy, where every pasture was full of them. You need a bulldozer to bury cows properly, unless you are going to take all day about it, and nobody had men to spare for a large-scale interment detail. They lay in the fields with their four legs pointing stiffly in the air, like wooden cows discarded from a child's Noah's Ark, and their smell hung over the land as the dust hung over the roads. Men are smaller than cattle and they are always buried first; we lived in the stench of innocent death. At our fourth command post, there were more dead cows than usual, because, the people on the farm told us, eighteen extra cows had arrived with the Germans a couple of weeks before. There had been two sets of Germans in the farm buildings—ten paratroopers who had showed up driving eight cows, and forty S.S. men who had appeared driving ten cows. The paratroopers, one of whom was a captain, had got there first and taken up quarters in the farmhouse. The S.S. men, arriving later, had billeted themselves in the outbuildings, but only after a noisy argument, in which they had failed to get the paratroopers out of the big house. The captain had too much rank for them. The paratroopers had been fighting a long time and were very down in the mouth, the people of the house said. A soldier who served as interpreter had told the French family that the war was over, that Germany was beaten. But the S.S. fellows, who had come from soft berths in Warsaw and Brno, were still *gonflés en bloc* (blown up hard) and talked as if they owned the earth. That was less than two weeks ago, but even the S.S. men, to judge by those taken prisoner, have changed now. The S.S. soldiers had brought a refugee family with them, to milk the cows, the people on the farm said. Every day the paratroopers drank the cream from their eight cows and threw the milk away. Both sets of Germans had departed abruptly, but the S.S. had left one man to guard the cows, presumably in case the reports of the Allied attack proved exaggerated. A shell had killed the cowtender.

I am sure that I will remember our two deserted command posts longer and more vividly than the two that were inhabited. Perhaps that is because you think more about people when they aren't there, and because you can be your own Sherlock Holmes and reconstruct them in accordance with your own hypothesis. The first deserted farm was a solid rectangle of stone and stucco buildings with walls nearly a foot thick. The farmyard, on which all the buildings fronted, could be reached only by narrow lanes that pierced the solid row of buildings at the front and at the back. It would have been a tough defensive position to crack if there had been any tactical reason to defend it. The farmhouse was very old and must have belonged to an aged, rich, crippled, bigoted woman or to a crippled man who had a fat old woman for a housekeeper. There was a crutch in the farmyard, lying as if it had fallen off a departing wagon, and in two of the bedrooms there was a pair of old, mended crutches that must have been discarded for newer ones. In the kitchen, by the great open hearth, there was a reclining chair with an extension on which to rest your legs, and in one bedroom there were several old and dirty corsets, whose whalebones, despite the garments' immense girth, had all sprung because of the continual effort to encompass a bulging body. There was a tall Norman clock in every room. Clocks of this sort are made in little towns, like Périers and Colombières and Marigny, which nobody outside Normandy ever heard of before this summer. Every crossroads seems to have had its clockmaker as well as its baker and its harness maker. The wooden cases of these timepieces are generally rather austere, but the dials are framed by hammered gilt sculpture; sheaves, golden apples, plows, and peasants in donkey carts are favorite motifs. The pendulums are vast, and they too are encrusted with ornament. A bride, I imagine, although no one has told me so, brings a clock as part of her dowry, and a house where there are many clocks has been ruled in turn by many women. This house was full of hideous modern religious images and of wax fruits and flowers under glass bells. There were no books except devotional ones and those that gave quick ways of making the computations a farmer must make in doing business with wholesalers. There were many of each kind.

The farmsteaders had left the place in a great hurry, and some soldiers, either German or American, had been there afterward and rummaged through the house, littering the floors with things, useless to them, that they had pulled from the cupboards—women's high-collared blouses, skirt hoops, dingy photographs of family outings and one of a man in a cuirassier's uniform, with breastplate and horsetail helmet, and three or four parchment manuscripts. One, dated 1779, was the deed of sale of a farm, another was a marriage contract dated the Year 3 of the First Republic. The contract enumerated the items the bride was to bring in her dowry, which included six pillowcases, one canopy for a bed, and ten handkerchiefs; the whole thing was to come to a thousand and fifty-seven francs. If the husband died before the wife, she was to be allowed to withdraw that much from the estate in consideration of her dowry. If the wife died first, the widower was to keep the pillowcases, handkerchiefs, and all the rest, probably to bestow on his next choice. I wondered, naturally, which of them had survived the other. There were canopies over the beds in all the bedrooms; one must have been the canopy listed in the contract. The house had stone floors that did not shake even when some guns just across the road were being fired, which happened for one entire night we spent there.

The guns were only three thousand yards behind the front line, but they were firing at a target—a railroad station or road junction—eleven miles away. They belonged not to division artillery but to a remote, unfamiliar entity called Corps. The battery commander, a harassed captain, called on our artillery general as soon as we moved in and said he hoped the general did not mind guns; there were a lot of generals who couldn't sleep on account of the noise and he had had to move twice already. He was like a man apologizing to his new neighbors for having noisy children; he was sensitive. Our general said that the guns were music to his ears, and we all smiled mechanically and obediently. The captain said, "I'm sure glad to hear that, because I feel I have an ideal setup here."

Across the yard from the house, in a small storeroom, lived a donkey so old that he had a gray beard. His hoofs were long and misshapen, like the nails of an old dog who gets no exercise, and he stayed in his gloomy cell, blinking out at the world, without enough energy to walk into the adjoining barn and eat the hay, although he would accept cabbages if they were brought to him.

From the crippled woman's, or man's, house we moved into a region that had been heavily bombed on the first day of the offensive and was completely deserted except for the surviving animals. An officer who had done some reconnoitering had found a hamlet, Chapelle en Litige* (Chapel in Litigation), which was intact. Bombs had fallen into all the adjoining fields and bomb craters had made the roads into it almost impassable, but its half-dozen houses and the dependent barns stood untouched. One officer, who considers the Air Forces a form of artillery totally lacking in professional direction, said, "If they had dropped hundred-pound bombs instead of five-hundred, they'd have killed just as many cows without spoiling the roads."** The façade of the granite house in which we set up shop was hidden by pear trees *en espalier*, laden with fruit and lush with leaves. An old hen had made a nest in a branch under the hayloft window and was rearing her chicks there; they were hard to find, buried among the pears, and produced a noise that was inexplicable to us until we discovered them. Some of the soldiers with us took up quarters in smaller houses, and once they had found niches for themselves, we all strolled about the village looking over the interiors of the houses. The owners had evacuated them in an orderly fashion, taking most of their belongings with them. There was not much left except furniture.

I found a pile of letters, most of them old, a few recent, lying on a dressing table in one of the houses. In a nearby cupboard was a long row of schoolboys' notebooks filled with exercises in drawing, arithmetic, and composition. All the books bore the inscription, written in a hand which became progressively less slack, "Cahier d'Albert Hédouin." A couple of recent business letters were addressed to Veuve Hédouin, and I assumed that Albert was the widow's son. There were also in the cupboard a

---

* La Chapelle en Juger, which is an older synonym for the same thing, was the right name.
** Brigadier-General (then) Clift Andrus, the First Division artillery commander.

number of the usual breviaries and cheap books of devotion, including a pamphlet of prayers for prisoners of war. Idly, because as a camp follower I had nothing else at the moment to do, I took some of the letters and, sitting down on the threshold of the plain little house I was in, started to read them.

One was dated September 25, 1914. It began, "My dear little Louise: I utilize a little moment to send you news of me. I am in good health and hope my letter finds you the same. I'd rather be at Chapelle en Litige than where I am, for it isn't nice to sleep outdoors. If this thing ends soon, I won't be sorry. I am with Anatole and Désiré, and they are in good health, too. Probably the buckwheat has been harvested, if the weather is as good there as it is here. I'd like to help thresh it and drink a big bowl of cider instead of being here, but it's useless to think about it. When you wean the little colt, leave him in the barn for two days, then turn him into the fields of broom, where the donkey is. Put some branches on top of the gate, so he won't try to jump over it. When you get this letter, send me some news of what goes on at home. Have you made a barrel of cider for Pannel yet and have the cows turned out well? Excuse me for being brief, my dear little Louise and cherished babies. I write this letter in the open air, sitting on my knapsack, and now I must go. Your husband, who loves you and kisses you again and again, Louis Hédouin, 336th Infantry. P.S. Put the donkey in Fernand's field."

The next letter was dated in November, 1914, and began, "My dear little Louise: It is with great pleasure I learn that you are in good health. I too am in good health. Dear little Louise, I think you should make at least three barrels of cider, although I know it will give you a lot of trouble. Considering the price of apples and the price of cider, it pays better to make cider than to sell apples. And make a good barrel for us, so that we can have the pleasure of drinking it together when I come home." ("Come home," I thought. "That war had four years to go then.") "My dear little Louise, you tell me that you have planted some wheat. Good. Prices are going up. I hope you have sowed oats, dear one. Dear little Louise, I hope you are well. Also the cows and calves. Butter is selling at a pretty good price, if it can only continue. I was glad to hear you had someone help you thresh the buckwheat. Dear little Louise, I wish I could have been there, but it's useless to think about it. Here one is and here one stays—until when, nobody knows. Your husband, who loves and will never cease to love you and the dear little children, Louis."

Looking up, I saw that four or five cows, probably wanting to be milked, were staring hopefully at me, and I wondered how Louis Hédouin would have felt if he had known that in thirty years not even a woman would be left to care for the cattle in Chapelle en Litige. There was another letter, also written in 1914, in which he said he had been to mass and then eaten some ham dear little Louise had sent him; he would rather have attended mass at home, but it was "useless to think of it."

"Dear little Louise," he went on, "you say you have had a card from Aimable and he is in good health. So much the better, for you can't imagine how unhealthy it is where he finds himself. I couldn't either, unless I had been there, but don't worry, I'm all right. Dear little Louise, you say that Marie has had a letter from Pierre and he is a prisoner. So much the better. That way he is sure to survive. I know that threshing must be a lot of trouble to you. I am sorry you are alone and have so much work to do. Do you remember, on that evening before I went away, Enée said that this business wouldn't be over before Easter? I am afraid he was right. It is sad when I think of it. Days are indeed long. Louis."

And on March 15, 1915, he wrote that he was sorry to hear that Louise was suffering but hoped she would soon be delivered—the first indication I had had that he knew she was pregnant. "My dear little Louise," he continued, "I had a letter from Papa the same time as yours. He says he has sold the old cow for three hundred and forty-five francs. It's not bad, when you think that she only had four teeth left. What about the black cow you thought was going to calve March 8th and what are you doing with the Jersey? Tell me in your next letter. Dear little Louise, you say you have threshed the oats. Good. There must have been some loss, but you did the best you could. The worst of it is we probably won't be home in time for the haying this season. Excuse me for not having written. We were taking ammunition up to the front lines. Lately things go badly. The regiment has refused to march to an attack. Everybody is sick of this business, and we lose courage and ask for an end of this terrible war. A sweet kiss from your husband, Louis."

Then, on the twenty-second of March, the latest date I found on any of his letters, Hédouin wrote, "My dear little Louise: I have received with great pleasure your letter of the eighteenth. Your mother writes to me that you have had a nine-pound boy and are doing well, and the boy, too. My dear little Louise, you did well to have a midwife from Remilly, and she didn't charge much, either—eight francs. My dear little Louise, I'd like to be with you, but it's useless to think of it. Distance keeps us apart. I hope God will help you in your troubles. My parents write me that at home people are saying this will end soon. So much the better. Dear little Louise, the boy will be called Albert. Before telling you, I waited to see whether you would have a boy or a girl. Your husband, who loves you, Louis. P.S. What about the black cow?"

Nineteen-fifteen. I did a bit of subtraction. Albert would have been twenty-four in 1939—just the right age. I thought of the graded notebooks and the pamphlet of prayers for prisoners of war.

# Letter from Paris

SEPTEMBER 1 (BY WIRELESS)

FOR the first time in my life and probably the last, I have lived for a week in a great city where everybody is happy. Moreover, since this city is Paris, everybody makes this euphoria manifest. To drive along the boulevards in a jeep is like walking into some as yet unmade René Clair film, with hundreds of bicyclists coming toward you in a stream that divides before the jeep just when you feel sure that a collision is imminent. Among the bicyclists there are pretty girls, their hair dressed high on their heads in what seems to be the current mode here. These girls show legs of a length and slimness and firmness and brownness never associated with French womanhood. Food restrictions and the amount of bicycling that is necessary in getting around in a big city without any other means of transportation have endowed these girls with the best figures in the world, which they will doubtless be glad to trade in for three square meals, plentiful supplies of chocolate, and a seat in the family Citroën as soon as the situation becomes more normal. There are handsome young matrons with children mounted behind them on their bikes, and there are husky young workmen, stubby little *employés de bureau* in striped pants, and old professors in wing collars and chin whiskers, all of them smiling and all of them lifting their right hands from the handlebars to wave as they go past. The most frequently repeated phrase of the week is *"Enfin on respire!"* (At last, one breathes!)

Happiest of all, in the French film manner, are the police, who stand at street intersections with their thumbs in their belts and beam paternally at everybody instead of looking stern and important, as they used to. Cyclists wave to them appreciatively. When, occasionally, a truck passes through a street, taking policemen to their beats, people standing on the café *terrasses* applaud and shout *"Vive la police!"* For Paris, where the street cry has always been *"A bas les flics!"* (Down with the cops!), this is behavior so unprecedented that the cops sometimes look as though they think it is all a dream. There is good reason for the change of heart; for the first time since Etienne Marcel led a street mob against the royal court in about 1350, the police and the people have been on the same side of the barricades. It was the police who, on August 15th, gave the signal for a mass disregard of the Germans by going on strike. It was also the police who, four days later, began the street fighting by seizing the Prefecture of the Seine, their headquarters, across the square from Notre Dame on the

Ile de la Cité. Three thousand of them, in plainclothes and armed with carbines, revolvers, and a few sub-machine guns, took the place over and defended it successfully for six days before being relieved by the arrival of the French armored division of General Leclerc. This was the largest centre of patriot resistance during the struggle. Because it is in the middle of the city, it was the knot that kept the network of patriot strongpoints together. The Germans held fortresses in the Place de la Concorde, the Place St. Michel, the Luxembourg Gardens, and along the Rue de Rivoli. Von Choltitz, the German military governor of the city, was finally captured by soldiers of the armored division in the Hôtel Meurice, and the Crillon was fought for as though it were a blockhouse. During the five days of fighting before the first elements of Allied troops began to penetrate the city, the Germans sallied from their strongpoints in tanks and systematically shot up the town. The Forces Françaises de l'Intérieur had erected barricades to stop the tanks, and boys fourteen or fifteen years old, with courage that was more than a riposte to the fanaticism of the Hitler Jugend, often destroyed tanks by throwing bottles of incendiary fluid through their ports. The bottles were usually filled with mixtures prepared by neighborhood druggists. The youngsters who did the fighting were not always of the type that is ordinarily on good terms with the police. They included the problem children of every neighborhood as well as students and factory workers. So the oldest of all Paris feuds has ended.

It has perhaps already been hinted in the New York press that our army had not expected to take Paris quite so soon. The city was to be bypassed and encircled to save it from street fighting, on the theory that the last elements of the German garrison would withdraw just before being cut off. Thus a certain amount of damage to the city's buildings would be prevented, unless, of course, the Germans mined them before departing. As it turned out, the Germans laid mines, all right, but they didn't set them off because they were caught sitting on them. There were ten tons of explosives in the vaults under the Senate alone. But none of this is so important for the future of the world as the fact that the French saved their selfrespect forever by going into the streets and fighting. The F.F.I.s were already in control of the city when the regular troops arrived, they like to tell you when you talk with them in the cafés. And, with a fine bit of military courtesy, the Allied Command, when it was informed that conditions in Paris called for an immediate move, sent in Leclerc's division first. Frenchmen had begun the liberation of Paris; other Frenchmen completed it. As a result, the Parisians are happy not only because of the liberation but because they feel they earned it.

The gratitude toward Americans is immense and sometimes embarrassing in its manifestations. People are always stopping one in the street, pumping one's hand, and saying "Thank you." It is useless to protest. To the Parisians, and especially to the children, all Americans are now *héros du cinéma*. This is particularly disconcerting to sensitive war correspondents, if any, aware, as they are, that these innocent thanks belong to those American combat troops who won the beachhead and then made the breakthrough. There are few such men in Paris. Young women, the first day or two after the Allies arrived, were as enthusiastic as children; they covered the cheeks of French and American soldiers alike with lip-stick. This stage of Franco-American relations is approaching an end. Children, however, still follow the American soldiers everywhere, singing the "Marseillaise" and hopefully eyeing pockets from which they think gum might emerge. And it is still hard for an American who speaks French to pay for a drink in a bar.

The city is resuming normal life with a speed I would never have believed possible. The noise of battle has receded and the only visible reminders of the recent fighting are some damaged buildings, holes in a few streets, and a considerable number of captured German automobiles dashing about loaded with F.F.I.s and their girls, all wearing tricolor brassards and festooned with German machine pistols, Lugers, and grenades. French adolescents have for years been deprived of the simple pleasure of riding about on four wheels, and if they seem to find an excessive number of military missions for themselves, all of which involve riding down the boulevards and cheering, nobody can blame them. Until very recently they seemed to have great difficulty in resisting the equally natural temptation to shoot off their new weapons, and every day sounded like the Fourth of July, but the F.F.I., whose officers are serious soldiers, is now being absorbed into the French Army and the promiscu-ous shooting has come to an end. On a shattered concrete pillbox in the Place de la Concorde some playful fellow has printed, in chalk, "Liquida-tion. To rent, forty thousand francs." And, as I write, a painter is reletter-ing "Guaranty Trust of New York" on the building next to the Crillon that the bank occupied before we went to war.

The physical conditions of life here are not too bad. Paris was spared the most uncomfortable experience a big modern city can have, for the water system has continued to work, a very important factor not only in sanitation but morale. Only a limited quantity of electricity is available; the power plants and distributing system are in good shape, but the hydroelectric power from central France is no longer coming in and there is a very small supply of fuel. Consequently, lights are on for only about two hours every evening, except in government offices. There is as yet no gas for cooking, but it has been promised that there soon will be. For that matter, there is not very much to cook; the city had no more than a two weeks' supply of strictly necessary foods when the liberators entered it, and though the American and French authorities have been steadily pumping food into the town, there is not yet enough for the reëstablish-ment of good eating at home, let alone good restaurant life. Only a few small black-market restaurants still exist. The price of *petit salé* (a kind of New England boiled dinner), one pear, and a half bottle of Bordeaux is seven hundred francs. This is the best fare you can get, and seven hundred francs, just to remind you, is fourteen dollars. Butter is four hundred francs a pound. However, the day of the black-market people is ending, because there are great quantities of butter, meat, and vegetables in Normandy, Brittany, and Anjou at about an eighth of Paris prices, and bringing them here is now simply a matter of transportation. Considering that all this food is only fifty to a hundred and fifty miles away, there is little reason to doubt that the problem will soon be solved. A decent pair of leather shoes cost a hundred dollars, a man's suit three hundred, and a portable typewriter five hundred and sixty. My advice to the Frenchman who wants any of these things is to do without for a few weeks, because such a situation can last only under the rule of the Germans, who drain a country dry of everything except grace, beauty, and good sense. The German occupation gave the black market a sort of moral sanction here. In Britain the feeling has been, ever since the blitz days, that a man who bought in the black market deprived other Britons of their share. Here people said, truthfully enough, that if you had money and didn't buy in the black market, what you wanted to buy would simply go to Germany. The black-market operators themselves are an unprepossessing lot, however, and a visit to a black-market restaurant will quickly convince anyone that a fair proportion of the patrons are engaged in other branches of the same racket.

The question of what is to be done with all this group is receiving considerable attention in the new French press. There are already eleven dailies in Paris, all almost direct offshoots of the clandestine resistance papers. Only three bear names well known before the war—the conservative *Figaro*, the Communist *L'Humanité*, and the Socialist *Le Populaire*. These three had been suppressed by Vichy, but *Populaire* and *Humanité* became as powerful as ever in their clandestine editions. Others, like *Combat, Libération*, and *Franc-Tireur*, are resistance papers appearing for the first time above ground and in full size. The editorial offices and printing plants of the big collaborationist papers have been handed over to the newcomers. *Populaire*, for example, is now published in the plant of *Le Matin*, on the Boulevard Poissonnière. The new papers have from the beginning taken divergent political lines; in the cases of *Figaro*, *Humanité*, and *Populaire*, it would perhaps be better to say that they have resumed them. They are in complete accord, however, on the prestige and position of General de Gaulle and his provisional government. So is every man, woman, and child I have heard speak of de Gaulle or his government in Paris. The man's prestige is so vast that it is slightly nauseating now to think of the "opposition" to him that rich Frenchmen were still telling credulous friends about in London and Washington only a few months ago. He put the seal on a personal legend last Saturday, when, on foot and towering above a couple of million compatriots, he led a parade down the Champs-Elysées and as far as Notre Dame, where he listened to the Te Deum while snipers and F.F.I.s exchanged shots around him. Such overwhelming popularity may in time prove to be a handicap to him; he must eventually disappoint some of the people who now expect irreconcilable things of him. His hold on the public could not possibly be greater. A united France has crystallized around him.

While de Gaulle led the march, a few Americans were otherwise engaged.

# Day of Victory

AUGUST 26, 1944, the day after the official Liberation of Paris, was a brilliant, sunny Saturday. Allardyce Meecham, a war correspondent who had once been a dramatic critic in New York, descended the fifth, and last, flight of steps between the floor on which he had been billeted and the lobby of the Hotel Scribe. Meecham, an awkward, red-haired man of forty-three, felt himself an unimpressive representative of a victorious army, and his futile wait for the lift, which was apparently out of order, had accented his sensation of inadequacy. He had arrived in Paris early that morning. All of his colleagues he had encountered since getting to the Scribe had, by their telling, acted as advance scouts for motorized-cavalry units and infiltrated into the city on Tuesday, Wednesday, or Thursday, before the surrender of the German garrison, which had taken place on Friday. Meecham had missed even that. He had gone off on a side trip into lower Brittany early in the week and had not known that Paris was going to be liberated until it was too late for him to precede even the Public Relations officers. On his way into the freed capital, with some officers from a corps in Brittany who had no real business in Paris but wanted to see the fun, he had felt guilty because, although he complained in a loud tone about having missed the big moment, he knew in his heart that he was content to have the combat troops go first. Not once, in two months of war, had he arrived in a town alone in time to receive the surrender of an S.S. Panzer division, an experience apparently banal for Hearst correspondents. When, on a single occasion, at St.-Lô, he had inadvertently got into a bad spot, he had been so shaken that he had been unable to write the story.

Meecham was dressed in a tanker's combat jacket and a pair of dress-pink trousers, an incongruity caused by the circumstance that he had left his Class A uniform blouse hanging in the closet of a hotel in Angers, while the G.I. pants he generally wore with the combat jacket were in his estimation too dirty to wear in Paris. He had been a bit muddled with drink on leaving Angers and had forgotten the blouse. On his head he wore a helmet liner. His only overseas cap was in the pocket of the blouse in Angers.

When Meecham reached the lobby, which was crowded with victorious correspondents and Public Relations officers, he pretended to be preoccupied and in a hurry, since he didn't want to hear them make light of their thrilling experiences and had none of his own to depreciate. As he made for the revolving door to the street, however, he was blocked off by Wallaby Bates, an Australian correspondent for a London newspaper, who was wearing British battle dress fronted by a landing net of ribbons from the last war. Wallaby shouted, in a concerned voice, "I say, Meech, haven't seen Larry Boddlebaum, have you? Our jeeps were cracking along on the way in from Chartres last week. Heard there were only a couple of middle-drawer Hun divisions left in Paris, so we thought we'd disregard them, what? Larry's jeep was behind mine, and as I went past an intersection, I saw a lot of their chaps around a dinkum super Mark VI tank—p'raps a Mark VII or VIII. I didn't have a chance for a proper dinkum look-see, what? I heard a spot of machine-gun fire behind me, and I wonder if poor old Larry copped it."

Meecham mumbled apologetically that he hadn't seen Mr. Boddlebaum, and hurried on toward the door. Just outside, he stepped on the heels of an oldish man in a costume that included a floppy garrison cap, worn fighter-pilot style, parachutist's boots, the patches of two armored divisions, one on each shoulder, and a new bit of purple ribbon. This was Larry Boddlebaum, war correspondent for a magazine popularizing scientific research and for another devoted to homemaking, to each of which he contributed one article a month. He had worn the purple ribbon ever since, in a blackout in Normandy, he had fallen over a latrine made from a packing box.

Boddlebaum turned in some irritation, but on recognizing Allardyce Meecham, he put on an expression of hearty good humor. "Why, if it isn't old Meech!" he shouted. "Haven't seen old Wallaby Bates, by any chance, have you? Wallaby and I were hightailing along a road near Fountainblue a few days ago, meaning to get under a parachute drop that we heard the boys were going to make behind the kraut line, him in one jeep and me in another. Next thing I knew, I was looking into the muzzle of an eighty-eight, but I ducked into the brush just as the thing went off. Haven't heard of poor old Wallaby since."

"He's just inside the door, looking for you," Meecham said.

Boddlebaum did not seem as pleased as one might have expected. He waved his hand, with a gesture which Meecham interpreted as a dismissal, and turned to a group of three women correspondents, whom he halted with outflung arms and shouts of greeting. Meecham, as he walked away, heard him shout, "Haven't any of you girls seen old Wallaby Bates, have you?"

The sidewalk and street in front of the hotel were crowded with cheering, chattering, happy people who enthusiastically waved their hands with fingers spread in the V sign whenever they thought they saw a correspondent or a jeep driver look at them. They left no path for jeeps and command cars, barely parting before each arriving vehicle. "*Vive l'Amérique!*" a man wearing a tricolor brassard marked "F.F.I." shouted. "*Vive Roosevelt!*" He rushed at Meecham and seized him by the right hand, which he clasped fervently. From the strength of the man's clutch, Meecham deduced that he must once have been a weight-lifter. Meecham's wife, a woman of such strong character that he never audibly disagreed with her, detested Roosevelt, so now he answered simply, "*Vive la France!*" Then, perhaps because he, too, had begun to feel liberated, he said boldly, "*Vive Roosevelt pour moi aussi!*" The man, still crushing his hand, said, "He speaks French admirably!"

A young woman with bare brown legs and green wooden earrings threw her bare arms around Meecham and forcefully kissed him on the left side of his face. A taller young woman, on whose equally brown limbs blond hairs glinted delightfully, closed on Meecham from the right and kissed him on that side of his face, pressing so hard he could feel her teeth through her lips and letting her mouth stay against his cheek for an extra second. The F.F.I. man cried, "Honor to the liberators!" Meecham started to say, "I have done nothing. I am only a journalist," but he couldn't speak French fast enough. By the time he had said "nothing," the first young woman cried, "He is modest! He is adorable!," and kissed him again, this time on the left temple, knocking the helmet liner over his right eye.

"How tall they are!" exclaimed a third woman, throwing her arms about Meecham's neck and pulling his head forward, while the F.F.I. man and the barelegged girls still hung on. The woman kissed him firmly on the forehead. "Look! He has lipstick all over!" a female voice farther back in the crowd squealed.

Meecham, feeling the man's grip ease, managed to break away and straighten the helmet liner. He grabbed a handkerchief from his hip pocket and made a motion to wipe the lipstick from his face, but there was a chorus of protesting voices—"No, no, don't do that." To humor his admirers, Meecham dropped his hand and stumbled on, the handkerchief still in his fist. He was exhilarated in a way new to him. He had never before experienced a manifestation of public approval, except after a lecture at a women's club in Greenwich. That, since he had been paid for his services, had been relatively tepid. None of the clubwomen had offered to kiss him, and he could not recall having regretted this omission.

As he turned the corner into the Boulevard des Capucines, his insufficiency as a newspaperman no longer weighed upon him. The press services would have kept his paper covered on the spot news of the liberation of Paris, he knew. What his editor wanted of him, he reflected with satisfaction, was something more subtle. This was the sequel to a Greek drama—this was "Prometheus Unbound." Replacing the handkerchief in his pocket, he stopped, took out a pencil and a Press Wireless blank, and wrote down the phrase. A woman grabbed him and kissed him before he had finished. Another, looking up at him, could not find a free space to leave her mark—she had, he noticed, a rather large mouth with flaring lips—so she took a handkerchief out of her handbag, spat on it, and scrubbed away at his face until she had cleared a sufficient area. Then she, too, kissed him.

Feeling pleased but silly, Meecham moved on to the front of the Café de la Paix. It was not open for business officially, but a number of American officers and several correspondents were already seated at tables on the terrace, and when he went to the door and talked to the manager standing there, he obtained the privilege of buying a glass of white wine for thirty francs. A waiter brought it to him at a table, and he began to think out a lead for his story—something about how it was the beginning of a return to normal when an American could again sit at a table at the Café de la Paix and wait for everybody he knew in the world to come walking by. He wrote it down.

When he had finished the glass of wine, he had another. He called over a news vendor and bought a paper, one of the new Resistance ones he had never heard of. General de Gaulle, he read, was to lead a great procession that afternoon down the Champs-Elysées and through the center of Paris to Notre Dame, where there would be a solemn Te Deum of victory. His French was really not too bad, especially after this two-month refresher course, which had begun in Normandy in June. The Te Deum would be the symbolic highlight of the liberation, Meecham decided, and he would build his color story around it. He had a third glass of wine and thought the story might turn out better than Will Irwin's account of the San Francisco earthquake. "Will Irwin once wrote a great story and called it 'The City That Was,'" he would begin. "This is the story of a City That Once Again Is." He had always liked newspaper stories that began "This is the story of" and then went on to whatever they were stories of. Stark. The lead about sitting at the Café de la Paix was less stark, but too good to throw away, he decided, so he might just as well use it further down in the story. Two women war correspondents from the Midwest walked up and looked at his lipsticked face disapprovingly. "Having a good time?" one of them said. He didn't ask them to sit down because they reminded him of his wife, a magazine executive who always referred to herself as a gal.

One of Meecham's chief talking points, in persuading his editor to send him to Europe, had been his familiarity with France, a theme on which he had expanded until even he had begun to forget that it was based wholly on a summer-vacation trip taken between his freshman and sophomore years at college. But he had now begun to feel quite honestly at home. After one more glass of wine, he started into the complex of streets that begins in back of the Grand Hotel and that he thought he remembered led off in the general direction of the Champs-Elysées, where he intended to arrive in time for the procession. On the way, he thought, he might be able to find a restaurant at which to eat. He could also stop in some *bistros* and collect some good quaint quotes.

All the shops and all the restaurants that he passed were closed. The proprietors had lowered the shutters during the sporadic street fighting, which had ended only on the previous day, and had not yet opened them again. But a number of the little bars were doing business. Meecham went into one near the Rue Caumartin. On the customers' side of the short metal counter at the front of the place he saw a small Chinese and a bulky Frenchman with a mouth that stuck out like a doorknob. The Frenchman wore a jersey and beret, and when Meecham entered, he was showing something to the proprietor, a little snipe-nosed man who, on his side of the bar, was wiping glasses. When Meecham came closer, he could see that the man held out on an upturned palm a very small automatic pistol. "It was tough on the Place de la République," the man was saying. "*Ça ratatinait.*" The word sounded so much like machine-gun fire that Meecham got the idea immediately. "*Ça ratatinait,* my boy," the man repeated, "but the boys of the République, huh, the little old kids of the neighborhood—well, *Ça ratatinait.* I got one *Schleuh* myself, species of a *Fridolin,* what! He was coming out of the subway station and he tried to run away, but I got him! Of course, there has been some criticism among the neighbors because he was so old and, according to what they say, inoffensive. Evil tongues—ambushed enemies of the Resistance. Nearly seventy years old he was, a sort of clerk. He had been billeted in a hotel in the neighborhood, it appears, for four years. But a Boche, what? How could I know he wasn't preparing something nasty? He could have turned on me, if he had been armed, huh?"

"You were right," the proprietor said. "You killed him with that gun?"

"And how!" the bulky man said. The Chinese giggled.

When Meecham ordered a glass of wine, the proprietor said it was on the house. The Chinese said, "Next one is on me. All Allies." The bulky man was cool for a moment, as if he feared the arrival of an American might divert attention from his recital. Soon, however, he sensed the new tactical opportunity and began to tell Meecham the story from the beginning. The proprietor and the Chinese looked as if they were trying to think of something else while he talked. Probably they had already heard him through several times. "*Ça ratatinait,*" the man said. And again, "*Ça ratatinait.*" While he was talking, they drank the Chinaman's round, and when the story was finished, Meecham bought one. Then the big man and the Chinese went out.

"He wouldn't buy a round, that one," said the proprietor, looking after the big man. "A dirty type. I'll bet he was a police spy before the Germans surrendered. He probably killed the old man to create himself a character as a patriot."

Meecham and the proprietor had another drink together. Meecham was now feeling the heat. It was high noon.

"I say, you're well arranged," the proprietor said, making his first allusion to the marks on Meecham's face. "The girls have been kind to you, what? You look like a real Red Indian in war paint."

"Perhaps I'd better wash it off," Meecham said.

"Sure. Then they can begin again. There's a washbasin in the back there."

After Meecham had washed, he felt a bit fresher, and asked the proprietor if he knew where there was a good restaurant open.

"It would be difficult to say, today," the proprietor said judicially, "but there is a black-market joint not far from here that I think will not be closed. The prices are horrible, of course. Take your right to the next street and then your right again until the next street and then your left for a hundred metres, and there you are."

Meecham had no trouble finding the place. It was a small restaurant with threadbare vestiges of chic. The plush on the divans was worn and footpaths were frayed across the pile of the carpets. The maître d'hôtel showed a black bow tie and a yellowish dickey under his white summer jacket. One American had already found the place before Meecham got there. Seated on the divan at the rear of the room, which was rather wide than deep, was a colonel named Rushby, one of the officers who had driven up from Brittany with Meecham. He was with a very pretty girl, Meecham noticed at once. The restaurant was full, and the maître d'hôtel said, "I regret, but we are complete for the moment."

"I will wait," Meecham said. "I have not seen any other restaurant in the quarter." He hoped Rushby would see him standing, since he might then feel obliged to ask him over. He felt sure that the Colonel did not want to be interrupted.

Before Rushby did see Meecham, a sleek Frenchman sitting alone at a table near the door rose and approached him. "Perhaps the gentleman would not mind sitting with me," he said. "It is ironic that on the day of victory one of our liberators should not find a place in a restaurant." The well-fed man was the only customer who had paid any heed to Meecham's entrance; the others—women of expensive appearance and men who looked as if they spent much of their time in barbers' chairs—seemed to pretend not to see him. "Certainly, M. Philippe," the maître d'hôtel said to the well-fed man, and Meecham said he would be delighted. When the two sat down, M. Philippe asked Meecham to share a bottle of non-vintage champagne that had just been opened for him. "It's not what I would have had with my lunch before the war," he said with resignation, "but *à la guerre comme à la guerre.*" Meecham smiled politely, and his host said, "You understand French admirably." When M. Philippe had filled Meecham's glass, he said, as if he were enunciating something startling, "To tell the truth, I am very glad to see American uniforms here. At least, you will be able to defend us from the Communists. The French, you know, Monsieur, are a very undisciplined people. They need a firm hand over them. The Germans could have taught us some valuable lessons, if we had been willing to learn."

"But Hitler—" Meecham began.

"Oh, I do not say there were not some portions of the doctrine that were perhaps excessive," M. Philippe said, refilling the glass the correspondent had just emptied. "But it is necessary to be a civilized being. Have you observed the condition of the streets, Monsieur? Paving stones torn up for barricades, burned-out tanks, barbed wire? All totally unnecessary."

Just as Meecham began to feel uncomfortable, he heard his name called in a loud voice. It was Colonel Rushby, yelling, "Hi ya, Meech! Come over here and help me talk to Michèle. She don't savvy coochy avec mwah."

Meecham got up and said to M. Philippe, "I am sorry, but I must go and have lunch with my friends. I had not seen them before."

"It is a pity," M. Philippe said with a wave of his hand, and went on placing creamed mushrooms inside his face.

Meecham, who was not quite sober, recognized without difficulty that Rushby was quite drunk. Michèle was a brunette with a triangular Hispanic face and a Lupe Velez coiffure. Girls in Paris, like those in New York, often styled themselves after Hollywood stars, Meecham already had noticed, but since they had seen no American films for five years, they imitated stars of an older vintage. He ordered food for three. Rushby had wanted only drink, and the girl had been afraid to order food for fear that the Colonel might not pay for it. The luncheon—roast pork, creamed mushrooms, and chocolate éclairs—was not the sort of thing Meecham would have expected in a good French restaurant, but it seemed to fit the pomaded clientele.* Rushby did not refuse to eat, and the food seemed to

---

* Fats and sweets were the rarest and dearest forms of food in a rationed society and were accordingly the most chic among profiteers and racketeers of the Occupation.

sober him somewhat. "Suppose we both got a girl," he said to Meecham. "You got to stick to me. I can't talk to these frogs. Maybe this babe has a friend." Michèle said all the girls she knew had by this time probably gone to watch the parade. "But there will be plenty in the streets," she said. "All you have to do is ask. You must stay with us, else I am afraid. I do not understand what he says. I thought it would be amusing not to understand, but it is rather frightening." Meecham had by this time decided that it was not essential that he literally see the parade. The feel of the city is what counts for *my* story, he told himself. He took the check, since it turned out that Rushby had only a few hundred francs. It came to about three thousand francs, which was sixty dollars of his newspaper's money. "They are giving you a special discount," Michèle said, seriously. "They are very decent." After the bill had been paid, they had a round of brandies on the house and then went out into the street arm in arm, Michèle between the two men.

The sun streamed down, the streets were full of holiday-makers, and Meecham, for the first time since he had left the Place de l'Opéra, was certain where he was—he could see the Madeleine. However the customers in the restaurant may have felt about the Liberation, these crowds in the street—parents with their children, girls with arms intertwined, larking young men in their shirtsleeves marked with tricolor brassards—were unaffectedly happy. They flocked down the Rue Royale and all the transverse streets leading to de Gaulle's line of march. Meecham could have found plenty of color to write about if he had any longer been looking for it. But now he was looking for a girl. There were, of course, hundreds, but they all seemed to be escorted or to be travelling in groups. He hesitated to approach a band and try to cut out one individual. Ordinarily, he would have given up the idea, but the drink, the sun, and the feeling of being a hero in the eyes of these happy people made him a man his wife would have recognized with difficulty. Rushby urged him on. "Go on and get yourself a number," he kept saying. "I'm going nuts out here in the sun."

Meecham fixed his attention on two tall girls, a blonde and a redhead, who were staring at his little group and smiling. They looked, he thought, like two unusually nice stenographers just back from a holiday at the seashore, brown and summery. The redhead was being Joan Crawford; the blonde was being either just herself or an imitation of some star Meecham did not recognize. "Come here!" he said to the blonde abruptly, remembering to use the familiar form of the imperative verb. "Come with us. It is the day of victory." Unhesitantly, the girl came to them. The redhead walked away into the crowd.

The girl took Meecham's arm, and now the four proceeded two by two, with Michèle and Rushby in front. "I know a hotel near here," Michèle said. "Lead on," said Meecham, now authoritative. He translated Michèle's remark to Rushby, who said, "That's swell!" The blonde said nothing, but clasped Meecham's arm as if she wanted to convert herself into a tourniquet.

In the hotel, it was cool behind Venetian blinds that had been kept closed against the sun all day. Meecham and the blonde had a room that was draped and furnished in imitation of the interior of a sheik's tent, but had a modern bed. There was a silver-framed photograph of Rudolph Valentino on a wall. To Meecham, the place seemed unconventional.

"What do you do when there is no holiday?" Meecham asked the girl, when they had become a little used to each other. "Do you work in an office?"

"No," the girl said. "I work in a house on the Rue Pigalle, and my sister, the redhead, and I had looked forward to twenty-four hours without men. Besides, I very much wanted to see General de Gaulle. But on the day of victory, I cannot refuse anything to one of our liberators."

Meecham had already begun to think of seeing the girl often during his stay in Paris, but a mistress in a brothel did not sound practicable. Afterward, though, he began to think of what a fine anecdote this experience would make, and was pleased.

Meecham ordered a bottle of champagne. It was brought up to the room and served by the housekeeper, a stout woman who was dressed in a kind of operetta maid's costume. After they had drunk a couple of glasses, they were tranquil, almost as if the champagne had been a sleeping potion, until what seemed a great noise of small-arms fire broke out over in the direction of the line of march. The sound was repeated and unmistakable. Yet inside the factitious Arab tent, war seemed a dream of the night before last. It couldn't be the Germans coming back, Meecham thought, reasonably. Even if the military situation had not precluded such a return, there would have been much artillery fire before they could reach the heart of the city. "It's the Militia, the murderers," the girl said. "There are plenty of them disguised with Resistance brassards now. They are shooting at the crowd because it is happy. And the real F.F.I.s must be shooting back. Stay here." Meecham had made no move to go.

In a couple of moments there came a burst of knocks at the door, and the housekeeper precipitated herself into the room without even asking pardon. "Come quick!" she cried. "Your friend the Colonel has gone mad. He will get us all killed!" She pulled Meecham by the leg. He reached for his trousers, but the woman said quickly, "There is no time for that. Have you gone mad, too? He has a revolver and he is trying to fire out of the window of his room at some F.F.I. guards on a roof who he thinks are snipers."

The blonde understood. Parisians appeared to react quickly to such situations, Meecham thought afterward. "He has no uniform on!" the blonde wailed. "They will see a man shooting and they will turn a machine gun on the house! Madame is right! We shall all be killed." The women ran out through the door, and Meecham followed them.

They entered another door, and he followed them again. The room in which he now found himself, he at once noted, was lined with mirrors. The ceiling and all the walls reflected a sculpturelike group of struggling figures, most of them nude. Rushby's was dominant. The Colonel, a tall man and an extraordinarily hairy one, was holding his Colt .45 at arm's length over his head to keep it away from the four women who surrounded him. Michèle had grabbed him around the knees and the housekeeper had tackled him waist-high—to prevent his progress to the window, Meecham supposed—while the proprietress of the establishment, a rather elegant female in an evening gown, had slipped her arms around his chest from the rear, and the blonde girl, who was tall for a woman, jumped again and again at the revolver hand. As Meecham watched, the whole mass swayed and went down, and there was an explosion comparable to that a howitzer might make in a less confined space. The pistol, describing a high arc, soared toward him and fell near his feet. There was broken glass around, some of it powdered so fine it looked like synthetic Christmas-tree snow. The bullet had hit one of the wall mirrors. Meecham stumbled toward the recumbent group and started to pull women to their feet like a football referee endeavoring to find who has the ball at the bottom of the pile. When he got down to Rushby, the Colonel was snoring peacefully.* Meecham and the women picked him up and laid him out on the bed, and a couple of hours later he was able to walk out almost sober. That must have been at about five o'clock, which was eleven A.M., Eastern War Time.

At 10 P.M., Eastern War Time, a copy boy began to lay takes of Meecham's story on the desk of his cable editor in New York.

"Will Irwin once wrote story called citythatwas," the lead began. "This is story of city that is again period bullets militia disguised as efefeye failed mar this sequel greek drama which originally never had such happy ending period this was prometheus unbound period it was throbbing heartwarming day of victory period burnedout tanks lay scattered about streets in front cafe de la paix bits broken glass."

* His head had hit the bidet.

# PART VI

## MASSACRE

I REMAINED in Paris, to report on political things, while my young friend David Lardner, who had come over for the purpose, relieved me as correspondent of *The New Yorker* with the Armies. Dave, extremely nearsighted, had been rejected from service, but was desperately keen to risk his skin. He was killed at Aachen in Germany when the jeep in which he was riding ran on a mine. He was one of the best.

With a photographer of a newly set up French War Crimes Commission, I made a trip to the Côte-d'Or, a region that, like Rennes, I had known in happier days. After I returned to Paris and wrote the following despatch, I went home, and missed the Battle of the Bulge. I never came back to the war. Before I could feel sufficiently ashamed for that, it was over.

# The Events at Comblanchien—

## November, 1944

THE COMMUNE of Comblanchien, in the Department of the Côte-d'Or, lies on the stretch of the National Highway that runs between Lyon, to the south, and Dijon, to the north. Comblanchien is six miles north of Beaune and three miles south of Nuits-St. Georges, in the Burgundy wine country. The commune has an area of a thousand acres; most of them are on the eastern side of the highway, falling away gently toward the railway that parallels the road at a distance of half a mile and forms Comblanchien's eastern boundary. A narrower strip of the village lies west of the highway, and in this direction the ground slopes up and more abruptly. A hundred feet above the road on this side there is a big, box-like, gray-and-white building which the people of the countryside call a château but which looks more like an old-fashioned American summer-resort hotel. From a small cupola on the roof of this building there is an excellent view of the surrounding country. The thousand acres are, except for a few fields of cabbages and sugar beets and the open mouths of four or five granite quarries, fairly well covered with grapevines, as one might expect in this region. The Comblanchien granite has more than a local reputation and when transportation was available it was sent as far away as Paris. The wines of Comblanchien are classed among the Côte de Nuits, but they are a secondary *cru* and have no such fame as those of Vosne-Romanée and Vougeot, both nearby communes. The wines bring good prices but not the extravagant sums that make the heir to a few acres in one of those more favored communities a rich man by birth. The village had five hundred and twenty inhabitants according to the last census, but it has rather fewer now. None of them are what the French call "rich rich," but a few are comfortably off. The proprietors of the Comblanchien vineyards work with their hands, like their hired help. The stone quarries are owned by outside companies and worked by employees who get modest wages. What distinguishes Comblanchien from other communities in the region is the burned-out shells of its houses.

There are perhaps a hundred houses in Comblanchien. About fifty of them are strung out along the highway; the rest are either scattered or grouped in clumps of two or three among the vineyards and fields that extend from the highway down to the railroad. Forty of the fifty on the highway are now in ruins. One of the town's three cafés and one of its three general stores have survived. Its one church is burned out, and so is the post office. The part of the community back among the vines and fields has suffered less; there are about a dozen charred ruins here and there. At one side of the road, as you come into town from the north, you see a rude sign that says, "Honor to all our liberators, who will avenge the martyrs of our dear village. Long live Comblanchien. Long live France. Long live de Gaulle."

"The events at Comblanchien" or the "things that happened at Comblanchien," as they are usually called by the people of the countryside, have some of the elements of a mystery story. Around nine-thirty on the night of August 21, 1944, about two weeks before the liberation of the region, some German soldiers disembarked from a troop train that had halted in the village and, together with the Germans from other detachments in the vicinity, set fire to many of the houses, after killing all the miserable people they caught in them. Most of the other inhabitants of Comblanchien had hidden in the vineyards, and toward morning the Germans went away. The German authorities never offered any explanation of the attack, and the Mayor of Comblanchien, a timid man, never asked for any. There was nothing to stop the Germans from coming back and completing the massacre by daylight, but they didn't. The people of Comblanchien continued to work in the vineyards by day and sleep there at night until the region was liberated. Then M. Jordan, a sergeant of the gendarmes in Corgoloin, a village near Comblanchien, started an investigation to establish what had happened. Comblanchien has no *gendarmerie* of its own, because it is not large enough; it has only a *garde-champêtre*, or constable. Jordan, who was in the Maquis, had been hiding in the vineyards on the night of the attack. He came out of his hiding place when he saw the fires and, slipping around among the Germans, he heard them crying, *"Hunde! Schweine! Schweine! Terroristen! Hunde!"* "I think it was because they were so frightened," he said afterward. "It is unimaginable how frightened they were." He has not been able to discover any other motive for the massacre.

*    *    *

Comblanchien, for four years after the Germans marched into Burgundy, in June, 1940, was without a history, but it was not happy. Like
thousands of other communities in France, it had an unending premoni-
tion of outrage. All through the land, fear was the most nearly intolerable
feature of the occupation. France was a kidnapped country; the kidnapper might let her live in a locked room, but when rescue seemed at
hand the kidnapper might try to kill her. Everyone had the feeling that
the Germans might arrest or kill anybody, at any time, for no reason that
would make sense to a civilized man. Materially, life was difficult. In
Comblanchien there was more food than in a big city, but only the
farmers really had enough. The quarry workers earned seven francs an
hour, but the purchasing power of the franc had almost vanished, so
textiles and matches and tools and clothing and tea and coffee, which
came from outside Comblanchien, cost incredible amounts. These workers, who had only little patches of ground in which to grow things, could
raise just a few vegetables and rabbits and chickens. They ate the vegetables and bartered their chickens and eggs and rabbits for such treasures
as spools of thread to repair their clothes, or bits of leather with which the
Comblanchien cobbler could patch their shoes. They seldom got meat
and, though they lived in a wine-growing district, they rarely could afford
to drink wine. The vineyard workers were in much the same predicament.
Many couples in Comblanchien serve both the regional industries; the
husband works in a quarry and the wife works in the vineyards. The
commune owns some woods, and on Sunday the laborers of Comblanchien would cut enough firewood to last them the week. The buses
which ran along the highway were infrequent and overcrowded; the men
and women who were employed in other villages of the region couldn't be
sure that they could ride to work. Only the relatively well-off owned
bicycles, so people often walked five or six miles to work every day and
back again at night, hurrying to get home before the nine-thirty curfew
the Germans had imposed. There was not much chance for the people of
Comblanchien to do any poaching; the Germans had attempted to confiscate all the sporting guns in the region, and the peasants who had defied
the order to disarm and had retained their weapons kept them carefully
hidden against the day they would have something more important than
partridges to shoot. Besides, the German soldiers, who were always
underfed, killed most of the game in the country. They shot at anything
edible and even dynamited streams and fish ponds.

There were, it is true, some residents of Comblanchien upon whom the
German occupation imposed no material privations. These were the
dozen or so well-to-do farmers who were getting such high prices in Dijon
that they were accumulating great wads of banknotes, although in a
currency that shrank in value every day. But even they felt the oppression
of something worse than want. The mere presence of Germans made
everyone feel subhuman. The sound of German voices filled the farmers

with a *malaise*, like the sound of rats scurrying within the walls of a house. The Mayor, M. Moron, was the wealthiest man of the commune. He owned a large pink building on the west side of the road, where he made and stored wine, and a good solid stone house on the east side of the road, where he lived. He was a tall, rather good-looking man, but no hero. *"Pas d'histoires"* was his motto, which might be freely interpreted to mean "For God's sake, no trouble." Moron is a common surname in Burgundy and has no pejorative connotation. The next wealthiest citizen was the deputy mayor and president of the communal council, M. Chopin. Chopin is also a Burgundian name. Chopin is a good solid chunk of a man with a bull neck and a strong, big-barrelled body like that of one of his prize plow horses. Both men regarded the Germans with a mixture of apprehension and dislike, the first sentiment dominating in M. Moron and the second in the more choleric Chopin.

One person in Comblanchien who did not seem to mind the presence of the Germans overmuch was Robert Ravigneaux, a café proprietor, whose bar was often filled with German soldiers who travelled the National Highway in convoys by night and stopped at Comblanchien to drink. Ravigneaux overcharged them for their drinks, and he told the townspeople that this was his form of resistance. The convoys didn't travel by day, because they were afraid of an Allied air attack. But even with their limited hours, they always seemed to have time to stop for refreshments, and there were no German equivalents of the "Off Limits" sign posted on the roadside cafés. Ravigneaux was a noisy, quarrelsome fellow who was not a native of the region—he had come to Comblanchien from the northeast of France five years before the war. He had an artificial left leg which was painted a pale flesh pink and on which he wore a sock and garter, just as he did on his other leg. When he got drunk, he would pull up the trouser of his amputated leg, slap the painted wood, and tell people that he had lost his leg in the last war, although everybody in Comblanchien knew that in 1944 he was only thirty-nine. Ravigneaux was drunk much of the time; it was his handsome, full-bosomed wife who watched the cash.

From time to time after the surrender of France, German soldiers were stationed in Comblanchien, in the Occupied Zone, and then withdrawn. In May, 1944, a new detachment arrived and moved into the château. This unit was known in Comblanchien as the Schoning Company, because it was commanded by Oberleutnant Schoning, a naval reservist who in civil life had been an architect in Kiel. The men under him were Marines. The Germans had found little for their Marine Corps to do aboard a portbound navy, so they had assigned detachments from it to various duties all over Europe. Schoning had about fifty men. Their job was to patrol the area, and chiefly the railroad, between Beaune and

Nuits-St. Georges, to guard against sabotage. The Oberleutnant was not much of a warrior. He was forty—just too young to have fought in the other war and just too old to have received any concentrated military training in the Nazi regime. He lived in fear that "terrorists" would attack the château, although the region is not really adapted to serious guerrilla warfare; it is too well cultivated and thickly inhabited. The vineyards would make excellent cover for a few snipers, but men cannot lie flat on their bellies for long. Schoning had been taken in by the Reich's propaganda. He saw terrorists everywhere. Soon after he arrived, he issued an order that every one of his men must learn to operate a field telephone so he could call the *Feld-gendarmerie* at Beaune immediately if the château were attacked. "The lives of each and all of us may depend on his comrades' presence of mind," Schoning's order read. What he lacked as a fighting man he made up for by abnormal arrogance, a phenomenon not confined to the German Army. He snarled and shouted constantly. Also, he never appeared outside the château without a machine pistol under his arm. As a joke, he invariably poked this weapon in Madame Ravigneaux's face when he visited the café. He was there often; he was an alcoholic, like Ravigneaux, himself a snarling man. There was something congenial to Schoning in the other disagreeable presence, although Schoning spoke no French and neither Ravigneaux nor his wife knew any German. The Oberleutnant's ignorance of French increased his suspicion of the citizenry. If anybody in Comblanchien laughed within his hearing, he was sure a joke had been made about him, and he would order the interpreter in his company, an Alsatian named Paul Zenses, to translate what had been said. Zenses had been drafted into the German Marines after the Nazis had "incorporated" Alsace and Lorraine into the Reich, in November, 1940. When Schoning was not with him, the Alsatian was on friendly terms with some of the local people. However, Schoning communicated his edginess to the rest of his men, and the groups that patrolled the railroad frequently fired at animals or shadows, thinking they were Maquis. People got used to hearing bursts of fire at night and thought nothing of them.

There had never been any special reason Schoning should fear an attack or the people of Comblanchien should have been subjected to any unusual repressive measures. There had been no acts of resistance in Comblanchien since the beginning of the occupation, although a number of the men there belonged to Maquis groups that operated elsewhere in the region. Some of these men had joined a group that had been established in a nearby district immediately after D Day, when General Koenig, in London, had called all the French Forces of the Interior to rise in active resistance, but after these orders had been countermanded, the Comblanchien men had returned to their homes, with the exception of two who had got themselves shot. Now the local Maquis affair had apparently blown over, and anyhow everybody was too busy in the vineyards and fields to worry about it. Protracted panic is a luxury beyond the means of working people. If the local Germans had wanted to make trouble, however, an opportunity lay at hand. All the men who had been in the Maquis could be distinguished by the new shoes that the resistance organization had distributed to them. The shoes were of Army issue and had been hidden from the Germans when the French military were officially disbanded, in 1942. The shoes were too good to give up, even if they did identify the wearers as men subject to the death penalty. Jordan used to go about telling the youths to stain their shoes and scuff them. But the Germans in the château were too stupid to notice such things, the men figured.

By late August the inhabitants of Comblanchien had almost forgotten the affair of the Maquis, except for the young blowhards, who sometimes drank and boasted about the feats they claimed they had brought off. The *garde-champêtre* of Comblanchien, who is not precisely Hercule Poirot, had been in the Maquis too, and he was soon going about telling people he had killed five Germans, which was, to put it mildly, inexact. Even M. Moron breathed easy. He had been summoned to the château to talk to Schoning three times, and each time he had gone in the fear that he would be held as a hostage. On the first occasion, Schoning had merely wanted to tell him that the water supply at the château was inadequate and that he would have to send a hogshead of water up the hill to him every day. The second time Schoning wanted to complain that the water had not been delivered promptly one morning. Schoning had been exceedingly nasty about it and had shouted even louder than usual. The third time Schoning was furious because a woman who had been doing housework for the Germans refused to come any more. She said she was sick, but the Mayor suspected that her husband, who worked in a quarry, had told her to give up her job at the château. The other workmen had probably threatened him. Schoning had ordered the Mayor to find a substitute, but he had been unable to find one. However, M. Moron had not been bothered again.

There was a great deal of work to do late in August. Most families, taking advantage of the double daylight-saving time, worked in their gardens right up to the nine-thirty curfew before going indoors to begin their suppers. A minute or two after curfew on the evening of Monday, August 21st, an hour easy to fix in the memory because the soup had just been put on everyone's table, a bell rang in the cottage of the watchman at the more southerly of the two grade crossings in the commune to warn of the approach of an unexpected train from the south. This crossing, No. 191 on the railway maps, is something less than a mile from the other, No. 190, and between them the rails run through a shallow cut. The passing of an unscheduled train was not unusual. The Germans had been using the railroad to move troops and matériel up toward Normandy. This sort of activity had increased since the Allied landings in the Midi on August 15th, because the Germans were systematically withdrawing from the south of France, evacuating base units as well as fighting troops. The watchman at No. 191 was, and is, Louis Maublanc, a youth of nineteen, who lives in the cottage with his widowed mother and a swarm of small brothers and sisters. A moment after the bell rang, Maublanc went out to close the swing gates of the crossing. He went over the track to close the farther gate and had just got back on his own side of the track when the train came along. It was a long train, he remembers—perhaps fifty cattle cars, filled with troops. French railroad cars are small, but even figuring only forty men in each, there were two thousand soldiers. They were carrying rifles, tommy-guns, and machine guns. The engine stopped on the crossing. Some officers got out of the cars, walked up to the locomotive, and spoke to the engineer. Maublanc says that he heard the man shout something about Comblanchien, so the officers had probably asked where they were.

There is a story in the countryside that the train was deliberately stopped at Comblanchien, but that is not true. The train stopped at Comblanchien because there was another train on the track at Nuits-St. Georges, three miles north. Many of the men in the cars were drunk and were singing and howling at each other. It is hard to tell when German soldiers are angry, the French say, because they are always howling anyway. The cars must have been well stocked with wine—the right of way where the train had stopped was littered with empty bottles next day— and the noncommissioned officers aboard were taking no notice of all the drunkenness. This did not seem unusual to Maublanc. German soldiers heading north were never happy; they undoubtedly sensed, despite their own propaganda, that things were going badly up there and that they might be killed. So they were generally drunk. Dusk was coming on, but there was still enough light, Maublanc noted regretfully, to work by in the gardens, if he hadn't had to go indoors because of the curfew. He was looking toward the west, where the sunset colors were fading in the sky. Suddenly he saw a burst of tracer bullets flying from the western slope. At once the Germans in the train started shouting much more loudly than they had done before. Some of them began firing machine guns in the general direction the bullets had come from. Others piled out of the cars and flung themselves flat along the tracks. Twenty of them poured into the Maublancs' cottage and pointed machine pistols at the widow Maublanc and her little children. Other soldiers grabbed Maublanc by his arms and throat. In all the things being shouted at him, he could distinguish one word again and again—"*Terroristen!*"—a word that even Frenchmen who speak no German understand. Meanwhile, somebody gave an order and the train moved past the crossing and into the cut, whose embankment offered some protection from the fire from the slope.

The train was so long that when it stopped the locomotive was almost at grade crossing No. 190. From the new position the machine gunners on the train laid down a real barrage. There was a volley of answering machine-gun fire from the west. Many villagers believe that the Germans attacked Comblanchien with malice aforethought and that they invented the story of the shots directed at the train. It has been established, however, that there actually was firing from the west. A few hundred yards west of the railroad line there is a poplar tree. When Jordan went over the ground, weeks later, he found bullets in both the east and west sides of the trunk and that many branches had been cut away from it. Lambert, the crossing watchman at No. 190, says that he saw five German soldiers on the train hit, but this testimony was impossible to check, because the train, when it did leave, carried away all the soldiers it had arrived with. Young Maublanc, who, like every other inhabitant of the region, knew that there was not a force of resistants within a hundred miles capable of attacking two thousand soldiers, was as puzzled as the Germans. The soldiers who had seized him finally flung him to the ground and left him there. Why they didn't kill him he doesn't know. As for his mother, she was so confused that she can recall almost nothing of what happened.

Nobody knows, and possibly nobody ever will know, who fired those first shots. Most probably, Jordan thinks, one of Oberleutnant Schoning's timorous, trigger-happy patrols let off a few rounds at a shadow in the vineyards, as the patrols often had before. It is known that two patrols were out when the shooting began. There is nothing to indicate that the first shots were aimed at the train or even came near it. The source of the heavier west-to-east fire which, a few minutes later, answered the barrage from the train is not mysterious. By what seems clearly to have been a coincidence, a German motor convoy had stopped on the National Highway in Comblanchien at the same time the train halted at the first grade crossing. It consisted of a dozen vehicles, each manned by a driver and a helper. There may have been in the group a couple of *Volkswagen* carrying officers, and perhaps some trucks had aboard a few hitch-hiking soldiers, but in all there could not have been more than fifty men. However, some of the trucks had machine guns mounted for use against strafing airplanes. The men in the convoy were scattered among the cafés of Comblanchien when the soldiers on the train began firing toward the highway. The convoy men, in their turn, shouted *"Terroristen!"* and ran to their machine guns. The fire was by now coming from two directions, most of it far overhead. Some of the convoy soldiers, therefore, fired to the east, toward the gun flashes they could see below them from the railroad; others fired west toward some flashes they saw.

Oberleutnant Schoning, who was finishing his dinner in the château when the firing from the train started, was immediately frightened. "Terrorists have begun their attack on the château!" he shouted to Zenses, who has since told Jordan what happened in the château that night. No one else had heard, or at any rate paid attention to, the first few shots from the slope. It was the shooting from the east that made the first impression. The machine guns at the château immediately began firing in the direction of the supposed attack. It is not known whether the fire from the château or from the trucks was responsible for the casualties—assuming there were any—on the train. The château was hit, but not many times. Jordan found a couple of bullet holes in it later, but it is not certain that Oberleutnant Schoning even knew the house had been struck. Zenses, who was sure that an attack on the château was beyond the means of the local resistance, felt that there was a horrible misunderstanding of some sort. The fire from the château, he feared, might hit the innocent people of Comblanchien, and he thought that perhaps Schoning could avert a massacre. After a couple of minutes of the firing, which did not seem to be directed at the château, Zenses suggested to the Oberleutnant that he be sent with a patrol down to the village to see what was happening. "I will take a patrol down there myself," Schoning said. "You will come with us." It was a heroic decision for the ex-architect; his pride had prevailed. The Oberleutnant and ten or fifteen of his men put on helmets, filled their belts with incendiary grenades, slung machine pistols over their shoulders, and went down to their usual destination, Ravigneaux's café.

Ravigneaux and his wife were in the café when the firing began. They heard the first burst and then the sustained fire. Some truck drivers from the convoy had been drinking there and they had run out without paying. That was all the Ravigneaux could tell Zenses. Schoning saw the convoy people firing from the trucks. There was still fire from the east, but it was going over their heads. Schoning said to Zenses, "There is some mistake, but I cannot do anything to stop it. You go back to the château. I have no more need for you." Zenses, before he went back to the château, paused in the village street and looked down toward the railroad, from which, he could readily see, many of the bullets were coming. It was now completely dark. As he looked across the vineyards, he saw a pillar of flame rise, halfway between the railroad and the highway, about where a peasant named Sergent lived. He realized even then that the Germans had begun to burn the village.

## II

MAX HENRY was one of the most respected citizens of Comblanchien. However, he had a hard time bringing up his family after the German occupation began. He was not a farmer but a salaried man, one of the few white-collar workers in the village, and he owned only the bit of ground surrounding his house. All prices were high in occupied France, and a man on a fixed salary was in a bad position, especially if he had to maintain appearances. M. Henry had two grown children to educate—a twenty-year-old son, Claude, and a sixteen-year-old daughter, Denise. Both went to the college in Beaune, six miles south of Comblanchien, and they continued to go despite the occupation. By August last year, Claude had finished a course preparing him to be an officer in the merchant marine. He must have been an optimist to choose that career, as he did, shortly after the armistice with Germany, when the French merchant marine had almost ceased to exist. He was to go to Paris on September 20th to take his final examinations for a commission.

M. Henry was a bookkeeper at the Comblanchien quarry of Civet, Pommier & Company of Paris, dealers in cut stone. He had worked for the company for twenty-five years, the last thirteen of them in Comblanchien. He was in his early forties. During the first year of the war he had been acting superintendent of the quarry, for a brief period, after the superintendent had been mobilized, in September, 1939. Then, in the spring of 1940, M. Henry himself was mobilized and a rigger in the quarry was made temporary superintendent. After the demobilization, the company took M. Henry back, but only as a bookkeeper, and kept the rigger on as nominal superintendent. The original superintendent, who had got a higher salary than M. Henry had, was not rehired. M. Henry had to take over all the correspondence, because the ex-rigger was uneducated. So M. Henry was something more than bookkeeper, and his chief was something less than superintendent, and neither of them got a full superintendent's salary, which was probably the company's idea in the first place. M. Henry was paid twenty-eight hundred francs a month. This would not have been lavish for a man with two children in school even if the franc had had its prewar value, but the franc had lost almost all its purchasing power. Fortunately, the Henrys had their house and chicken yard and vegetable garden and enough vines to provide them with family table wine, and Mme. Henry was an excellent manager. She was a thin, worn-looking woman with high color in her cheeks and black hair drawn tight in a bun behind her head. She came from the Department of the Meuse, and her husband from Reims. Madame was decidedly better educated than the farm women of the community, but she worked as hard as any of them, and Claude and Denise worked too, when they were home. M. Henry was very tall and thin, so thin in proportion to his height that when he was a young man he had been excused from military service; in 1940 the Army was less particular and he was mobilized as a private.

Monday, August 21, 1944, was a hot day, and Claude and Denise, who were home from college, went swimming in a stream with friends. One of the friends took a picture of Claude posed on a diving board. Mme. Henry still has it. It shows a tall, long-legged boy with heavy eyebrows, a straight nose, and the French variant of the crew haircut. On the evening of August 21st, until nine-thirty, when the curfew imposed by the Germans compelled everybody in Comblanchien to go indoors, the whole Henry family picked string beans in the garden. Because of double daylight-saving time, it was still light at curfew, but they had to go into the house just the same. They washed up (there was a bathroom in the Henry house, which was one of the most modern in the village) and sat down to supper. Like many of the buildings in the commune, the house fronted on the National Highway, which ran through the village; it was on the east side of that thoroughfare. M. Henry had built it himself in 1931. The exterior was of simulated gray-stone, an unconvincing concretish substance, and the house had six rooms, four on the ground floor and two in a kind of turret above. The front door was in the middle of the house and opened into a hall. M. and Mme. Henry's bedroom was at the right on the ground floor as you went in. Denise's bedroom was behind theirs. The dining room was on the left side as you entered, and the kitchen and the bathroom were behind that. The staircase leading to the turret was in the hall, and a shorter flight of stairs in the back led down to the basement. Claude's bedroom was on the second floor, in back; at the front of the turret was a spare bedroom.

The family had begun supper in the dining room when, Mme. Henry told me several weeks ago, while I was in Comblanchien, they heard two shots which, she said, sounded "like a signal." The sounds did not alarm them, because the patrols from the company of German Marines frequently fired shots for trivial reasons; the idea that these shots were a "signal" is undoubtedly purely retrospective. Then there was a real outbreak of shooting. It seemed to come from the southeast and it was so loud that all the Henrys dropped to the floor. Mme. Henry remembers that as the family lay on the floor her husband pulled her away from the window. After a while there was a pause in the firing. M. Henry, perhaps to reassure the others, said that there was no accounting for Germans; he was going to bed. He went into his bedroom and began to undress. Mme. Henry followed him and sat down on the bed, but she was afraid to take her clothes off.

It happened that Claude Henry was a member of the Forces Françaises de l'Intérieur, and an effective one, but he had kept his activities so secret that not even his parents knew of them. He lived at home only during the college vacations and on weekends. He had helped in *coups de main* and acts of sabotage in parts of central France less accessible to the Germans than the Côte-d'Or, in which Comblanchien is situated, and had organized resistance groups in several villages. He had also tended a parachute strip on which Allied planes dropped arms for the Maquis. Claude, driving an old truck, would pick up the weapons and distribute them to comrades.

When, on the night of August 1st, his parents went to their bedroom,

Claude went upstairs to his room, which faced east and south. Denise followed him after a couple of minutes. Looking out a window, they saw, through the gathering darkness, gun flashes down along the railroad, which was half a mile away, and then Claude pointed out to her what he said were groups of Germans moving up along the two roads that wound through the Comblanchien vineyards toward the village. Some of the men had flashlights, which they swung about as if they were looking for something. They stuck pretty well to the roads; the Germans were always timid about going into the vineyards, where, they fancied, the broad leaves might conceal snipers. Then Claude and Denise saw a house, midway between the railroad and the highway, begin to burn. The flames rose very high in an instant; the Germans were undoubtedly using incendiary grenades, which are usually effective immediately. "They are coming this way!" Claude said, and he hurried Denise down into the basement, shouting to his parents to join them. Mme. Henry hastened downstairs, but M. Henry, the methodical, bookkeeping kind of man, stayed in his room to dress.

A moment later there was a great crash on the ground floor. Some of the Germans had hurled grenades through the window of the dining room, setting fire to the house, and others had fired machine pistols and automatic rifles through the front door, their favorite way of breaking a lock. The three in the cellar heard boots and gunstocks on the floor over their heads, and then they heard the soldiers shouting at Henry. Claude, who had had six years of German at school and college, knew that the intruders were questioning his father. Claude also knew that his father did not understand a word of the language, so he ran up from the basement. His sister went up the basement steps behind him, but ran out the back door into the garden, where she threw herself down among the vines. Mme. Henry remained in the basement, too frightened to move.

Before his son had appeared, Max Henry had come out into the hall from his bedroom, although he had not finished dressing. The Germans presumably pushed him back against the wall and poked the muzzles of their automatic weapons against his body. He must have waved his hands in protest; he must have heard again and again, without understanding, the German words for "concealed arms." Denise, lying in the garden, saw the window of her brother's room, on the second floor, light up and Claude appear, followed by three or four Germans. He was gesticulating, evidently trying to convince them that there were no weapons concealed there, and he was talking fast. "He was talking the entire time I could see him," Denise told me when I was in Comblanchien. "Then they all went out of the room."

The house was already burning, and a minute later the flames mounted high in the sky. A dozen Germans ran out the front door, shouting and laughing. The night should have been growing darker rapidly now, but there was still light in the village, because the Germans had set fire to a score of houses, and the highway was illuminated by the fires in the houses lining it. Neither Max nor Claude Henry came out of the house. Denise, cowering among the vines, heard her mother call her name. She called back, and Mme. Henry crawled through the garden to her daughter's side. She had come up from the basement and out the back door the moment the Germans left the house. Flames were roaring in both the dining room and the bedroom at the front of the house, but they had not got into the hall between them, Denise said. Mme. Henry, who earlier in the evening had been the most timid member of the family, now found a courage that still astonishes her. "Claude and Papa must be in there," she said to her daughter. "Let us go in and find them." The two women went into the house through the back door. Max Henry lay in front of the door to his bedroom. His head had been severed from his body, apparently by a burst of machine-gun bullets. His blood puddled the floor of the little house he had built for his family. Claude Henry was lying at the foot of the staircase, his feet resting on one of the lower steps. He lay with his once handsome face among his brains. The Germans had probably killed M. Henry while Claude was still frantically talking upstairs; Claude must still have hoped to save the elder Henry when Denise saw him in his room with the Germans. When Claude had reached a point on the stairs from which he could see his father's body, a German behind him had presumably shot him in the back of the neck with his revolver. Then another German, apparently, fired a redundant shot into the boy's head as he lay dead. "We must put the bodies in the basement, where they will be preserved from fire," the mother said. The slight woman and the strong girl picked up the butchered bodies of their men—first the father and then the son—and carried them down into the basement. One of them must have made a third trip for Max Henry's head. The bodies were not touched by the fire and later received a proper burial. The women went outside again, but Mme. Henry, acting as incomprehensibly as people often do in crises, said, "The fire hasn't caught upstairs yet; maybe we can save some bed coverings and a mattress. They will be almost impossible to replace." So they went in and got some blankets. The flames reached upstairs before they could make another trip for a mattress.

Mme. Henry and her daughter lay in the garden all night. Houses were burning everywhere and there were intermittent bursts of gunfire. German soldiers passed back and forth on the highway a few yards from the two women, carrying things they had stolen from wrecked houses—quilts and chandeliers and chamber pots. They loaded them onto the dozen or so trucks of the convoy that had halted in the village that night. The magpie compulsion of a German soldier is hard to believe unless one has seen German trucks overflowing with a ragman's treasure of miserable household wares, wrecked along a roadside after a strafing.

The Henry house was one of a row of four on the highway that stood a little apart from the rest of the village. A woman named Gabut was in the house next to the Henrys', with her four children, when the enemy came. The Henry women heard her shrieking to the Germans not to kill her after her house had been set afire. She said afterward that she thought she had been spared because she had a crippled, subnormal child that could not stand up. A German pulled the child from its crib, and when the child fell to the floor he became interested in it. The crisis of blood lust past, he ran out of the house without killing the woman.

On the other side of Mme. Gabut's house was the house of a man named Salomon, a Communist who had led an abortive Maquis uprising near Comblanchien in June. Salomon had left the village some time ago, but his wife and her sister had lived in the house during most of the summer. This night, however, they, too, were away. It is logical that if this outbreak of arson and murder had been a premeditated punitive expedition against Comblanchien the Germans would have gone immediately to Salomon's house, since he was a known "terrorist." But they did not. The fourth house in the row was inhabited by a sixty-three-year-old man named Joseph Blanc, a retired postal employee living on a pension, and his wife and daughter. The Blancs, like their neighbors, must have trembled when they saw the Gabut and Henry dwellings burning. They ran to the basement of their house, but the Germans left them alone, at least for the moment. Two widows, mother and daughter, who lived not far from the Henrys but on the other side of the highway, were less fortunate. One of these women, Mme. Chapuzot, the mother, was sixty-eight. She worked in the vineyards when there was work for her and made mattresses at home when there was none. Her daughter, Mme. Voye, was forty-six, a cheerful, hardworking woman who hoed in the vineyards, did housework, and washed bottles for the wine merchants whenever she had a chance. The Henry women heard these two widows shrieking and begging the Germans to spare them, but the soldiers killed them both. It is hard to imagine that the Germans thought the two women dangerous. They were killing now simply because they had had a taste of blood, like weasels loose in a chicken yard.

At a farm in the commune they killed a young farm laborer named Marcel Julien. He was a pleasant, uneducated boy of eighteen who, unlike many Frenchmen of his age, had never been in the Maquis or done anything untoward. The Germans spared the other men on the farm, however. Their choice of victims that night was entirely capricious. The men who saw Julien killed say that the German who shot him was wearing shorts and an undershirt, carried a carbine, and was "slobbering" with fury. This led the people who later tried to reconstruct the massacre to think that this particular murderer must have come from the German truck convoy and not the troop train. German Army truck drivers were known to discard their outer clothes in hot weather. After some of the soldiers from the train had reached the National Highway and encountered the men from the truck convoy, who numbered about fifty, both parties must have realized that they had been firing at each other and not at an attack of what they called *Terroristen*. At any rate, the exchange of shots between the two groups ceased. The killing and burning, however, went on uninterrupted. In fact, it was now on a partnership basis. Some of the inhabitants of Comblanchien say that they recognized, among the soldiers attacking the houses, several of the Marines in Oberleutnant Schoning's detachment, but identifications in such circumstances are undependable. It is certain, however, that at eleven-thirty, an hour and a half after the murder of the two Henrys and the two widows, a band of Germans went to the Salomon house and began shouting for the "terrorist women" to come out. They must have meant Salomon's wife and sister-in-law, and this indicates to the man who has made the most careful study of the massacre—M. Jordan, the sergeant of gendarmes from Corgoloin—that officers from the troop train must have made contact with Schoning sometime between ten and eleven-thirty and asked him to point out the houses of people he suspected of "terrorism." In the absence of the Salomon women, the Germans set fire to the house and then went on to Blanc's, next door. They demanded that Blanc hand over the women, whom they said he was sheltering. The old man shook his head helplessly, and they shot him to death. They also fired at and wounded his wife and daughter, but the women escaped and managed to hide in the vineyards.

M. and Mme. Blaise Lieutard were a couple of retired railroad employees who had built themselves a house not far from the Henrys', fifty yards back from the road. They had lived in Comblanchien nine years. They had both worked in the Gare de Lyon, in Paris, for thirty years, he as an electrician and she as a messenger in the railway offices, and they had a joint pension of a thousand francs a month. The Lieutards had come to Comblanchien after their retirement because Mme. Lieutard's sister, Mme. Gauthron, lived there and Mme. Lieutard wanted to be near her. Mme. Gauthron was the village dressmaker and was married to a stonecutter in one of the quarries. M. Lieutard was a wiry little southern Frenchman of sixty, but, as his wife says when recounting her story of the dreadful night, "he looked older because he had had so much trouble." In Comblanchien the Lieutards had practiced severe economies, like all French couples of their type, who save throughout their working lives for the house they will build when they reach the pension age. Their pink stucco house—four rooms and a kitchen—might have seemed exiguous and jerry-built even to a promoter of Long Island building developments, but to Mme. Lieutard it was the fulfillment of a lifetime's hopes. She is a short woman with a broad, flat face and straggly, faded blond hair. Her eyes are blue-white and she has stubby little hands and feet; she could not have been pretty even when she was young, but her face, when she talks of the past glories of the little house, is radiant. On the ground floor there were two rooms and a storage "cellar." There was no inside staircase; to get to the second floor you walked up stone stairs on the outside of the house. The Lieutards had what Mme. Lieutard called a Louis Quinze bedroom, on which they had spent twenty thousand francs. In a corner of this room, and in a corner of the living room, which adjoined it, there were green-enamelled fireplaces. In the kitchen was a magnificent green metal salamander for heating water and a sink into which water ran from a long, convoluted pipe about as thick as a strand of macaroni. They had fine curtains on all the windows, and two overstuffed chairs which would have attracted attention in the window of any furniture store on the outer boulevards of Paris. Madame is in despair when she thinks of it. They were very comfortably off before the war, when the franc still had some value. Besides their pension, they had the usual chicken yard and garden and cages of fat rabbits, which were a joy as well as an auxiliary source of nourishment. Like all rustic French workers who have had to live in the city for a long time, they took immense pleasure in their return to the country. They had but one cause for anxiety: their only daughter, a Mme. Pascal, was a widow, her husband having died shortly after the Lieutards retired. She had two children, a boy and a girl. Her husband had left her no money and she had had to go back to her old job in the material office in the Gare de Lyon. Her parents, however, were able to help her out now and then with a few hundred francs or a fine hamper of country *charcuterie*.

Living conditions did not become difficult for the Lieutards until after the armistice. Under the Germans, it was impossible for them to live on their pension and send anything to their daughter and her children, so M. Lieutard went back to work, as chief electrician at the railroad station in Beaune. His salary was seventeen hundred francs a month, but his pension stopped, since he was now working again, so his income was only seven hundred francs a month more than it had been. M. Lieutard had no bicycle and could not afford to buy one, so he walked the six miles to Beaune and back every day. "And he had slightly flat feet," Mme. Lieutard recalls. Walking made him very hungry, but food was even more expensive in Beaune than in Comblanchien, so he had to eat in the workmen's restaurant there. It served nothing but vegetables and noodles, and all the cooking was *à l'eau*, which is repugnant to most Frenchmen, who believe that boiling takes all the nourishment out of food. When he got home at night, he was sometimes so hungry that there were tears in his eyes. He often ate bread with mustard on it, for lack of meat. When the chickens laid, the Lieutards had to barter the eggs for thread or salt or other necessities they could not afford to buy, and when they killed a chicken it went into the package they sent to Paris every week for their grandchildren. Sometimes M. Lieutard did not dare look at the rabbits, for fear he would be impelled to kill one and stew it, and thus enrage his wife. Cigarettes were of course beyond his means, so he planted a little tobacco in the garden. He had heard that it should be dried in the sun, but he never had the patience to wait; he would put the green leaves on the stove and try to toast them dry, so that he could smoke them immediately. Early in 1944, the Lieutards' daughter, who had saved up some money, decided that it would be easier to feed and lodge the children in the country than in Paris, even without her job, so she came to join her parents and brought the children with her. The girl was fifteen, the boy thirteen. She confided her savings—twenty-five thousand francs—to her mother for safekeeping. Mme. Lieutard hid the money in one of her overstuffed chairs, one that had cost three thousand francs. The Lieutards were happy to have their daughter and her children with them. Mme. Pascal helped her aunt, Mme. Gauthron, with the dressmaking, and the children went to school. It was no longer necessary to send packages to Paris, so M. Lieutard got a taste of meat once in a while now. During the summer the old electrician watched the German troop trains that passed through the station in Beaune and drew his own conclusions about how the war was going for *"ces messieurs."* He talked to the train crews, who told him about air bombardments and sabotage along the line. He became optimistic, and used to say to his wife, "When this is over, we will offer ourselves a nice faceful of food and then we will repaint the house."

When Lieutard heard the firing begin on the night of August 21st, he summoned his family into the storage "cellar," a windowless part of the ground floor. The women were in their slips—they slept together upstairs —while Lieutard, exiled from his Louis Quinze room, shared a room on the ground floor with his grandson. "It was a genteel little room with green walls and folding beds," Mme. Lieutard says with infinite regret. The Germans ran up to the house and entered it. The Lieutards and Pascals slipped unnoticed out the back door of the "cellar" and into the garden, but there they were trapped, for they were fenced in by chicken wire except at the front of the house, and if they went out that way, they would run into the Germans. M. Lieutard tried to tear his way through the wire at the side of the house. A German soldier, coming from Mme. Lieutard does not know where, turned a flashlight on him. Mme. Lieutard, Mme. Pascal, and the two children took refuge behind a hen coop and lay flat on their bellies. Mme. Pascal's legs are long and her feet extended beyond the shelter. It was mere chance that the German didn't see them. M. Lieutard turned toward the light and said, in a faint voice, *"Qu'est ce que c'est?"* "He sounded as if his throat was stopped up, my little man," Mme. Lieutard says. The German fired—an explosive bullet that went in at Lieutard's right collarbone and came out the middle of his back, leaving an opening as big as a saucer. The inoffensive little man crumpled on the bit of garden earth he had spaded up so many times in the past nine years. "He bled! he bled!" Mme. Lieutard says. "He had planted celery on that spot, but he bled so much the celery never came up. They killed him like a wild boar." Mme. Lieutard's comparison seemed to accentuate the difference rather than the similarity between poor Blaise Lieutard and a savage beast. The German leaned over the stricken man and put his weapon to the victim's head and blew it to bits. Then he went away, shouting for his companions, probably to show them what he had done.

The women, clawing at the fence behind the chicken coop with a strength they had never suspected they had, were able to make a small opening between the wire and a fence post, and through this the children and then the mother and grandmother succeeded in wriggling. They crawled on all fours through a field of wheat stubble, lacerating their hands and knees and tearing their light garments to shreds, before they reached the nearest vineyard, where they hid under the leaves like vermin. And from between the vines Mme. Lieutard saw her small house, her treasure, burn. The overstuffed chair with Mme. Pascal's twenty-five thousand francs in it burned, too. Some of the chickens and rabbits survived, and Mme. Lieutard, who now lives with her sister, visits the ruined house morning and evening to feed them. I discovered her there when I visited Comblanchien. "I found a fork among the ashes today," she said, "but it was all black and twisted. We had such pretty tableware! Oh, Monsieur, if they had not burned the house, I would have had a roof to shelter my head and I would have had all our things to remind me of my poor husband! Or if they had not killed him, we could have got along without the house; we would have had each other! But this way they have left me nothing."

The Germans also killed a seventy-two-year-old man named Simonot, a stonecutter, but no witness to the crime remains in Comblanchien. Simonot lived with a spinster sister even older than himself, and she has moved away from Comblanchien.

Not even the bar of the irascible Robert Ravigneaux escaped. When Schoning and his interpreter, Paul Zenses, visited the café early that evening, as the trouble was just beginning, Schoning advised Ravigneaux and his wife to close their shutters and stay indoors. But at midnight the couple, in their bedroom, heard someone shouting, "Robert! Robert!" Whoever was calling sounded the final "t," which is silent in French but is pronounced in German. With that they heard a crashing in of shutters and windows, as if gun butts were being used on them, and then grenades exploded on the first floor. The house caught fire immediately and

Ravigneaux and his wife barely had time to save themselves. "It must have been the *salauds* from the château," the surly innkeeper says, "because the others wouldn't have known my name. That's what you get for treating the Germans decently. Not that I was ever friendly with them!" he adds hastily when other villagers are listening. He is not a popular man.

The Mayor of Comblanchien, M. Moron, was more fortunate. The Germans came to his house, said they were going to burn it, and ordered him and his wife to get out. Mme. Moron told them that her little girl was ill and had a high fever, and Moron's son, a classmate of the unfortunate Claude Henry at the college in Beaune, talked to them in German. They finally left the house without setting fire to it, but they carried away a small barrel of wine. The survival of the Mayor's residence and his wine warehouse, across the road, did nothing to increase his popularity with his less fortunate fellow-citizens, but it seems to have been sheer chance. Of a hundred-odd buildings in the village, the Germans burned fifty-two, and their decision to spare some was apparently as haphazard as their decision to destroy the others. In addition to killing eight people, the Germans arrested twenty-four men and boys. They put these prisoners aboard the troop train, announcing that they would carry them away as hostages. The selection of the hostages was as inexplicable as everything else about the affair. One of them was a boy of fourteen, and none of them were important citizens—not, for example, the Mayor, the deputy mayor, or the town clerk. Next day, at Dijon, the Germans released twelve of the hostages. All had expected to be shot. The Germans put the twelve others aboard a train for Germany, but when the train was bombed by American planes, two more of the prisoners escaped. They eventually made their way back to Comblanchien. The remaining ten have not been heard from.

The shooting, burning, and looting continued until dawn. In the middle of the night, a truck rolled up from the *Feld-gendarmerie* at Beaune, hauling a field gun. By that time it must have been obvious to all the Germans that they had not been attacked, as they may have thought at first, by the resistance forces, but the gunners fired a dozen rounds at the town hall and church. They hit the belfry of the town hall, knocking off a piece of stone bearing the letters "R.F." (République Française), but did no other damage. Shell cases found on the highway show that the gun was a thirty-seven-millimetre piece. This shelling was probably done for "moral effect." At dawn the truck convoy went on its way, the soldiers in it singing happily. The Germans from the troop train marched back to their cars in cadenced step, singing manly songs about morning in the forest and village maidens with dewy eyes. Oberleutnant Schoning had already gone to the château. In the vineyards, haggard women peered through the leaves at the smoking sockets of their houses.

Toward eight in the morning, it was discovered that the church was burning. The iron grille at the entrance had been locked, and the Germans, after firing a few ineffective shots at the lock in an attempt to break it, had gone off on some other drunken inspiration. But probably an incendiary bullet or grenade, going through a window, had started a smoldering fire that burst into flames hours later. M. Gilles, chief of the commune's volunteer fire company, and M. Chopin, the deputy mayor, went to the Mayor and asked for the key to the engine house, so that they could get out the fire engine. The Mayor said that the Germans had started the fire and might renew the massacre if an attempt were made to save the church. He refused permission to take out the engine, and the church burned to the ground.

Later in the day some of the Germans from the château appeared on the highway. They pointed to the ruins of the town and shouted, "*Boom boom kaput! Terroristen kaput!*" They seemed to find the scene amusing and laughed a great deal, but they made no move to attack any of the people they saw rummaging in the ruins of their houses. Schoning communicated with nobody in the village from then on. During the first week in September he and his Marine detachment evacuated the château and left town. French and American troops arrived in Comblanchien on September 7th.

While the fires were still at their height on the night of the massacre, M. Jordan, the gendarme from Corgoloin, came secretly to Comblanchien to see what was happening there. M. Jordan is a sallow, long-faced man with a hawk nose and a grizzled mustache. He is intelligent and logical and has a professional fondness for phrases like "reconstitution of the crime," since for the past sixteen years he has been a police officer. Until he fled to join the Maquis a couple of weeks before the massacre, M. Jordan had been a *maréchal des logis,* or sergeant, of the national gendarmerie. For the sixteen years of his service he had been stationed at the *gendarmerie* nearest Comblanchien, in the neighboring commune of Corgoloin, so he was intimately acquainted with the district and all its people. During the occupation he had pretended to help the Germans, but he had consistently forewarned everybody he was instructed to arrest. He had salvaged a few weapons so damaged that the Germans had thrown them away, and he had painfully and ingeniously repaired them, so he and the three gendarmes under him were armed with carbines and a submachine gun in addition to the gimcrack revolver and nine rounds per man the Germans allowed French gendarmes to retain. The four gendarmes had gone into the Maquis after they had been warned of an impending raid upon their cache of arms. On the night of the massacre, M. Jordan remained in Comblanchien for an hour watching the Germans. He realized by then that he could do nothing to amend matters, so he crawled off through the vineyards until he got well away, because, even though there was no moon, the flames cast a brilliant light. After the liberation, he returned to the *gendarmerie* at Corgoloin. As soon as he had cleared up a few routine matters, like the arrest of a couple of Germans in civilian clothes who remained in the region, he began a careful investigation of the slaughter of his fellow-citizens at Comblanchien. His findings have not pleased all his neighbors, for people everywhere like to believe in diabolical plots, and M. Jordan has not been able to establish that there was one.

When he began his inquiry, there was already a story in the countryside that the arrival of the train and of the truck convoy at Comblanchien had been coördinated that night for the purpose of making an attack on the village. It had become an article of faith that the few shots before the massacre were a prearranged signal. "The few shots, of course, might have been a signal," Jordan says, "but there had been shots like them in the night on dozens of previous occasions, always proceeding from those nervous Marine patrols. As to the thesis that there really was an attack on the train by men of the resistance and that the Germans fired in defense, I am in a position to say that it cannot be sustained. There were no F.F.I. patrols in Comblanchien that night. Moreover, if the handful of men of Comblanchien had meditated anything so mad as an attack on a two-thousand-man troop train, would Claude Henry, an F.F.I. officer, have been picking string beans in the garden when the train arrived?"

M. Jordan also heard in the countryside a story that people had seen rockets fired from the château before the attack began, but he could never actually find these people. There was also a story that Schoning's Marines had appeared, completely equipped for battle, at the Ravigneaux café an hour before the first shots, but M. and Mme. Ravigneaux and Paul Zenses, the Alsatian interpreter, who subsequently deserted from the German Army and joined up with the French, agreed that Schoning had appeared in the café *after* the firing started. There was also a very persistent report that the German commander of the troop train had insisted, at Corgoloin, the station below Comblanchien, that "the train must go through because we have to get to Comblanchien this evening." The Corgoloin station-master told Jordan that the officer had wanted to get as far as Dijon, not Comblanchien, and that the train had stopped there only because another one was ahead of it. "The strongest argument against the thesis of a deliberate punitive attack on Comblanchien," Jordan says, "is the fact that if they had wanted to kill all the people, the Germans could have remained on the scene the next day and killed them at their leisure. But they didn't. Well, then, there was no premeditation. Well, then, what happened?

"This is what happened. Two detachments of Germans, arriving here simultaneously from two directions, with their customary brutality exacerbated by fear and chagrin, frightened each other into an exchange of shots. The precipitating influence was probably one of the patrols from the château, which were always frightened. The patrol fired two or three shots and soldiers on the train replied with a massive fusillade. Those of the truck convoy replied to this fusillade with a nourished fire. The château joined in. Train and convoy fired on the château. This I know because I have found imbedded in the château two machine-gun bullets that came into it through open windows. No glass is broken, but remember that it was a hot night. One bullet had entered at such an acute upward angle that it was lodged in a ceiling. It must therefore have been fired from the road directly below the château. The other had lodged in a wall almost on a level with the window sill and therefore must have been fired on an only slightly rising trajectory—from the train on the other side of the village. The evidence of a poplar tree, standing between train and convoy, and blasted by fire from the two directions, proves that the Germans fired on each other.

"Now, however, please remark that I do not exonerate these brutes for what they did. Mistakes sometimes occur, even in armies which, like the German, propagate a legend of their own perfect discipline and skill at warfare. If some innocent inhabitants of the village had been caught in the crossfire and wounded, that would have been regrettable but not a crime of war. But notice—the Germans descended from the train and killed eight persons in their houses, firing point blank. These persons were not only unarmed; of the eight, three were men more than sixty years old and two were women, persons unlikely to be dangerous. They did not kill only in the first access of fury, because it was an hour and a half after the first attack that they killed old man Blanc. Long after they discovered their mistake, they continued to burn houses. What was their crime? In my opinion, any court would convict them of murder."

# Afterword

I have been advised to write an epilogue to this book to "give it unity" and "put it in perspective," but I find this difficult, because war, unlike drama, has no unities, classical or otherwise. It is discursive, centrifugal, both repetitive and disparate. Also, I have never got it into perspective myself— It is sometimes as much part of now as then, particularly the moment when I saw the blood mixed with milk. ("The symbolism was too obvious," a literary friend said to me afterward, mistaking me for a creative writer.) Also, although I am a rationalist without belief in the hereafter, some of the pieces are irrationally filled with spooks, like the dead airplane crew in "Run," that wanted me to fly with them, and this makes it hard for me to write about these stories—they must speak for themselves.

A.J.L.
1964

ABBOTT JOSEPH LIEBLING (1904–1963) was one of America's finest and most influential journalists. For over forty years he wrote on such diverse subjects as boxing, gastronomy, World War II in Europe, and, perhaps most importantly, on the press itself: his "Wayward Press" columns in the *New Yorker* established him as the pioneering critic of American journalism.

# WITNESSES TO WAR
## FROM SCHOCKEN BOOKS

## LIVING THROUGH THE BLITZ
### Tom Harrisson, 0-8052-0892-5, paper

"As near an objective history of people at war as we are ever likely to get."
—*Times Literary Supplement*

## THIS IS LONDON
### Edward R. Murrow, 0-8052-0882-8, paper

"This book is in the full sense the stuff of history—not only to be read now but to be kept for rereading later."
—*New York Times*

## ORWELL: THE WAR COMMENTARIES
### W. J. West, ed., 0-8052-0889-5, paper

"The clarity, the care with which Orwell expresses every nuance, and the tone of evident common sense, are masterful."
—*Library Journal*

## INTO THE VALLEY
### John Hersey, 0-8052-4078-0, hardcover

A minor classic of war reporting by the Pulitzer Prize–winning author of *Hiroshima*.

"A terse, faithful, moving narrative good enough to remind you of Stephen Crane."
—*New Yorker*

## MOLLIE & OTHER WAR PIECES
### A. J. Liebling, 0-8052-20957-3, paper

An eloquent and engaging collection of Liebling's classic war writings from the *New Yorker*.

## THE RED ORCHESTRA
### Gilles Perrault, 0-8052-0952-2, paper

"One of the best pieces of reportage on an espionage network to appear in a very long time."
—*New York Times Book Review*

# OTHER SCHOCKEN AND PANTHEON
# TITLES OF INTEREST

## NEW YORKER BOOK OF WAR PIECES

*Schocken, 0-8052-0901-8, paper; 0-8052-4049-7, cloth*

Perhaps the most distinguished collection of World War II journalism ever compiled. —*Just published*

## THE GOOD WAR

**Studs Terkel,** *Pantheon, 0-394-53103-5, FPT*

"Tremendously exciting and very illuminating . . . It will give historians a lot to write about. And for the general reader it will be a revelation." —William L. Shirer

## TOTAL WAR

**Peter Calvocoressi, Guy Wint, John Pritchard,** *Pantheon, 0-394-57811-2, cloth*

"Remarkable for its enormous wealth of information, its organizational clarity, and the spare simplicity of the writing." *Just published.* —*Publishers Weekly*

## IN HITLER'S SHADOW

**Richard J. Evans,** *Pantheon, 0-679-72348-X, paper; 0-394-57686-1, cloth*

A brilliant critique of recent attempts by some West German historians to reinterpret and distort the history of the Nazi past. —*Just published*

## NAZI GERMANY

### IN HITLER'S GERMANY

**Bernt Engelmann,** *Schocken, 0-8052-0864-X, paper*

"It conveys the everyday climate of life in the darkest of times. It is a valuable and absorbing addition to the history of the period." —*New York Times Book Review*

### FACES OF THE THIRD REICH

**Joachim Fest,** *Pantheon, 0-394-73407-6, paper*

"Fest has pulled together in a single volume more details of the lives of his subjects than are included in any other book I can think of." —Christopher Lehmann-Haupt, *New York Times*

### CRISIS OF GERMAN IDEOLOGY

**George Mosse,** *Schocken, 0-8052-0669-8, paper*

"A milestone in the study of National Socialism." —*New York Review of Books*

## NAZI CULTURE

*George Mosse, Schocken, 0-8052-0668-X, paper*

"A full picture of the scope and methods of the anticultural vandalism of the Nazis."
—*Christian Science Monitor*

# THE WAR IN THE PACIFIC

### BY THE BOMB'S EARLY LIGHT

*Paul Boyer, Pantheon, 0-394-74767-4, paper*

"A pathbreaking study . . . the first to document in detail just how the bomb figured in the nation's public discourse and popular mythology between 1945 and 1950 . . ."
—*Newsweek*

### WAR WITHOUT MERCY

*John Dower, Pantheon, 0-394-75172-8, paper*

"May well be the most important study of the Pacific War ever published."
—*New Republic*

### PACIFIC WAR

*Saburo Ienaga, Pantheon, 0-394-73496-3, paper*

"No one can really understand contemporary Japan and its policies unless he is acquainted with the grim story Saburo Ienaga presents."
—*New York Times Book Review*

### UNFORGETTABLE FIRE

*Japan Broadcasting Corporation, ed., Pantheon, 0-394-74823-9, paper*

Over 100 vivid color drawings, and brief accompanying descriptions, by survivors of Hiroshima.

"More moving than any book of photographs of the horror could be."
—John Hersey

# MEMOIRS FROM THE WAR IN EUROPE

### THE WAR

*Marguerite Duras, Pantheon Modern Writers, 0-394-75039-X, paper*

"More than one woman's diary . . . a haunting portrait of a time and place and also a state of mind."
—*New York Times*

### MEMOIRS 1925–1950

*George Kennan, Pantheon, 0-394-71624-8, paper*

"A remarkably candid, beautifully written and utterly fascinating autobiography."
—*New York Times*

### NAPLES '44

*Norman Lewis, Pantheon Modern Writers, 0-394-72300-7, paper*

"A British officer's vivid, lucid, eloquent journal of a year in Allied-occupied Naples."
—*New York Times Book Review*

## WAR DIARIES

*Jean-Paul Sartre, Pantheon Modern Writers, 0-394-74422-5, paper*

"An extraordinary book . . . His mental agility here is dazzling."
—Alfred Kazin

## A WOMAN'S PRISON JOURNAL

*Luise Rinser, Schocken, 0-8052-4045-4, cloth*

At last available in America, Rinser's account of her year as a political prisoner in Nazi Germany was the first document of its kind published there after the war.

## WORLD WAR II FICTION

### THE BLOOD OF OTHERS

*Simone de Beauvoir, Pantheon Modern Writers, 0-394-72411-9, paper*

"One of the few books which depicts the atmosphere of Paris during its occupation." —*New York Times*

### THE ASSAULT

*Harry Mulisch, Pantheon Modern Writers, 0-394-74420-9, paper*

Probes the moral devastation following the Nazi's slaughter of an innocent family in retaliation for the assassination of a Dutch collaborator.

"A beautiful and powerful work . . . takes its place among the finest European fiction of our time." —Elizabeth Hardwick

### THE OGRE

*Michel Tournier, Pantheon Modern Writers, 0-394-72407-0, paper*

A riveting story of fascism and obsession.

"The most important book to come out of France since Proust."
—Janet Flanner

## HOLOCAUST

### UNANSWERED QUESTIONS

*François Furet, ed.,*
*Schocken, 0-8052-0908-5, paper; 0-8052-4051-9, cloth*

The first systematic investigation by an internationally acclaimed group of historians and scholars of the unanswered questions surrounding the Holocaust. —*Just published*

### CENTURY OF AMBIVALENCE

*Zvi Gitelman, Schocken, 0-8052-4034-9, cloth*

Nearly 400 rare photographs document Jewish life in the Soviet Union over the past century.